Metamodernism in Contemporary British Theatre

Methuen Drama Engage offers original reflections about key practitioners, movements and genres in the fields of modern theatre and performance. Each volume in the series seeks to challenge mainstream critical thought through original and interdisciplinary perspectives on the body of work under examination. By questioning existing critical paradigms, it is hoped that each volume will open up fresh approaches and suggest avenues for further exploration.

Series Editors

Mark Taylor-Batty
University of Leeds, UK
Enoch Brater
University of Michigan, USA

Titles in the series include:

Contemporary Drag Practices and Performers: Drag in a Changing Scene
Volume 1
Edited by Mark Edward and Stephen Farrier
ISBN 978-1-3500-8294-6

Performing the Unstageable: Success, Imagination, Failure
Karen Quigley
ISBN 978-1-3500-5545-2

Drama and Digital Arts Cultures
David Cameron, Michael Anderson and Rebecca Wotzko
ISBN 978-1-472-59219-4

Social and Political Theatre in 21st-Century Britain: Staging Crisis
Vicky Angelaki
ISBN 978-1-474-21316-5

Watching War on the Twenty-First-Century Stage: Spectacles of Conflict
Clare Finburgh
ISBN 978-1-472-59866-0

Fiery Temporalities in Theatre and Performance: The Initiation of History
Maurya Wickstrom
ISBN 978-1-4742-8169-0

Ecologies of Precarity in Twenty-First Century Theatre: Politics, Affect, Responsibility
Marissia Fragkou
ISBN 978-1-4742-6714-4

Robert Lepage/Ex Machina: Revolutions in Theatrical Space
James Reynolds
ISBN 978-1-4742-7609-2

Social Housing in Performance: The English Council Estate on and off Stage
Katie Beswick
ISBN 978-1-4742-8521-6

Postdramatic Theatre and Form
Edited by Michael Shane Boyle, Matt Cornish and Brandon Woolf
ISBN 978-1-3500-4316-9

Sarah Kane's Theatre of Psychic Life: Theatre, Thought and Mental Suffering
Leah Sidi
ISBN 978-1-3502-8312-1

For a complete listing, please visit
https://www.bloomsbury.com/series/methuen-drama-engage/

Metamodernism in Contemporary British Theatre

A Politics of Hope/lessness

Tom Drayton

methuen | drama
LONDON • NEW YORK • OXFORD • NEW DELHI • SYDNEY

METHUEN DRAMA
Bloomsbury Publishing Plc
50 Bedford Square, London, WC1B 3DP, UK
1385 Broadway, New York, NY 10018, USA
29 Earlsfort Terrace, Dublin 2, Ireland

BLOOMSBURY, METHUEN DRAMA and the Methuen Drama logo are trademarks of
Bloomsbury Publishing Plc

First published in Great Britain 2024

Copyright © Tom Drayton, 2024

Tom Drayton has asserted his right under the Copyright, Designs and Patents Act,
1988, to be identified as author of this work.

For legal purposes the Acknowledgements on pp. xii–xiii constitute
an extension of this copyright page.

Series design by Louise Dugdale
Photograph © Alex Brenner

All rights reserved. No part of this publication may be reproduced or transmitted in any
form or by any means, electronic or mechanical, including photocopying, recording, or
any information storage or retrieval system, without prior permission in writing from
the publishers.

Bloomsbury Publishing Plc does not have any control over, or responsibility for, any
third-party websites referred to or in this book. All internet addresses given in this
book were correct at the time of going to press. The author and publisher regret any
inconvenience caused if addresses have changed or sites have ceased to exist, but
can accept no responsibility for any such changes.

A catalogue record for this book is available from the British Library.

Library of Congress Cataloging-in-Publication Data
Names: Drayton, Tom, author.
Title: Metamodernism in contemporary British theatre :
a politics of hope/lessness / Tom Drayton. Description: London ;
New York : Methuen Drama, 2024. | Series: Methuen drama engage |
Includes bibliographical references and index.
Identifiers: LCCN 2024007975 (print) | LCCN 2024007976 (ebook) |
ISBN 9781350286429 (hardback) | ISBN 9781350286436 (epub) |
ISBN 9781350286443 (pdf)
Subjects: LCSH: Post-postmodernism (Literature) | Postmodernism (Literature) |
English drama–21st century–History and criticism. |
Theater–Great Britain–History–21st century. | Aesthetics.
Classification: LCC PR744.P67 D73 2024 (print) | LCC PR744.P67 (obook) |
DDC 822.9208–dc23/eng/20240515
LC record available at https://lccn.loc.gov/2024007975
LC ebook record available at https://lccn.loc.gov/2024007976

ISBN: HB: 978-1-3502-8642-9
ePDF: 978-1-3502-8644-3
eBook: 978-1-3502-8643-6

Series: Methuen Drama Engage

Typeset by Newgen KnowledgeWorks Pvt. Ltd., Chennai, India

To find out more about our authors and books visit www.bloomsbury.com
and sign up for our newsletters.

Once again to Bibi

Contents

List of Illustrations   xi
Acknowledgements   xii
Notes on the Text   xiv

Introduction   1

1   (Already) beyond the postmodern   13
    Mapping metamodernism: Traces of a new paradigm   22
    Notes on metamodernism: Traces of theatre   36
    Notes on theatre: Traces of metamodernism   41

2   Metamodernism   49
    Origins and definitions   49
    Oscillation   55
    Aesthetic strategies   57

3   The children of postmodernism: Hope/lessness   69
    The millennial (as a) generational demographic   70
    The millennial (as a) structure of feeling   72
    'Follow your passion': New Labour's impact on the British theatre scene   82

4   Metamodern theatre: A spotter's guide   89
    Overarching sensibilities   90
    Aesthetic strategies   95
    Themes   109

5   Metamodernism in contemporary British theatre   119
    Treading the line between fact and fiction: Eager Spark's *Beneath the Albion Sky* and The Gramophones' *End to End* and *Wanderlust*   120
    The sound of lost futures: Middle Child's *All We Ever Wanted Was Everything*   132

I want to believe (all of this is true): Poltergeist's *Lights Over Tesco Car Park* — 141

Playful participation and (im)possible political realities: Feat.Theatre's *The Welcome Revolution* and Hidden Track's *Drawing the Line* — 150

The (meta)narrative you can(not) stage: Arinzé Kene's *Misty* — 158

The audience as storytellers at the end of the world: YESYESNONO's *we were promised honey!* and Nathan Ellis's *work.txt* — 163

Conclusion — 173

Afterword: (Im)Possible Futures — 177

References — 181

Index — 205

List of Illustrations

4.1	Diagram based on Greg Dember's 'tent-like' structure	94
4.2	Diagram illustrating levels of metatheatricality in metamodern theatre	101
5.1	Ria Ashcroft (centre) with audience members onstage at the end of The Gramophone's *Wanderlust*	131
5.2	Joshua Meredith as Brian (left), Alice Beaumont as Holly (centre, silhouette) and Bryony Davies as Leah (right) in Luke Barne's *All We Ever Wanted Was Everything*	138
5.3	(L–R) Rosa Garland, Alice Boyd, Julia Pilkington and Callum Coghlan in Jack Bradfield and Poltergeist Theatre's *Lights Over Tesco Car Park*	144
5.4	Stella Marie Sophie (left) interacts with a participant in Feat.Theatre's *The Welcome Revolution*	152
5.5	Nisha Cole (far left) as Lineswoman with audience participants in Elliot Hughes's and Hidden Track's *Drawing the Line*	156
5.6	Sam Ward in *we were promised honey!*	165

Acknowledgements

Writing a book is at once a solitary endeavour and one wholly supported by a loving and dedicated community of friends, family and colleagues. I am incredibly privileged to be able to have worked on this volume for the last few years, and even more privileged to be surrounded by some of the best supporters anyone could ask for. I am unbelievably grateful to everyone who has helped, in some way, to produce this book. I want to give special thanks to Dominic Hingorani, who has supported my research from the beginning, as well as my other colleagues at the University of East London – particularly Kate Hodgkin and Sarahleigh Castelyn, who have each supported this project in their own ways. I also want to thank my colleagues Pavlos Christodoulou and Benjamin Archer for holding down the fort during some of the more intensive writing periods. My sincere gratitude goes to the late Martin Heaney, who I was fortunate enough to have on my PhD supervisory team and whose influence will always be felt in my research.

I am incredibly grateful to the theatre makers who gave up their precious time to me over the past few years, particularly Hannah Stone, Ria Ashcroft, Corrinne Furness, Paul Smith, Jamie Potter, Jack Bradfield, Josie Davies, Stella Marie Sophie, Anoushka Bonwick, Elliot Hughes, Sam Ward, Emily Davis and Nathan Ellis. I am also very grateful for the support of a community of academic colleagues who are simultaneously attempting to work all this metamodern stuff out and wish to express particular gratitude to Greg Dember and Linda Ceriello for continually – and critically – supporting this community and to Antony Rowland for his development of the AHRC Metamodernism Research Network. Thanks, too, to Marissia Fragkou for initial support and belief in this book.

I am also incredibly grateful to series editors Enoch Brater and Mark Taylor-Batty whose advice and guidance has made this book so much stronger. Anna Brewer and Aanchal Vij at Bloomsbury have been guiding lights throughout this process, and I am very grateful for their support. A special thanks goes to Alex Brenner, who allowed us to use his beautiful shot of Danny Vavrečka's lighting for Nathan Ellis' *work.text* at Soho Theatre in 2022 as the cover image for this book.

Thanks, too, to the students across the years who have been enthusiastic, questioning, critical and excited about this research when applied to their teaching. Additionally, periods of teaching remission granted by the School of Arts & Creative Industries at the University of East London, and their

Acknowledgements xiii

support in attending a writing retreat, were also of invaluable help. Thanks also, as always, to my parents, Jean and Rodney, for their unwavering belief and genuine interest in my work.

I also want to take this opportunity to thank my brilliant, beautiful sons Bodie and Otis, who have both come into the world during the writing of this book, for every moment away from it. And finally, for the support, encouragement, hard-work, laughter, care, kindness, strength and everlasting patience of my wife, Bibi – thank you. I owe you one.

Notes on the Text

Part of Chapter 2 and part of Chapter 3 have been revised and expanded for this book from a previous version published as: Drayton, Tom. (2018) 'The Listening Theatre: A Metamodern Politics of Performance', *Performance Philosophy Journal*, 4 (1): 170–87. https://doi.org/10.21476/PP.2018.41200.

Parts of Chapter 4 and part of Chapter 5 have been revised and expanded for this book from a previous version published as: Drayton, Tom. (2020) 'Towards a Listening Theatre: Metamodernism, Millennials and Contemporary Political Theatre'. PhD Thesis, University of East London, School of Arts and Creative Industries. https://doi.org/10.15123/uel.88208.

Excerpts from MISTY copyright © 2018 Arinzé Kene. Reprinted with permission from Nick Hern Books.

Introduction

I confess I was hesitant to begin this book with the following anecdote. I am aware that, in telling it, I might make myself quite unpopular in certain circles. However, I feel that it is important to begin by recounting a moment that serves to illustrate some of the catalysts behind my decade-long preoccupation with attempting to unravel, map and understand the shifts in contemporary performance that I locate within this volume. As such, I would like to pre-emptively provide an apology to whoever feels they are owed one and emphasize that the following does not intend to detract from the quality of this company's work or their inarguably overall important contribution to the field of theatre within Britain and beyond over the best part of forty years. That being said, back when I was an undergraduate drama student, I couldn't *stand* Forced Entertainment.

To explain, we – a coterie of drama undergraduates who had been wedged into a coach before sprawling across the back of the cheap seats in the upper circle of a local theatre – had been taken on a trip to see the company's latest production as part of a module that focussed on postmodern performance. Whilst student engagement across the module itself had been largely positive, it became clear whilst watching this production that something about Forced Entertainment's application of the strategies we had been learning about just didn't *work* for us. One by one, my fellow students began to switch off. Some simply walked out during the performance (a protest hitherto unheard of by a cohort who had spent precious student-loan funds on subsidized tickets). Our tutor did not appear happy with these deserters and explained to us, in an exchange that I will never forget, that if we didn't *like* the performance, then we didn't *understand* the performance. It was our fault if we didn't find it entertaining. Our inadequate comprehension of the piece made it inaccessible. We simply weren't clever enough to enjoy it.

Whilst I naturally focus on my own experience for the purpose of this anecdote, this student-focussed walk out was not, in fact, a one-time occurrence. In his 2010 review of this performance – *The Thrill of It All* (2010) – at Riverside Studios in Hammersmith, London, Steve Carsmile (a self-proclaimed long-term fan of the company itself) notes that he was fascinated by the number of walkouts – particularly from students – which he contrasts with his own experience of seeing Forced Entertainment during his own studies in the early 1990s:

> There's always one or two [audience members who walk out] who have seen a non-specific review or come along with their mates and expect A Play, which it isn't, but there were probably twenty who were mainly, according to my sources, students from one particular performance course … which I find mind-boggling. When we first saw forced ents in 92 (possibly 93) we spent the rest of our time at college shamelessly ripping them off because they opened so many new doors for us, so to walk out an hour in … is, at its basest, to miss stuff you can nick. If there are more exciting and innovative companies out there I really want to know about them, is it just because the performers are mainly in their 40s now? That The Kids don't get it? (Carsmile 2010)

Whilst I refuse to subscribe to the idea that 'The Kids' simply didn't 'get' the work of Forced Entertainment in the early 2010s, or that the age of the performers or company is a deciding factor in such a reaction from the students, there is a pertinence in Carsmile's shocked comparison between the continual relevance of such work from the early 1990s onwards for himself and the apparent disregard displayed by this new generation of theatre makers. It also legitimized my own concerns regarding this reaction – in that my immediate peers were not the only group of students who behaved as such in reaction to this show. Of course, as a reviewer of the show for online magazine *A Younger Theatre* pointed out, in previous decades, Forced Entertainment – '*the* experimental theatre company of the 80s and 90s … revelled in their mid show walkouts and their letters of complaint from "Outraged! Of Oxfordshire"' (A Younger Theatre 2010). The same reviewer, however, goes on to explain how, for them, rather than outrage, the audience's dissatisfaction of this piece came from the fact that 'there was something desperately incomplete about the show. It felt thin and unoriginal … Perhaps', they go on to question, 'Forced Entertainment have lost their touch, perhaps with so many new and exciting theatre companies on the scene nowadays they have become outdated. Or perhaps, heaven forbid, I simply didn't get it' (A Younger Theatre 2010).

In returning to the memory of my own experience of *The Thrill of It All* again and again, I am sure that I have embellished, romanticized and 'cleaned up' certain elements in my remembering. As such, I cannot be certain that the following happened exactly as described – or even occurred during a different exchange entirely, perhaps in a follow-up seminar – or, in all honesty, is entirely fictitious. However, in my (probably edited) memory, what happens following this performance is this: a fellow student pipes up – possibly standing, revolutionarily, on a table – and exclaims,

> It's not that we don't understand it. We get it – it's literally *forced* entertainment. It's not meant to be entertaining, per se, and it's forced on us as an audience that, maybe, *expected* entertainment. Great concept – must have been ground-breaking at one point, surely. It disrupts the traditional theatrical expectations a typical audience will have. But why do we have to sit through it *now*? I have a slight suspicion that people are sitting there, annoyed at the experience, and pretending – to each other and themselves – that they're enjoying it. But they feel like they *should* enjoy it – otherwise they're just not cultured enough. Maybe that's the point, but I think that says more about the state of the British theatregoing public than of the company and their intentions … Anyway –

[Here, the student – who has admittedly spoken incredibly fluently for someone making this up on the spot – waves their hand dismissively and stands a little taller]

> My point is that the *forced entertainment* point's already been made. Great job all – and, now, we can move on. Now, we should move on. Now, we *want* to move on. Now, we *want* to be entertained. We want stories. We want connection. We want empathy. Yes, we want deconstruction and an end to the High Art/Low Art dichotomy.

['But isn't this kind of thing just *becoming* high art?' interjects another student, 'I mean, just look at who the audience were!']

> and we understand [*the first student continues, with an appreciative nod to the interjector*] the application of Barthes or Baudrillard to the realm of performance in a post-televisual culture. But – and here's the thing – it's got to be worth our while, doesn't it? It's all well and good saying this is postmodern performance, but who is it for? Who does it speak to? What, I dare say, is the point?

In my mind's eye, this rallying cry (itself a vast oversimplification and misrepresentation of Forced Entertainment's methodology) sends us – a legion of prospective performance makers in our own right – into battle; immediately charging into studios and developing new performances to challenge the work we supposedly weren't clever enough to enjoy. In reality, this speech was probably only a weakly proffered response during the coach-ride home and any effect upon me or my fellow students was largely brushed under the carpet when we went on to write the assigned critical essays in response to the piece. Despite my narrative embellishment, the point still stands; whilst, as undergraduates, we were engaging with what was considered contemporary performance methodologies, companies and theories – largely coalescing around both the postmodern and/or postdramatic (Lehmann 1999) – the strategies of creation and reception that we were being taught made sense at a historical and theoretical level but did not relate to our own – then current – lived experiences. Back in 2006, Alan Kirby noted the beginnings of this issue when reflecting on the fact that most of the students undertaking a module entitled 'Postmodern Fictions' that year

> will have been born in 1985 or after, and all but one of the module's primary texts were written before their lifetime. Far from being 'contemporary', these texts were published in another world, before the students were born … It's all about as contemporary as The Smiths, as hip as shoulder pads, as happening as Betamax video recorders. These are texts which are just coming to grips with the existence of rock music and television; they mostly do not dream even of the possibility of the technology and communications media … which today's undergraduates take for granted. (Kirby 2006)

Of course, the year after Kirby's observation saw the release of the iPhone, heralding instant, pocket-sized access to Web 2.0 across the world. The technological changes that Kirby was concerned with the year prior escalated at speed, and by the peak of the 2000s, the 'offstage' lived experience of my peers and I already blurred the boundaries between the offline and the digital space; our personal relationships being formed and developed as much – or even more so – online as they were in real life. Although, as millennials (which this book defines as those born between roughly the early 1980s and mid-1990s, but further clarification on this is detailed in Chapter 3), we had not reached the current level of digital integration that subsequent generations have been born into, we were the first early-life adopters of social medias in our teenage years – or even latter stages of childhood – the digital natives of the early 2000s (Bolton et al. 2013). To spend the night sharing details of your personal life with relative strangers over Tumblr whilst watching YouTube videos of intricately choreographed recreations of *High School Musical* (2006) dance sequences entirely performed by avatars in *The Sims 2* (2004), only to venture into a seminar the next day and be told that a performance in which avatars on online role-playing game *Second Life* (2003) clumsily and slowly recreate a scene from *Hamlet* whilst audience members awkwardly comment via a textbox is the height of cutting-edge performance technology and communication or a revolutionary trajectory for contemporary theatre seemed at best contradictory, if not already completely outdated. At the time, both performance theorists' and certain companies' respective focus on the complexities around the digitization of theatre at the turn of the twenty-first century through methods of integration between online technologies and the stage were labelled as emerging but were quickly becoming outmoded.

I am aware of my own oversimplification of (the teaching of) postmodern performance practice in this example, particularly through the above focus on inter-medial and digital performance. As Nick Kaye warns, any attempt at defining the characteristics of postmodern theatre 'must consider first all the difficulties that intrude upon any categorical definition of what the 'postmodern' actually is' (Kaye 1994: 1). As such, I offer a precis of postmodernity at its height by applying Victor Turner's 1990 analogy in which he locates the modalities of postmodernism as providing an impressive and exciting toolbox for theatre makers – postmodernism's liminality implying 'chaotic, fertile nothingness, that is potentially full of possibilities, that strives after new forms and structure' (Turner 1990: 12) – in order to encapsulate such a broad range of modalities, strategies and techniques. Whilst this is detailed further in Chapter 1, for the purposes of this introductory anecdote, a generalized overview of postmodern performance practice at the time included, but was not limited to, a non-hierarchical multiplicity of understanding, aesthetics and methodologies; a collaborative and participatory understanding of authorship; and an essential decentring of established (read: white, male, heterosexual, cisgendered and Eurocentric) theatre practice – all of which was essentially liberating in its catalysing of a myriad of aesthetic and practical performance methodologies that had, over the past few decades, broken the theatrical mould. However, certain foci within the teaching, research and performing of such strategies – during the time of my undergraduate degree at the turn of the 2000s – appeared outdated to my peers and I compared to our immersion within the early stages of Web 2.0. The apparent originality of a multi-authored text was lessened due to our everyday engagement with multi-authored online spaces. The integration of digital technologies into performance practices seemed arbitrary rather than groundbreaking as that was how we were already regularly communicating outside of (and often within) the theatre space. Even the implied open-ended multiplicity of semiotic meanings afforded to a text through a Barthesian lens (Barthes 1967) reflected the development of an endlessly self-referential (but primitive) online meme culture. As a generation, we could not escape (and perhaps even resided comfortably within) the irony, cynicism and open-ended meaninglessness that, somewhat inevitably, followed the deconstruction postmodernity facilitated – as that was the paradigm in which we were born and raised. However, it appeared to me at the time that my peers and I – whilst admittedly a very small pool of reference – desired something else from the performance practice that we were both creating and engaging with. Notwithstanding our understanding of the historical situatedness of postmodern deconstruction – as well as its cultural, political and philosophical value and impact – the artistic strategies, aesthetics and companies that fell under the postmodern bracket did not (and do not) reflect our current lived experience. Instead, certain artistic and aesthetic strategies within the work we began enjoying, viewing and engaging with – and the work some of us were creating – could not be suitably placed within the terminology of what has generally become labelled as postmodern performance. It felt like theatre was on the cusp of something – a turn, or a shift, towards something new – something beyond postmodernism.

 This book is about this shift into post-postmodern theatre practice. It is about work that appears to move beyond the realms of what can be comfortably labelled postmodern whilst continuing to trade in some of the elements and aesthetics that we would continue to consider postmodernist. It is about companies working on the fringes of the British theatre circuit who, in their own ways, have created work that exhibits something that feels new, distinct and different – whilst still, somewhat contradictorily, embracing and utilizing certain tropes, techniques and sensibilities attributed to postmodernism. These companies' works are concerned, for instance, with (a return to) storytelling, affect, engagement, connection and authenticity whilst continuing to – paradoxically – be disaffected, disengaged, disconnected, critical of (meta)narratives and overtly aware of theatre's inherent inauthenticity. Such shifts are therefore oscillatory and paradoxical – at once in/authentic, ironic/honest – or 'ironest' (Dember 2017b) – and hope/less. I am not the first to notice such trends throughout the past few decades, and it is through tracing the observations of similar or related trends made by other theatre scholars that, whilst these shifts towards paradoxical concerns appear at first to be independent aesthetic and methodological choices made by disparate theatre companies, when observed together, the interconnectivity between them becomes clear. Building from previous work that similarly argues that theatre is moving/has moved beyond postmodernity, this book argues that, far from being isolated aesthetics, choices or preoccupations made within a theatre-focussed vacuum, these changes are reflective of a wider cultural shift through and beyond the postmodern paradigm which affects, and in turn is affected by, these theatrical modalities – a wider cultural shift called metamodernism.

As an attempt at describing a cultural episteme or structure of feeling (see Chapter 1), the term metamodernism – as popularized by Robin van den Akker and Timotheus Vermeulen in 2010 – provides a language for the developing spate of cultural works that appear to embrace elements of the postmodern whilst also – simultaneously and even paradoxically – exhibiting a desire for, or strive towards, elements that seem antithetical to what we have come to see as 'traditional' postmodern preoccupations, aesthetics and practices. Turning towards the realm of theatre, this book locates such preoccupations within performances that oscillate between postmodern and seemingly modern preoccupations – between the silly and the serious, the ironic and the sincere, the hopeless and the hopeful; that appear to extol the power of participation, of storytelling and of the communal act of performance, whilst also remaining critical of the effectiveness of each; that are interested in the concept of authenticity – not in the sense of what we might traditionally refer to as an 'authentic' performance from a particularly skilled actor, but through, for instance, the authentic 'real' lives of the performers or audience becoming part of the performance – as well as embracing and exploiting the inherent inauthenticity of the theatrical medium; that are inherently metatheatrical but, rather than such metatheatricality being used to critique the theatrical medium, use metatheatrical devices to centre, strengthen and solidify the felt experience of the audience/performers/participants engaging in the performance; that embrace the paradoxical nature of performance being at once un/real and, rather than emphasizing the disconnect that this can cause in the audience, make use of such a paradoxical nature to re-centre the simultaneous un/reality of our feelings and emotions whilst experiencing a performance; that celebrate the inherent ridiculousness of theatre alongside the power of the communal act of audience and performers coming together to share an experience; that move beyond the ironic disconnect and disillusionment of postmodernity to offer a (tentative) (re)turn to sincere connection and engagement whilst remaining sceptical of such; that are silly, yes, but are also serious; that are ironic, yes, but also sincere; that are fake, yes, but also, somehow, very real.

Whilst scholars across other cultural fields have embraced metamodernism as a way to define an interconnected developing aesthetic or set of preoccupations within art (Turner 2015; Kovalova et al. 2022), film (MacDowell 2010, 2012, 2017; Flight 2023), music (van Poecke 2017; Dember 2019), literature (Gibbons 2017; Abramson 2018), poetry (Rowland 2021) and popular culture (Ceriello and Dember 2013), theatre scholarship has been largely hesitant to embrace this term. Over the past few years, a small number of theatre scholars have begun to (albeit sometimes hesitantly) envelop the term into their thinking as a way of beginning to devise a shared terminology for certain theatrical shifts within the wider cultural paradigm – including, but not limited to, Kemi Atanda Ilori (2014), Daniel Schulze (2017) and Benjamin Broadribb (2022). Additionally, the often-under-looked work of postgraduate students – including Nele Frieda Beinborn (2016), Nathan Sibthorpe (2018) and Nina Mitova (2020) – has also been pivotal in developing the thinking around how metamodernism can be located within contemporary theatre and where contemporary theatre sits within the wider metamodern paradigm. *Metamodernism in Contemporary British Theatre* builds on the work of these scholars to argue the case for the mainstream use of the term metamodernism within theatre scholarship. It proposes that the term can be used as a heuristic label through which to discuss specific contemporary shifts in post-postmodern theatre practice as well as to acknowledge that these shifts within contemporary theatre are, in fact, part of (by which I mean are reflective of and affected by, as well as influence and, in turn, develop) a broader shift happening within wider culture that has already been labelled metamodernism. As such, this is the first book to focus solely on the connectivity between contemporary theatre and the metamodern and offer a framework from which to understand what metamodern theatre is and can be. To achieve this, the volume builds a theoretical framework from the ground up – initially locating the links between theatre scholars' separate observations of shifting trends in contemporary performance, before illustrating how these trends fit within the framework of the metamodern as defined in wider cultural studies, and then reapplying both aspects towards a model through which we can define metamodern theatre. Through a specific focus on the experimental and genre-defying work created by millennial-led companies across Britain over (roughly) the past decade, including those who have been creating work on the fringes of the fringe theatre circuit, this book demonstrates how certain theatre practice across the country has shifted towards metamodernism, illustrated by the innovative work of a range of companies and theatre makers often under-represented within academic writing. As such, *Metamodernism in Contemporary British Theatre* builds a thesis from current literature on performance, develops this into a concise theoretical framework encompassing wider cultural studies and then provides detailed illustrations of the concepts in action in order to provoke further discussion.

Partly because the impetus for my focus on this topic came from my experience as an undergraduate, this book is written in such a way as to be accessible to students as well as researchers and theatre makers who are approaching the concept of the metamodern for the first time through a theatre- and performance-focused lens. Embracing a continual centring of felt-experience and embodied understanding, which – as will become clear – is central to the metamodern structure of feeling, I have threaded my own particular experience and understanding throughout this book. This introduction, for instance, began with an attempt at putting to words my initial *feeling* of experiencing Forced Entertainment's *The Thrill of It All* in 2010, and, throughout this book, I continue to build the academic analysis on, through and beyond my embodied experience as an audience member, a millennial, a theatre maker and performance scholar. As further detailed in Chapter 1, our experiencing of a theatrical production is inherently embodied. We encounter performance physically as well as (or as much as) cerebrally. As such, and in keeping with a similar focus within the definition of metamodernism in this volume, the writing in this book aims to oscillate, in some ways, between the personal and the academic, the embodied and the intellectual, the felt and the thought. Chapter 1, '(Already) beyond the postmodern', builds on the opening of this introduction's focus on Forced Entertainment, through my own embodied reflection on my peers' waning interest in 'postmodern strategies' across our own studies in the late 2000s, towards an illustration of how this embodied experience links to more recent observations of contemporary performance theorists who locate and describe the development of post-postmodern aesthetics and methodological strategies within contemporary performance; drawing on, for instance, the work of Anne Bogart, Daniel Schulze and Andy Lavender. Chapter 1 also traces instances of scholarly writing around the possibilities of metamodern theatre, compiling an essential catalogue of how metamodern theatre has begun to be understood by others through an analysis of the observations of both scholars who are focused on metamodernism in other cultural fields writing about theatre and scholars who are focussed on theatre, in turn, writing about metamodernism.

Chapter 2, 'Metamodernism', works as an introduction to metamodernism within broader culture. Through cataloguing several metamodern methods, strategies or aesthetics as defined by theorists across other cultural studies, this chapter develops a detailed definition of metamodernism both for the purposes of this volume and for further use within the field of performance studies. In part, this chapter aims to demystify the somewhat complicated development of the terminology, from Timotheus Vermeulen and Robin van den Akker's pivotal article 'Notes on Metamodernism' in 2010, which speculatively named the developing post-postmodern paradigm as metamodernism, and the somewhat contradictory definitions that have developed through this. It also, crucially, distances this volume's definition of the metamodern from social movements, manifestos and political ideologies that have appropriated the term alongside its use within cultural studies. The chapter defends metamodernism as the preferred understanding of the developed/ing post-postmodern structure of feeling, touching on alternative nomenclatures, and also offers an important clarification on how postmodernism is defined within this post-postmodern context, as well as the problematics regarding that in mapping what succeeds postmodernism, the postmodern itself risks becoming moulded to retroactively fit the map.

As the development from postmodernity to metamodernity is inherently linked to the development of the permacrisis throughout the 2000s–10s (cf. van den Akker and Vermeulen 2017: 17), the development of metamodern theatre is in turn affected by the generational experience of these 'emerging' companies which I locate as clearly exhibiting the metamodern theatrical shift. Specifically, how these theatre makers', performers', writers' and directors' economic, cultural, educational, political and sociological experience as millennials in Britain over the past two decades has influenced the development of the theatre that they (are able to) create as well as limited who is able to create any theatre in the first place. Chapter 3, 'The children of postmodernism: Hope/lessness', therefore focuses on understanding the role of the millennial generation in the context of both metamodernism and contemporary British theatre. After an initial breakdown of what the term millennial actually denotes – working through and beyond the negative connotations of the term as a media-based diatribe – the chapter argues that the millennial can instead be understood as a structure of feeling (Williams [1961] 1969). It contends that certain interconnected experiences specific to the millennial generation – including particular issues of precarity within employment and housing – combined with the generation's specific childhood experience within the relative peace and prosperity of the 1990s before entering their formative adult years in the emergence of the permacrisis (and development of Web 2.0) in the mid-2000s has developed a generational structure of feeling that centres around our being haunted by the prior promises of futures that can no longer come to be. Theatre has always been affected by, and reflective of, the political, economic, and cultural structures of the relative time, and the contemporary British theatre detailed within this book is likewise fundamentally connected to the generational experience of these millennial theatre makers. In the subchapter, "'Follow your passion": New Labour's impact on the British theatre scene', I further detail the experience of British millennials who found themselves studying theatre and performance in the 2000–10s and the effect that their emergence 'into an adult world where only one rule exists – the certainty of uncertainty' (Huntley 2006: 15) following this has affected their theatrical practice and, in turn, affected/s the development of metamodern theatre.

Chapter 4, 'Metamodern theatre: A spotter's guide', offers the first detailed catalogue of metamodern theatrical methods, aesthetics and strategies in order to define metamodern theatre. By focusing on three levels of analysis, this 'guide' continues with the focus on felt (or embodied) experience – detailing, in the first section, the overarching sensibilities that make a piece of theatre initially *feel* metamodern and which, I argue, are found infused throughout all metamodern theatre. The second section catalogues the theatrical aesthetics and forms of performance that emulate metamodern aesthetics as defined within other cultural practices and therefore serve to create, develop and/or strengthen the overarching metamodern sensibilities. Following this focus on form, the third section addresses examples of both the narrative themes and intertextual topics explored through these strategies that also, separately, emulate metamodern sensibilities in their textual make up. The chapter is subtitled 'A spotter's guide' to indicate how I hope it can be used – to provide a shared language and framework through which others can begin to pinpoint, discuss and define why a particular production feels metamodern rather than postmodern. Importantly, however, this is offered as a 'guide-in-progress' – a proposition for others to offer further development, debate and dialogue around what constitutes metamodern theatre practice.

Following this, the final – and largest – chapter of this book (Chapter 5) focuses on illustrating instances of metamodern theatre throughout Britain between 2012 and 2022 – concentrating specifically on productions developed by millennial-led companies that exhibit the metamodern sensibilities, aesthetic strategies and narrative themes as defined in Chapter 4. This chapter uses the 'spotter's guide' from Chapter 4 in order to analyse how ten productions from nine different companies exemplify the millennial and the metamodern as inherently symbiotic structures of feeling and illustrate how, over the past decade, theatre makers mostly working in Britain's vibrant Fringe Theatre scene are developing work that breaks the previous mould of postmodern practice in ways that reflect, build upon and – in turn – affect, the wider shift into the metamodern episteme. Whilst metamodernism – and metamodern theatre – is not purely exclusive to the theatre of the millennials, I offer that it is through the experimental, genre-defying work of these 'emerging' companies that real innovation – which both reflects and creates the metamodern theatrical form – is particularly evident.

Lastly, I offer an overview of (im)possible trajectories for such metamodern theatrical forms as new crises are laden on the incoming Gen Z theatre makers, with the caveat that this book is not a manifesto, nor a 'how-to guide' for those wishing to 'make' metamodern theatre. Rather than proposing a set of methodologies, strategies or aesthetics that I think theatre should embrace, *Metamodernism in Contemporary British Theatre* is an attempt at cataloguing and defining changes that have already happened, whether we label them metamodern or not. I do not suggest that the theatre makers in this volume go into the studio with the express desire to create metamodern theatre – in fact, most – if not all – of them had never heard of the term until I introduced them to it and, in some cases, are completely indifferent to any such label. Instead, this volume aims to offer new and timely documentation and analysis of pre-existing shifts in contemporary performance practice by drawing together and building upon recent theorists' observations to discern how metamodernism, as already determined in other cultural fields, can be used to gather-together, explain and contextualize these shifts. It illustrates how these shifts can be seen in action through new analyses of previously undocumented companies, whose position as millennials is intrinsically linked to the post-postmodern shift both politically and culturally. Through this, I aim to provide an important starting point for further, vital enquiry and analysis of metamodernism within the field of theatre and performance.

1

(Already) beyond the postmodern

This volume is concerned with what exists beyond postmodern performance practice. As such, it is inherently intertwined with the postmodern, as to define the *post*-postmodern requires an inescapable comparison *to* the postmodern. But just what *is* postmodernism? What is postmodern performance? And, if something exists beyond, or follows, postmodern performance practice, *when* did this change happen? When did postmodernism end? *Has* it ended? The answers are, of course, complicated – in part because the meanings of the terms 'postmodernism' and 'performance' are so malleable and ever-shifting. As Phillip Auslander notes, 'The conceptual complications of the relationship between postmodernism and performance derive from the instability of both terms, neither of which has a single, universally agreed-upon meaning' (Auslander 2004: 97). As such, any definition of the interstitial relationship between postmodernism and performance negotiates a particularly liquid, ever-shifting framework. This book is not the place to attempt to solidify such a definition. However, I am acutely aware of the trappings of generalizing the discourse surrounding postmodernity and performance. Even back at the turn of the century, Dave Robinson noted the liquidity of postmodernity as a critical or cultural frame of reference or understanding, claiming that 'nobody really knows' (Robinson 1999: 35) what the term meant as it had become 'perhaps just a convenient label for a set of attitudes, values, beliefs and feelings about what it means to be living in the late 20th century' (ibid.). In an attempt at reconciling this problem, I share Robin van den Akker and Timotheus Vermeulen's understanding of the nomenclature of postmodernism (and metamodernism) as an attempt to put to words a rhizomatic structure that is (or was) manifest in a form of 'cultural logic, a certain dominant ideological patterning that leaves its traces across culture' (Vermeulen and van den Akker 2015a). Throughout this volume, as detailed in the next section, Raymond Williams's application of the term 'structure of feeling' (1969) is used as a way of negotiating this liquidity – enabling a verbal understanding of a modality that is both 'as firm and definite as "structure" suggests, yet ... based in the deepest and often least tangible elements of our experience' (Williams 1969: 18). Whilst the term structure of feeling can be a mouthful, it is used within this volume – in part – to continue to centre the focus on felt-experience as central to my understanding of metamodernity and metamodern theatre. However, this understanding of a dominant cultural logic within a shifting time-frame can also be understood through Michel Foucault's epistemes (1970), through which he developed a language by which to discuss the implicit 'underlying code of a culture or epoch that governs its language, its logic, its schemas of perception, its values and its techniques' (O'Leary and Chia 2007: 392). For Foucault, each historical period has its own epistemological conventions, ways of thinking and cultural possibilities. Whilst *The Order of Things: An Archaeology of the Human Sciences* (published in the original French in 1966) was primarily concerned with modernity (following Foucault's analysis of the renaissance and the classical era), his epistemological model has been adapted towards postmodernism (and post-postmodernism) by Greg Dember and Linda Ceriello, who translate Foucault's model onto contemporary epistemes, defining the shift from tradition to modernism to postmodernism and to metamodernism as an epistemological development. For Dember the 'pre-modern' episteme is tradition – in which the focus within culture is 'the transmission of crucial knowledge and culture from the past' (Dember 2018), with cultural artefacts of this period working to 'reify the unassailable wisdom of the old and the cyclical nature of reality' (ibid.). The episteme of modernism (which differs from Foucault's understanding of 'moder*nity*' emerging around the 1500s) began in the nineteenth century, breaking from tradition by 'emphasizing invention, intention, seeing below surface layers to (what are perceived as) essential structures, and making clear delineations by ranking, rating or typologizing things' (ibid.). In theatre, the modern episteme is largely said to have become evident in a shift towards performance that interrogated traditional theatrical methodologies, as dramatists started to prioritize the inner workings of their characters and how to best reflect them on stage – in response, in part, to developments within the field of psychology. This is not to imply that all modernist drama was naturalistic or realistic, but that theatre within modernism was concerned with how *best* to portray this new way of looking at (often inner) reality. Modernist theatre, in this sense, includes 'the Symbolists, the Futurists, the Expressionists, the Surrealists' (Leach 2004: 1) and the varied work of dramatists such as 'Stanislavsky, Meyerhold, Brecht and Artaud' (ibid.). In the mid-twentieth century, however, the postmodern episteme emerged, which, as according to Dember, sought to 'correct modernism's hubris through irony, playful juxtaposition, bringing attention to subcultures that are outside the dominant, [and] the re-elevation of traditional patterns rejected by modernism' (Dember 2018). Further detail on theatre within the postmodern episteme follows further on but can be summarized, for now, as performance within the latter half of the twentieth century that attempted to 'dissolve existing ways of perceiving the world and one-self' (Saner 2001) through such strategies as pastiche; parody; critique; fragmentation and randomness; a lack of optimism; a destabilizing of the playwright and/or director's authorial intent alongside an acceptance that every audience member's 'reading' (or experience) of a piece will, of course, be different because it will be based on their own individual life experiences; as well as a deconstruction of (the performance of) character, (the structure of) narrative and the 'expected' audience-performer relationship. As further detailed in the following section, *A Structure of Feeling*, when understood as parts in a series of continually developing structures of feeling or epistemes, the terms modernism and postmodernism (and metamodernism) refer to respective assemblages of almost intangible, and yet experiential, modalities apparent within a particular cultural time-frame that are 'essentially related, although in practice, and in detail, this is not always easy to see' (Williams 1969: 17). As Vermeulen and van den Akker recapitulate from Williams, this application of the term *structure* of feeling refers to a 'sensibility that is widespread enough to be called structural … yet cannot be reduced to one particular strategy' (Vermeulen and van den Akker 2015a).

When taken this way – without intending to reduce the scope of performance practices that fall within the bracket of postmodernism – we can broadly consider specific, interconnected and experiential modalities that make up the main elements of the postmodern structure of feeling within theatre and the performing arts as outlined by previous scholars throughout the latter stage of the twentieth century. In attempting to define the impact of postmodernism within theatre, for example, Phillip Auslander turns to Elinor Fuch's 1983 treatise *The Death of Character* in which she defines the 'harbinger of postmodernism in theatre [as] a de-emphasis of the modern concept of psychologically consistent dramatic characters in favour of fragmented, flowing and uncertain identities whose exact locations and boundaries cannot be pinpointed' (Auslander 2004: 103). As Fuchs explains,

> The result, seen in a decade of experimental group work, and in a number of striking new plays and adaptations of classics, has been a stage turned curiously in upon itself, blurring the old distinctions between self and world, being and thing; and doing so not through a representation of the outside word but through the development of a performance art 'about' itself. (Fuchs 1996: 170)

It is the 'collapse', for Fuchs, of particular 'traditional' boundaries 'between cultures, between sexes, between the arts, between disciplines, between genres, between criticism and art, performance and text, sign and signified' (ibid.) that exemplified the postmodern within theatre and performance at the end of the previous century. Phillip Auslander goes on to marry such collapse, or fragmentation, with his definition of postmodern theatre, drawing on the concept of cultural collages – with specific reference to Elizabeth LeCompte's New York-based company, The Wooster Group, 'juxtaposing texts and performance elements in various styles and connecting the play with other cultural texts to produce a hybrid' (ibid.: 106). As Judith Hamera posited around the time of Fuchs's dying character, postmodern performance is 'often both fragmented and highly subjective' (Hamera 1986: 18), drawing on Richard Schechner's earlier defining of postmodern performance practice as nonnarrative (Schechner 1979: 21). Hamera posits that Schechner, here, is 'making a focused application of a fundamental "tenet" of postmodernism' (Hamera 1986: 15) onto the critical study of performance practice – that of Lyotard's defining of the postmodern as an 'incredulity towards metanarratives' (Lyotard 1984: xxiv) reflected, in the performing arts, 'in the dissolution of narrative continuity and narrative forms [to be replaced by] a plural, fragmented reality' (Hamera 1986: 16). This effect is then amplified when taken alongside Roland Barthes's (1967) removal of authorial authority in appreciation of the multiplicity of readings of a given audience. If the naturalism favoured by narrative-driven modernist drama strove to be representational, states Auslander (2004), (some) postmodern performance practice can therefore be identified as being non-representational or *anti*representational. 'Just as Character once supplanted Action', writes Fuchs, 'so Character in turn is being eclipsed' (1996: 171). Perhaps, she muses, instead of Character and Action 'holding dominion over Music, Diction, Thought and Spectacle' (ibid.: 176), postmodern theatre replaced narrative drama with a 'flux' – an anti-hierarchical mixture of Aristotle's six elements of Drama (ibid.: 175). As Henke and Middeke proffer, through such amalgamation, postmodern artworks (often) embrace 'a fascination for self-reflexive, metadramatic modes which reflect on epistemological uncertainty [and] ambiguity [;] fragmented formal structures: collages, cut-up forms, paradox, pastiche, parody – signifiers that [in contradiction to traditional drama] disperse unidirectional attributions of fixed meanings, intentions, or propositions' (Henke and Middeke 2007: 13).

Of course, as Karen Jürs-Munby explains, Hans-Thies Lehmann's pivotal appropriation of the term 'postdramatic' in 1999 articulated 'the relationship between drama and the "no longer dramatic" forms of theatre' (Lehmann 2006: 1) – providing a new terminology for performance studies that has become ingrained within analysis of contemporary performance practices in the postmodern paradigm. Whilst Fuchs's focus was largely on text,

Lehmann also considered the aesthetics of time, space and body with equal weight in understanding how theatre had moved through and beyond the dramatic. In doing so, Lehmann also situated this shift in theatrical aesthetics in conjunction with the wider shift from a text-based culture to a mediated one throughout the twentieth century. And yet, given the wider situatedness offered by Lehmann, this volume is not primarily concerned with building on, or deviating from, the postdramatic as a frame of reference. There is a contention, here, in regard to how the postdramatic has become so intertwined with discussions around the postmodern within performance studies that there becomes an uneasy inability to speak of postmodern performance – or performance that includes postmodern modalities, aesthetics or trends – without explicitly referring to the postdramatic. However, in defining postdramatic performance, Lehmann was particularly concerned with, as Jürs-Munby explains, 'tracing a trajectory from *within* theatre aesthetics' (Lehmann 2006: 14; emphasis in original) rather than, as Jürs-Munby quotes from Wessendorf (2003), 'the application of a general cultural concept [i.e. postmodernism] to the specific domain of theatre'. Whilst the performance methodologies, aesthetics and modalities explored throughout this volume's focus on metamodern theatre come from an attempt to explore how metamodernism – a trend that has been traced as a wider cultural concept as per Wessendorf's misgivings – is manifest, too, within contemporary performance, this volume does not attempt to apply a general concept onto the field of theatre and performance. However, neither is it wholly analogous to Lehmann's tracing of modal shifts solely from within theatre aesthetics. Instead, I aim to explain and explore how certain shifts through and beyond postmodernity – that have been located as part of the metamodern shift within wider and popular culture – are *also* happening within the fields of theatre and performance. It is an unpacking of both contemporary performance practice and the wider metamodern shift so as to illustrate the interstice between these two frames of reference and to demonstrate how aesthetic, methodological and political shifts within contemporary theatre practice exemplify the metamodern shift within wider culture.

My focus on postmodernism over the postdramatic in defining what metamodern performance both builds upon and grows beyond depends then, too, on an essential understanding of the wider epistemological shifts occurring around developments in theatre from modernity, through postmodernity and into metamodernity, whilst centring how these communicate with particular shifts in theatre and performance. In the next section, I offer a brief echo of Lehmann's 'tracing from the inside', detailing how certain shifts in practice that have been located and defined by performance scholars, including Andy Lavender and Anne Bogart, are examples of such communication – in that their location of changing modalities and aesthetics from the turn of the century to the present coalesce around the wider cultural framework of the metamodern (as defined in Chapter 2). For now, however, it is important to note that my focus on the post*modern* in this volume over Lehmann's post*dramatic* enables a wider frame of reference to be employed and also serves to illustrate the point that metamodern theatre does not, per se, supplant postdramatic forms of practice but, instead, continues to engage in postdramatic strategies. In this sense, metamodern theatre is inherently postdramatic, as it does not revert (back) to dramatic drama. But not all (contemporary) postdramatic theatre – as defined by Lehmann and his contemporaries – is metamodern. Therefore, in the context of this study, post*modernism* refers to an '*age* of simulation and fragmentation' (Schulze 2017: 13, emphasis added) in which the '"classic" postmodern tropes of detachment, irony and contingency' (Lavender 2016: 3) permeate both wider (and popular) culture as well as performance practices. It is an understanding of postmodernity as a 'cultural logic' (Vermeulen and van den Akker 2015a) – embracing Lyotard's 'simplifying to the extreme' of the postmodern as 'incredulity towards metanarratives' (1984) combined with Vermeulen's 'ironic detachment' (Gorynski 2018). This definition does not intend to detract from the understanding of postmodernism as a critical methodology or an important emancipatory movement (ibid.) but to emphasize that postmodernity's 'ground tone [is of] irony and relativism' (ibid.).

To return to my theatre-undergraduate-based anecdote about Forced Entertainment's *The Thrill of It All* (2010) which opened this book, if, back then, I had such a reaction to the piece – which, on reflection, has something to do with it being situated in a soon-to-become if not already outmoded postmodern paradigm – how exactly was the piece exemplary of postmodern performance practice? In 2010, *The Thrill of It All* was familiar Forced Entertainment territory (Taylor and Roberts 2010); 'as with much of the work that has preceded it,' noted Alexander Roberts in his review, the company 'creates a world that enjoys the beauty of failure and the accomplishments and creativity that come from that' (Taylor and Roberts 2010). The piece itself is built around the idea that the audience are invited to experience a 'good time', to be entertained – Elvis-style quiffs and blonde wigs adorn a cast dressed in sparkly suit jackets and flapper dresses. However, as Lyn Gardner's (2010) review of the piece explains, 'It soon becomes clear that everything is fake and rubbish ... Even the dancing is [purposefully] crap: people bump into each other; scuffles and fights break out. The fixed smiles crack and turn venomous' (Gardner 2010). The piece is

(Already) Beyond the Postmodern 19

exemplary of the company's 'impulse towards a self-reflexive emancipation from a dependence on conventional strategies of narration and reception' (Gritzner 2008: 338) in their use of fragmented structures, a dissolution of narrative forms, an interest in performing a dissection of what 'performing' is and of what an expected relationship between performers and audience is over the performance of character, story or entertainment. If the ground tone of postmodernity is irony and relativism – of cynicism even – *The Thrill of It All*'s use of such structures is exemplary of postmodern performance. The show questions the idea that a theatre company has a responsibility to provide entertainment to an audience in such a way that diminishes the entertainment factor of the piece. Disconnection, failure and cynicism prevail.

In a 1998 interview, Forced Entertainment performer Claire Marshall expressed a view that would disagree with my application of the term postmodern onto the work of the company, in that she thinks it 'has become a bit of a dirty word ... that suggests that everything is very ironic, very cynical and very removed' (McGuire 1998: 11). She suggested, twelve years prior to *The Thrill of It All*, that postmodernity might not be a 'good description [of their work] because a lot of what we do contains a lot of cynicism, a lot of anger, and there is also a lot of naivete and hope and innocence in the things that we want to make happen onstage' (ibid.) and that the company 'don't set out to make a Postmodernist piece of work' (ibid.). It is an interesting outlook – particularly when, as will become clear over the following chapters, such oscillation between cynicism and hope is exemplary of what has become labelled metamodernism as it developed out of postmodernity. However, despite the company's previous intentions, *The Thrill of It All* does not exemplify such a post-postmodern dichotomy and, instead, revels in the cynicism, irony and deconstruction of what I see as postmodern performance practice's climatic last hurrah – a bookend to a paradigm manifest as performance that is 'contemptuous towards both the cast that performed it and the audience' (Taylor and Roberts 2010). Whilst Jürs-Munby suggests that the company's name 'leaves it open whether it is us or them who are being 'forced' to entertain or be entertained' (Lehmann 2006: 5), *The Thrill of It All*'s conceit being based around a failing performance in which, because of how the show is intentionally structured, the audience experience is one of disconnect and contention means that the 'show unravels [and] the spectacle of theatre is revealed and examined', as Bryony Byrne (2010) states in her review; '[as such ... t]his is indeed "forced entertainment"'.

Some may see my issues with this as a disavowal of postmodern performance practice (and/or a company that has delivered inarguably important contributions to the field for several decades) that deals at once in the broadest strokes and offers an example of a single production that is itself over a decade old. I am aware that in choosing to begin this volume largely through my own embodied reaction to a singular performance, I therefore become vulnerable to specific criticism regarding the validity and wider applicability of such an argument. And yet, so much of what is to come throughout this volume is purposefully based in embodied understanding. This is for three main reasons. Firstly – it is through such embodiment that we experience and understand theatre; performances are not only experienced cerebrally but physically and emotionally. As such, any understanding or meaning making that comes from interrogating such practices comes from a position of embodied understanding. Secondly – such embodiment is extended to the specific historical situatedness of my peers and I as what I have come to label the (British) Children of Postmodernism and how particular cultural, economic and political structures that have coalesced throughout our childhood and formative adult years have had an integral effect upon our embodied understanding of performance. To ignore such positioning of our readings of performance within these wider structures – and how this positioning in turn affects our art – is to omit an integral aspect of understanding, particularly in regard to a post-postmodern structure of feeling. Thirdly – as will become clear throughout the following chapters, in opposition to the ever-disconnected, cold deconstruction of postmodernity, the affective post-postmodern turn allows space for emotions and affect to return as central motifs and important foci in the reading of performance. As film theorist Pansy Duncan makes clear in her unravelling of emotion's re-emergence through and beyond the postmodern, 'Where the critical stocks of affect and emotion are on the ascendant, those of postmodern theory and aesthetics must be on the wane' (Duncan 2015: 37) – a sentiment echoed by performance theorist Andy Lavender, when he observes a development towards performances that 'connect more overtly with social process [and] a pronounced form of personal experience' (Lavender 2016: 3). Of course, in summarizing (the problematics of) postmodern practice through broad strokes and offering only one example of such practice, I have simplified a wide-reaching field of thought and performance culture to an extreme. However, it is not the role of this volume to further detail postmodern practice. Rather, this volume attempts to unravel what is developing/has developed post postmodernism's reign. To summarize, however, for the purposes of the following discussion, postmodern performance practice builds through Barthes's killing of the author towards a disavowal of narrative and character-driven drama (Fuchs 1996), often deconstructing traditional notions of what an audience would come to expect from a performance towards anti-representational, often trans-mediated, cultural collages. In simple terms, postmodernity offered a fertile playground (cf. Turner 1990) for performance makers – by breaking down the traditional rules and cultural boundaries into interconnected and moveable pieces. As Lavender states, 'Theatre has been exploded' (Lavender 2016: 9) and, following this explosion, the '"classic" postmodern tropes of detachment, irony and contingency' (ibid.: 3) became, in some ways, the new normal. However, as Lavender continues, following theatre's destructive explosion, 'it has regathered' (ibid.: 9) and, instead of such sensibilities reigning supreme, we find work that values and extols the power of terms and sensibilities that oppose these 'classic' postmodern tropes – work preoccupied with terms such as connection, empathy, authenticity and narrative. Whilst at first glance such focus might seem like a cyclical return to the trappings of modernism or a simple rejection of the complexities of postmodernity, this is (as will become clear) not the case but, instead, a vacillation between aspects of the two without negating one another. A new paradigm of performance is being (re)built from the fractured pieces created through postmodernist performance modes – something not wholly resembling the old but not wholly new either. As such, the work of concern in this volume doesn't indicate a return to modernism. Nor does it indicate a complete departure from the postmodern. Instead, this volume is concerned with work which indicates that pure reliance on 'classic' postmodern tropes doesn't seem to hold the same overarching relevance within both contemporary performance practice and the wider cultural structure of feeling that has emerged throughout the 2010s. As my peers and I made clear following our theatre trip at the turn of that decade, we both wanted to see (or experience) and create something *more* – something *beyond* what we were sold as contemporary (read: postmodern) performance practice. Over the next ten years, it would become clear that other students, companies and artists were doing the same and that – additionally – performance theorists were beginning to notice different shifts through and beyond the 'classic' postmodern tropes. If Judith Hamera's 1986 unpacking of postmodern performance practice can be seen as a hermeneutics of such, the following is my similar attempt in regard to collating a hermeneutics of contemporary performance – in that such scholars are, separately, noticing newly developing trends within contemporary theatre over the past decade. When these observations of such trends are taken individually, they are fascinating examples of developments beyond certain postmodern practices. It is when they are observed collectively, however, that it becomes clear that these developments are parts of an interconnected structure of feeling developing within contemporary theatre that clearly echoes what scholars outside of performance studies – particularly in the fields of literature and popular media – have defined as the structure of feeling that is succeeding/has succeeded the postmodern as the dominant cultural paradigm – metamodernism.

Mapping metamodernism: Traces of a new paradigm

Three women jump around the small, brick-walled basement that serves as the stage of the Bike Shed Theatre in Exeter, Devon. Lights flash along to thumping bass as moisture collects on the bare walls. The women wear brightly coloured balaclavas and shout – no, scream – protests through megaphones. The sound of their chanting bounces loudly around the confined space. The audience, who have only just sat down, are acutely aware of the group's homage to the Russian activist punk band Pussy Riot, two members of which had been arrested for their protest action in Moscow only the year before in 2012. In a moment, the vibe of the performance will shift to one of calm conversation, as the women on stage take off their disguises and talk to us. One of them will tell us the story of the nervousness they experienced in attending their first protest at a G8 gathering. Another will hold up a sign that simply proclaims, 'I feel ignorant'. The third will share some pictures of cats that they have recently fostered. They will ask us about our own relationship with political activism, about what would make us want to protest. As female-led company The Gramophones' *Playful Acts of Rebellion* (2013) continues, it is revealed that one of the usual company members is absent from the performance. For a show whose premise is built around a discussion between the tight-knit group of performers and the audience regarding our experiences of protest and activism, the fourth member's absence starts to become noticeable. And then, in a moment that provides a glimpse outside of the space we are currently sharing, the fourth company member *does* join the other women on stage. There is no 'enter stage left', however. Instead, video feed is projected onto a large placard – allowing us to see her from the comfort of her own home, which, at this point, becomes part of the performance space. We see her bookshelf behind her, the sun on the wall, a radiator. She now has the opportunity to tell us about her own complicated relationship with political activism and reveals that she couldn't join the rest of the company on this tour in person as she is currently on maternity leave.

There are glimpses, here, beyond the red-bricked basement of The Bike Shed theatre (which sadly closed in 2018) and beyond the theatricality of this performance – beyond, even, the inherent inauthenticity of performing a facsimile of Pussy Riot – towards a sensation of 'real world' authenticity permeating the theatrical space, with both the performers' and audience's own lives outside of the theatrical event becoming integral to the content and aesthetics of the performance itself. Seven years later, amidst the backdrop of the Covid-19 pandemic, the theatre-going audience (and general public), of course, became all-too-familiar with the image of someone joining a performance, a meeting or even just a family get-together, virtually – from their own home – via a webcam. As the country went into lockdown, work, socialization and entertainment moved online. In the British theatre scene, whilst there was an effort to provide recorded and livestreamed versions of stage performances to the locked-in public, such as the National Theatre's *NT at Home* project, there were also significant developments in utilizing video conferencing software such as Zoom as a mode of performance, rapidly repurposing its 'Gallery-View' interface as a virtual theatrical space.

In June of 2020, I found myself sitting in my living room with my wife, staring at a laptop screen, on which was a collection of other audience members in their own living rooms, bedrooms and kitchens – all facing each other in our little Zoom boxes. Joining us from separate spare bedrooms or home offices were two performers from Bristol-based company Uninvited Guests. The group has been performing their show *Love Letters Straight from Your Heart* to audiences round the country in an in-person capacity since 2007, and in the midst of the first 2020 lockdown had repurposed the show towards a Zoom-based, online form. The format of the piece involves each audience member submitting anonymous song dedications prior to the performance, with the two performers playing these songs and reading out the dedications of love – in its many forms – throughout the show. The experience for an audience, here, is built around the possibility of having your own choice of song played and dedication read whilst also knowing that every anonymous submission – some of which are incredibly touching, funny, personal or even heart-breaking – has been written and submitted by another audience member who is currently in the performance space with you. Every performance of the show is filled with different songs and dedications that are unique to that particular audience, in that particular space and at that particular time.

The company's transferral of this format to Zoom within the context of nationwide lockdown – retitled *Love Letters at Home* – transposed the physical intimacy between the audience members to a virtual space. Despite the physical distance between us as an audience, whilst we watch each other react to the dedications or nod our heads to the music from across unknown distances (instead of across a long, banquet table as per the original, onstage show), the perceived *feeling* of intimacy is still there. As Joanne Scott describes in regard to similar, Zoom-based, lockdown era performances, such works are computationally centred in that the space and locus of the encounter between audience and performance/performer is a networked application accessed through a computational device. The device and its processes necessarily sit at the centre of the work as a node of connection between the physically distant bodies at play [and yet there] are degrees of co-presence here. (Scott 2022: 73)

Regarding *Love Letters at Home*, these degrees of co-presence are heightened in the emotionality of the performance process. These are intimate moments of our real lives that we are sharing together. One member of a couple suddenly becomes embarrassed, or giggles uncontrollably or begins to cry as it becomes clear that their counterpart has written a dedication to them. We then listen to a beautiful dedication to someone's late mum. We scour the faces of the audience members in their living rooms. We may never know who wrote it, who chose to share this grief with the company and, by extension, us. And yet, we have all shared in an act of listening together – attending to what these audience members wanted to say about the person/s that they, in some way, love. Benjamin Broadribb labels this feeling of 'concurrent togetherness and separation' (2022: 45) imbued through such Zoom-based performances as *together-apartness*, suggesting that the pandemic 'amplified and catalysed this sensibility which already defined the opening decades of the twenty-first century' (ibid.) and that, perhaps, 'the defining signifier of our together-apart existence during the pandemic is the stratospheric rise of Zoom' (ibid.: 51) which, paradoxically, both 'simultaneously facilitat[es] affective connection ... *and* reduc[es] our friends, our families, ourselves, into depthless low-definition digital duplicates' (ibid.: 52; emphasis in original). As Uninvited Guests' show reaches a climax, we digital duplicates are asked to dance. We (whether easily or begrudgingly – for me, I admit, it is the latter) stand up and shuffle awkwardly in our own rooms. But, slowly, the performers – and the music – encourage us further; we have, after all, started to become comfortable in this virtual space built out of disparate and yet somehow connected living rooms. The screen soon becomes a blur of tiny dancing figures: a couple in a ballroom-dance embrace, a family doing the twist, an older woman nodding her head on a sofa. We, in our own ways, dance along to a song at once both cringe inducingly cliched and beautifully perfect for the moment – Joy Division's *Love Will Tear Us Apart*, possibly, or Madness' *It Must Be Love*. I can't quite remember the song – just the feeling of Broadribb's together-apartness as we danced along in our own little Zoom boxes – physically distanced, yes, but joined together in a shared experience.

Then, suddenly, the space on screen is disrupted. The performers grab their laptops and remove them from their desks. Our views of them on

Zoom dramatically shift as the stationary webcam angles that we had become accustomed to over the past hour change and become mobile. There's a sudden sense of freedom – the Zoom-based frames of their existence quite literally opening up. As they dance with their laptops around their rooms, they give us glimpses of their separate 'backstage' spaces – cables, microphones, a cup of tea. They spin us around – their Zoom-box a jumble of extended arms, beaming smile and blurred, spinning background. And then – with the lovesong still playing from their laptops and ours – they leave their rooms, but they take us with them. We are carried down flights of stairs, through living rooms, into kitchens. One performer's family is clearing up after dinner, and we join them in the kitchen – still dancing. The performer brings their child into an embrace – puts the laptop on the kitchen counter and (forces) encourages their child to dance with them. The child is sheepish, but they join in. We see the performer's fridge, the dishwasher halfway loaded, the child naturally embarrassed by having to join in with their parent's work. Not only have Uninvited Guests facilitated a space in which we – as an audience – were able to share glimpses into our own lives outside of the theatrical event, but they now open up their own homes to us – bringing themselves and their lives, not just their performance-focussed personas, into the piece. As we see them embrace – and dance with – the people that *they* love, their lived reality – their authentic lives – become a central part of the performance experience.

The Gramophones' *Playful Acts of Rebellion* and Uninvited Guests' *Love Letters at Home*, of course, reflect Lehmann's understanding of postdramatic performance practices in that they are examples of theatre that is no longer concerned with a focus on the dramatic (cf. Lehmann 2006). Neither shows include traditional ideas of character, plot or dramatic tension in their makeup. Whilst both include elements of storytelling – *Playful Acts of Rebellion* in its focus on the company members telling the audience the stories of their protests and *Love Letters at Home* in articulating stories donated by the audience in the form of song dedications – the foundation of each piece is not dramatic narrative, but is, rather, reflective of Hamera's understanding of the postdramatic as a 'plural, fragmented reality' (1986: 16). In fact, the focus of each piece appears to be facilitating some sort of emotive connection between those in the 'room' (whether virtual or in-person), with a heavy focus (whether directly intentional or not) on authenticity (the slippery terminology of which will be addressed soon). This authenticity manifests itself within both shows through the authentic personas of the performers (over their performative selves) becoming an intrinsic part of the performance – of the Gramophones' fourth company member's living room being 'beamed' onto the stage, of Uninvited Guests' children getting dragged into a dance party. It manifests itself, too, in the material generated by the audience (although there is the possibility, of course, that certain audience members' input could be intentionally inauthentic). This authentic 'feel' is heightened by our being able to, in the case of *Love Letters at Home*, see the responses of other audience members to this material as their dedication to a loved one gets read out, or they are surprised to hear a dedication read about them. Throughout both pieces are threaded aesthetics of care, of connection, of – dare I say it – love. These are postdramatic pieces in that they no longer concern themselves with dramatic conventions, but their key aesthetics mark a differentiation from the irony and depthlessness (Jordan 2019: 2) associated with postmodern performance practice. This is not to say that these performances are wholly sincere or entirely concerned with facilitating depthiness (cf. Gibbons, Vermeulen and van den Akker 2019) over irony and relativism. Instead, they offer fluctuations between sincerity and irony, between depth and depthlessness, between engagement and disconnect. Participating in *Love Letters at Home*, we fluctuate between feeling disconnected from each other through the webcam-focused, boxed-off nature of our existence as an audience 'within' this digital space and feeling incredibly connected with each other through participating within the structure of the performance that Uninvited Guests provide. It is an oscillation between connection and disconnection – a feeling of being dis/connected that permeates our theatrical experience. This oscillation between seemingly opposing or disconnected states, as will become clear, is threaded throughout the performances examined within this volume: a 'heightened separateness and connection' (Broadribb 2022: 47), a fluctuation between seemingly postmodern predilections and … something else. In my own watching of, and participating in, performances by predominantly 'emerging' (to use the flawed industry terminology) companies[1] around Britain in the past decade, it became clear that my perspective on these works, and how they related to each other, did not fit comfortably within the 'tradition' of postmodern or postdramatic performance practice. Yes, they exhibited postdramatic and postmodern elements in their make-up, but the oscillation between paradoxical aesthetics gave me pause. Put simply, these works just didn't 'feel' postmodern. Whilst they shared some similar postdramatic and postmodern aspects with, say, Forced Entertainment's *The Thrill of It All*, the disconnection used within such performances also shared space with an attempt at sincere connection, the irony swung towards sincerity and back

---

[1] Whilst Uninvited Guests are not one of these companies, their inclusion serves to illustrate that metamodern theatre practice is not explicitly confined to work created by the millennial generation.

again, the inherently inauthentic theatricality met with an attempt towards facilitating some form of authenticity.

In *The Death of Character*, Elinor Fuchs describes her own struggles with identifying what was going on in her own experience as an audience member, critic and theorist in New York City in the early 1990s. She mentions how seeing new work across the city and, in turn, writing reviews about that work for newspapers, teaching students and reading 'theory' (the brilliantly slightly sarcastic quotation marks are hers) instigated and developed her thinking on theatre *after* modernism (Fuchs 1996: 1). She describes the driving force behind this, however, as embodied in herself and her own experience, relating her 'search for a language in which to describe new forms, forms that have appeared both in actual theatres and in the theatricalized surrounds of contemporary public life and discourse' (ibid.). The theatre she was experiencing at the time did not fit into what had been labelled modernist theatre or modernism more generally. However, even more 'known' oppositions to modernist theatre practices, the 'older categories of fantastic, theatricalist and the "absurd", whose effects realism underwrites through contrast, had little explanatory power' (ibid.) either. Fuchs details how this 'vertiginous new perspective [was] at once artistic and broadly cultural' (ibid.), existing both within the theatre and theatre practices, but also expressed in wider, more general cultural shifts outside of the theatrical bubble. But, she states, 'I lacked a name, much less an adequate vocabulary and grammar' (ibid.) through which to discuss, explore and explain this shift. That is, it seems, until she 'had fallen into the mental swoon of postmodernism' (ibid.).

I return to Fuchs, here, as a reflection across time and space of my own experience in searching for an adequate vocabulary and grammar to explore and explain the methodological and aesthetic shifts I have experienced across the theatrical landscape that, just as Fuchs experienced in regard to postmodernism in the 1990s, I also see as an interconnected part of a wider structural shift across the cultural and political landscape in the 2010s. In a continuation of both Fuchs's and my own focus on an embodied understanding of these cultural and theatrical shifts, whilst I refer to a structural change, I specifically relate this to Raymond Williams's understanding of a 'structure of feeling' (Williams 1969: 17).

A structure of feeling

Raymond Williams's concept of a structure of feeling develops a framework of understanding in order to examine shifts in cultural aesthetics that, when examined in isolation, may seem disparate and unrelated, but when examined as an embodied and overarching 'feeling', allow for a panoramic understanding of such shifts as interconnected through a framework that is 'as firm and definite as "structure" suggests, yet ... based in the deepest and often least tangible elements of our experience' (Williams 1969: 18). It enables an understanding of how some almost indefinable, and yet experiential, modalities apparent within a particular cultural time-frame or context are 'essentially related, although in practice, and in detail, this is not always easy to see' (ibid.: 7) but are, therefore, part of a wider cultural change. The terminology stems from Williams's *Drama from Ibsen to Eliot* (1952) and the more renowned revision of this text, *Drama from Ibsen to Brecht* (1961), in which Williams analysed the shift from naturalistic to expressionistic forms within his own contemporary theatrical landscape. As he looks back over historical shifts within dramatic practice and theatrical convention, he notes that 'while it is possible to see this [clear shift in convention] in retrospect, it could never have been easy, and it is not easy now, to see such a situation with sufficient clarity, in the flux of the present experience' (Williams 1969: 16). It is here that a (difficult and messy and interconnected) line is drawn between conventions and structures of feeling, in that an artist may have followed particular *conventions* of the time period they are creating work within, but at the time these conventions are being followed, we may not have, to return to Fuchs, an 'adequate vocabulary and grammar' (Fuchs 1996: 1) for such shifts. As Williams describes,

> In the [retrospective] study of a period, we may be able to reconstruct, with more or less accuracy, the material life, the general social organization, and, to a large extent, the dominant ideas. It is often difficult to decide which, if any, of these aspects is, in a way, arbitrary, and an important institution like drama will, in all probability, take its colour in varying degrees from them all. But while we may, in the study of a *past* period, separate out particular aspects of life, and treat them as if they were self-contained, it is obvious that this is only how they may be studied, not how they were experienced. We examine each element as a precipitate, but in the living experience of the time every element was in solution, an inseparable part of a complex whole. (1969: 17–18; emphasis added)

Williams's structure of feeling attempts to capture these interrelated aspects within the (relative) current period of examination rather than retrospectively. He notes that whilst we are often able to see such a structure (perhaps manifesting as theatrical conventions of a particular period) when studying theatre of the past, 'it is precisely the structure of feeling which is most difficult to distinguish whilst it is being lived' (Williams 1969: 18). However, it is through examining these interrelated shifts in theatre (and wider culture if required) within the framework of the structure of feeling that allows for an analysis of 'dramatic methods with a clear technical definition, and yet know ... that what is being defined is more than technique; is indeed the practical way of describing those changes in experience – the responses and their communication; the "subjects" and the "forms" – which make the drama in itself and as a history important' (ibid.: 20). My application of Williams's framework, here, is to connect – in the time that such shifts are occurring as much as possible within the context of a scholarly review – particular elements, both through my own embodied experience of theatre as well as the observations, from a range of contemporary theatre scholars, of current performance practices and how they – in their interrelation – are part of a wider post-postmodern structure of feeling that, I contend, can be best described as metamodern. As Williams puts it best,

> As we collect our experience of particular plays, we see the structure of feeling at once extending and changing: important elements in common, as experience and as method, between particular plays and dramatists; important elements changing, as the experience and conventions change together, or as the experience is found to be in tension with existing conventions and either succeeds or fails in altering them. (ibid.)

Believing in stories (as if they were true)

I am far from the first theatre scholar to notice how performance practices over roughly the past decade have exhibited a shift through and beyond the irony and detachment of what we have come to understand as part of postmodern aesthetics and methodologies towards something that, whilst not wholly removing itself from such aesthetics, is also (contradictorily in some cases) imbued with aesthetics of care, authenticity, hope and engagement. In 2014s *What's The Story: Essays about Art, Theater and Storytelling*, theatre director and performance scholar Anne Bogart described her own observations of what she saw as shift within theatrical practice and wider culture, proposing that 'we have reached the end of postmodernism [and] are on the cusp of a new paradigm, as yet unnamed, only partially inhabited, unfamiliar and novel' (Bogart 2014: 5). Bogart is particularly interested in the re-appreciation of narrative – of *storytelling* – in contemporary performance practice and relates this shift both periodically and politically to the mid-2010s, discerning that it 'is becoming increasingly clear that the hegemony of isolation is not a solution to our present global circumstances ... In moments such as these, of upheaval and change, stories become necessary to frame our existence' (ibid.). Interestingly, Bogart positions this shift in relation to her previous cultural understanding in a historic and generational sense when she describes herself and her work thus:

> I am a product of postmodernism, of deconstructionism, of a general rejection of hierarchical narrative and objective truth. For much of my life in the theater I have resisted the comfort and tyranny of stories. But the times are shifting. (ibid.: 4)

Importantly, this re-appreciation for narrative detected by Bogart doesn't indicate an unmitigated return to an acceptance of overarching metanarratives or pre-deconstructivist dominance of authorial intent. Instead, Bogart champions a participatory and individualistic storytelling both within our own lives and within the theatre. As will become clear in Chapter 2, this is inherently linked to the 'as if' nature of our metamodern experience, in that, whilst postmodern deconstructivism revealed the falsity of certain metanarratives, we still exist within, and tend to have some form of contradictory belief in, certain structures *as if* they are true – whilst, at the same time, understanding them to be false. We may understand the falsities and failings of capitalism, yet we still have a bank account. We may critique the inherently patriarchal flaws of the system of marriage between partners of the opposite sex, but roughly half of millennials continue to tie the knot (ONS 2022), albeit around a decade later than their parents' generation (Harrison 2021). On a personal level, whilst I am acutely aware of the increasing effects of global heating and the impending crises that we will, inevitably, have to deal with in our lifetime and therefore I increasingly worry about the fragile state of the world which future generations will be forced to inhabit within the immediate future, I still actively chose to bring children into this world with some sort of hope that they will be able to have a 'good' life[2]. British artist Luke Turner describes this current post-postmodern structure of feeling (which he defines as metamodern) as centred around a certain pragmatic idealism, or informed naïveté (Turner 2015), which Seth Abramson expresses as 'knowing your optimism is naïve – but plowing [sic] on anyway' (Abramson 2018). Abramson contends that we understand that our metanarratives are 'insufficient, they're fragile, they're false – but they

---

[2] I am aware, too, that I write this from an extraordinary position of privilege in the Global North and that, largely, the current effects upon mine and my family's lives have been incredibly minimal in comparison to those communities acutely affected by the impacts of global heating at the current time.

help us' (Owls at Dawn 2017) and that the current paradigm is 'very much about living as if something were true' (ibid.). After all, he states, 'we still have to make breakfast and go to work and have some sort of hope that things can work out and that there's some meaning' (ibid.). Bogart's understanding of the importance of stories – inherently connected, here, to the idea of metanarratives – reflects our individualistic construction of narratives, and our *choice* to adhere or believe in such narratives, as we exist through and beyond postmodern deconstruction. She links this, inherently, to individual power within global politics and culture and emphasizes that 'more important than the facts of any life is the meaning and significance that we attribute to those facts' (Bogart 2014: 3), relating this to Polish philosopher Zygmunt Bauman's concept of liquid modernity (2000). At the turn of the century, Bauman's portentous understanding of the beginning of a shift beyond the postmodern placed specific importance on the move away from a hardware-focussed paradigm towards a more liquid software-based paradigm, the effect of which on both the collective and the individual is that our lives become more unpredictable and insecure. As Bogart explains, 'It is the onus of each one of us to adjust, shift and adjust again to [Bauman's] constant liquid environment of fluid and unending change' (Bogart 2014: 2). In response to this, Bogart focuses re-appreciation on the importance and effect of narratives but emphasizes that, rather 'than mechanically allowing other people's stories to guide our lives, it is possible to get involved and narrate from a state of passionate participation' (ibid.). In this sense, when refocussing on theatrical practice within a post-postmodern paradigm, Bogart calls for theatre makers to 'begin to think of ourselves, rather than stagers of plays, as orchestrators of social interactions in which a performance is part, but only a fragment of that interaction' (ibid.).

An age of engagement

In *Performance in the Twenty-First Century* (2016), performance theorist Andy Lavender argues that our contemporary cultural space 'has the look and feel of one that is now definitely beyond the postmodern even while it continues to trade in certain postmodern strategies' (Lavender 2016: 10). In a post-mortem-like timeline of postmodernism, Lavender refers to Hal Foster's 1983 treatise on modernism's subsummation of mainstream culture, in which Foster proclaims that 'modernism is now [in 1983] largely absorbed. Originally oppositional ... today, however, it is the official culture' (Foster 1985: ix). For Lavender, the official culture of postmodernism centred around Lyotard's 'incredulity towards metanarratives' (Lyotard 1984: xxiv) whilst embracing the 'rhetoric and practices of fracture, detachment and irony'

(Lavender 2016: 18) and, whilst such strategies began as oppositional to cultural norms, Lavender argues – quite rightly – that the cultural absorption of the postmodern was so all encompassing that, by the end of the twentieth century, postmodernity had become the overarching cultural norm itself.

In the 2010s, however, Lavender observed the emergence of performative modes that 'mark a break from the decenterings of postmodernism' (ibid.: 20), noticing a developing (re)appraisal of particular aesthetic and methodological concerns within contemporary performance practice around issues such as narrative, responsibility, authenticity, care and – a particularly striking break from postmodernism – the *real*. Lavender asserts that by around the mid-90s, 'Postmodernism had performed the healthy function of destabilizing assumed norms and notions of the real [but since the turn of the millennium] the tools that it introduced proved limited in dealing with new scenarios that changed our relationship … to realities and their expression' (ibid.: 19). For Lavender, contemporary performance continues to exhibit many of the attributes of Lehmann's postdramatic theatre, or Henke and Middeke's (2007: 13) assessment of contemporary drama's application of postmodern aesthetics. But, Lavender contends, the continual application of such strategies is also entwined with a 'new fascination with authenticity' (Lavender 2016: 23) and *engagement*. He uses this latter term to encompass theatrical process that, 'subsequent to the "classic" postmodern tropes of detachment, irony and contingency … entail altered modes of engagement on the part of both practitioners and spectators [, connecting] more overtly with social process [and] involv[ing] a pronounced form of personal experience' (ibid.). Such performances exhibit an antithesis to the earlier mentioned 'classic' postmodern tropes, in that they aim towards attachment, sincerity and the *real*. Lavender's *Theatres of Engagement* 'describe performance after postmodernism [as they] face outwards rather than inwards, albeit they might also involve the most intimate personal sharing [, they] ask commitment [and they] depend on and produce feelings and experience' (ibid.: 27).

Lavender's *Theatres of Engagement* reflect a number of aesthetic and methodological issues across recent shifts in contemporary performance practice throughout Britain that I, too, am concerned with in this volume. His understanding of these shifts being inherently connected to a wider cultural shift through and beyond the postmodern is particularly pertinent. However, the shifts that Lavender describes as part of a decentring of postmodernity within contemporary performance practice are inherently connected to, and encompassed within, what we can comfortably frame as metamodernism – as will become clear in the next chapters. In the introduction to his book, Lavender proclaims that 'we find ourselves in a cultural space that has the look and feel of one that is now definitely beyond the postmodern, even while it continues to trade in certain postmodern strategies' (Lavender 2016: 10). This both/and nature (both postmodern and post-postmodern – or even both postmodern and modern) is central to the wider cultural understanding of metamodernism as an emerging cultural sensibility fast replacing postmodernism. Lavender just falls short of mentioning metamodernism by name. Perhaps he, in 2016 – just like Fuchs in the 1990s – didn't quite have the words.

The return of the real

One last word on Lavender. In *Theatres of Engagement*, he points to Jeffrey Melnick's assertion that 'once we [as a culture] loved irony and took refuge in that distancing strategy: now we are earnest and authentic' (Melnick 2009: 20). Lavender positions a 'new fascination with authenticity' (Lavender 2016: 23) as integral to understanding this current paradigm shift. He states that any 'significant shift in representation is usually a return to the real' (ibid.: 19). Only a year later, Daniel Schulze's *Authenticity in Contemporary Theatre and Performance* (2017) provided a fascinating and detailed analysis of the contemporary concern with authenticity, seeing this resurgence in interest in the authentic as arising as a direct response to postmodern existence. 'Assuming that for the layman in postmodern society, postmodern theory is perceived as scary rather than liberating,' states Schulze (2017: 25), 'it becomes evident that the search for authenticity – in other words, a flight from the unwelcome truth of fragmentation and uncertainty – is the only viable option'. For Schulze, the postmodern condition drove humankind to feel 'far-removed and isolated from nature and its own origins, sentenced to live in a world which is perceived as fake and superficial' (ibid.: 26). Deconstruction, mediatization and poststructuralism led to an inevitable superficiality that 'creates a sense of loss in a complex world' (ibid.) and the rise of 'authenticity is the counter movement to these profound feelings of uncertainty and instability' (ibid.: 23). In Chapter 3, I detail how concerns regarding the concept of the authentic within the work of the companies I am concerned with can be traced to my own generation's particular uncertainty and instability, millennials' longing for the authentic developing from an inherent feeling of generational loss. This desire is manifest in a 'pragmatic idealism' (Turner 2015) that engages with a revival of the strive for authenticity and progression whilst not 'forfeiting all that we've learnt from postmodernism' (ibid.). As such, the contemporary (re)engagement with the concept of the authentic, as music theorist Niels van Poecke discerns, oscillates 'between a modern enthusiasm for authenticity and a postmodern "sense" about authenticity's artificiality' (van Poecke 2017: 58). The aesthetic and performative modalities employed by the performances in this volume clearly exhibit an endeavour towards forms of authentic connection and representation of the 'real' whilst being simultaneously critical and quizzical of such an attempt. Of course, any analysis of authenticity inhabits a paradoxical terminological area, in that, in defining the authentic as a quality, it ceases to hold its 'claim to being unmediated, genuine or real' (Schulze 2017: 39). As Susanne Knaller explains, the authentic exists in a paradox 'between subjective legitimisation and objective certification' (Knaller 2012: 70) and as Timotheus Vermeulen expands, authenticity 'aspires to unformed immediacy and non-fictive truth but can only ever manifest in and as a fictive form' (Huber and Funk 2017: 155). Its autological nature means that when the authentic is verbalized, 'the concept collapses like a soap bubble' (Schulze 2017: 39). Taking a cue from Schulze – and continuing my focus on embodiment as laid out at the beginning of this chapter – in order to attempt to verbalize the notion of authenticity, I see authenticity as based on a tacit understanding embodied within the audience and artists' individual experience of a performance; the authentic is intuitively understood through embodied experience. Through this, I aim to 'subject [such definitions] to some conceptual elaboration' (Kester 2009) whilst remaining aware of the paradoxical, slippery nature of such an endeavour. In ways, however, this is reflexive of the particular methods in which the companies and performances explored in this book are addressing their own attempts to develop or portray or utilize authenticity in that they are simultaneously sceptical, critical and questioning of their own endeavours. Throughout this book, I use Schulze's designation of 'mechanisms of authenticity' (2017: 29) employed within theatre as manifest in a 'longing for something that is not a simulacrum' (ibid.: 34), that can, however paradoxically, stake 'a claim to being unmediated, genuine or real' (ibid.: 39).

The Gramophone's *Playful Acts of Rebellion*, or Uninvited Guests' *Love Letters at Home*, exhibit such aesthetical concerns and would comfortably fit within Lavender and Schulze's frameworks. The projection of The Gramophone's missing company member, or Uninvited Guests' dancing with their children, particularly, pinpoint a fascination with the *real* that is central to each. Importantly, though, this post-postmodern fascination with 'the real' is not a return to modernist attempts towards real*ism*. Performance practice has not returned, naïvely, to attempted authenticity in its representation of reality. Instead, this fascination with portraying the 'real' in performance is also combined with previous postmodern concerns with the *un*reality of it all. Uninvited Guests taking their laptops downstairs into their kitchens and dancing with their children doesn't attempt to perform authenticity, or replicate the real; it simply *is* authentic. These are the performers' real

(Already) Beyond the Postmodern 35

children, in their real kitchens. The embarrassment on their kids' faces, too, is real. Their breaking out of the initial performance frame, by showing us the 'real life' continuing around them as they do their jobs, also reminds us of the (unreality of the) performance frame.

Schulze's stance on a contemporary focus on authenticity mirrors Lavender's, in that he sees it as important evidence that there is a cultural shift – specifically within theatre and performance – beyond postmodernity. For Schulze, 'Postmodernism as a cultural *modus operandi* is dead' (ibid.: 55), and authenticity is one of the new foci that offer proof of its demise. As he explains,

> Authenticity is an important factor in today's culture. It is the first strong clue that the postmodern age of simulation and fragmentation has been replaced with mechanisms of authenticity and, thus, possibly even new forms of essentialism. I am not arguing in favour of dismissing Postmodernism and its practices altogether. On the contrary, it is clear that many forms of postmodern practice have achieved great merit and are still in practice. But, it is evident that new practices, while still conscious of the old ones, have superseded them (Kirby 2009: 6). They have built, as it were, on the sandy foundations of Postmodernism a new and more stable house. (Schulze 2017: 13)

Importantly, Schulze is one of the first theatre and performance scholars to connect this 'new and more stable house' to the term metamodernism. He directly relates his understanding of a post-postmodern cultural shift to Williams's structure of feeling, and states that although 'many terms have been proposed for this ... none of them have stuck so far' (ibid.: 54). Whilst he recognizes the issues regarding 'finding a label for an ongoing process' (ibid.), Schulze decides to use the term metamodernism as a 'shorthand for contemporary structures of feeling without allowing it to become set in stone' (ibid.), emphasizing that, 'in order to spark debate, a clear description and even a label will prove helpful in order to refine concepts and encourage further discussion' (ibid.). Chapter 2 will detail what the label metamodernism denotes, and this will be expounded upon within the field of contemporary theatre and performance throughout the rest of this volume. However, I feel it important to note here that Schulze's use of the term metamodernism is a way *into* his primary focus on authenticity within contemporary performance. He rightly locates an interest in the authentic – however impossible and paradoxical within the inherently inauthentic artistic medium of performance (cf. ibid.: 58) – as part of the wider metamodern cultural shift – using the term as a (possibly temporary) label to refine concepts and encourage further discussion.

Whilst this book is the first volume dedicated to exploring the metamodern within contemporary theatre, there have been a number of notable mentions of metamodernism within recently published theatre and performance research (and vice versa) that have begun to – when plotted together – map out how recent trends within theatre reflect the wider metamodern sensibility. The following two sections offer the first mapping of such material published over roughly the past decade in order to build an interrelated framework of understanding.

Notes on metamodernism: Traces of theatre

From 2009 to 2016, the website *Notes on Metamodernism* published peer-reviewed writing by various cultural theorists and critics concerning the metamodern cultural paradigm. Founded by Timotheus Vermeulen and Robin van den Akker, the project included three short articles published on theatre and performance which, in various ways, began to plot the developments within contemporary theatre that indicated a shift away from postmodern performance practice and towards something that appeared to align with what other cultural theorists were describing as the metamodern.

Birgit Schuhbeck's 'Less Art, More Substance: New Tendencies in Contemporary Theatre' (2012) may be the first examination of contemporary theatre through a metamodern(-aligned) lens. In the article, Schuhbeck argues that the 'mosaic structure of postmodernism is not appropriate anymore to represent the current developments in culture, the "new" theater feels the need to turn to seemingly "old" traditions like mimesis, and the pristine urge to tell stories' (Schuhbeck 2012), reflective of Bogart's renewed interest in narrative only two years later. She focuses largely on her own observation across contemporary German theatre of a shift away from a postmodern theatre 'marked by association, citation and intertextuality' (2012) towards a renewal of *dramatic drama* – a term she translates from Birgit Haas (2007). Through this, theatre returns to 'clear-structured storylines – a set beginning and a definite ending – [which] seems to be a return to traditional elements, but is, in fact, a very contemporary tendency' (Schuhbeck 2012). Rather than representing a 'step back' within theatrical representation, Schuhbeck argues that the tendency she is observing differs from Aristotelian drama in that, within such narratives, the 'individual was only the victim of fate and had no possibility to act in a self-determined way' (Schuhbeck 2012) and, in this contemporary drama, such individually limiting metanarrative is non-existent – characters (and performers) have individual agency within a narrative, rather than some god-like fate. However, this renewal of narrative 'also differs from a psychological theatre with a social background – as German drama was characterized around 1910 – which concentrated on an exact, detailed and subjective representation of reality without referring to its own limits' (Schuhbeck 2012). Instead, Schuhbeck connects such (re) centring of narrative to theatre's inherent connection to political and cultural shifts. Whilst she argues that these new tendencies imply that 'the stage is not an open (postmodern) stage, rather it serves as a virtual closed space [and] fiction is separated from reality again' (2012), this separation, for Schuhbeck, enables a form of politically and ethically driven work in which 'theatre understands itself again as a critical force that reveals and deals with society's hidden power-structures, instead of simply giving up in face of an overcomplicated world' (2012). I critique Schuhbeck's focus on the metamodern stage being 'closed' and, through the productions detailed in this volume, it will become clear why. However, her appraisal of a renewed interest in narrative and engagement rather than open-ended mosaic and disengagement is a particularly pertinent foundational understanding of how elements within contemporary theatre were shifting beyond postmodernity towards something new, reflecting the later interests of Bogart, Lavender and Schulze detailed earlier on. Her understanding of theatre's position as a critical and political force, too, is particularly important to understanding a metamodern shift within contemporary theatre – implying that theatre does not remove itself fully from postmodern strategies but builds on certain structures within this framework whilst removing itself from any apathetic disconnection to, instead, 'incorporate an ethical perspective again' (Schuhbeck 2012) *at the same time* as remaining somewhat, inescapably, *also* apathetic.

Later in 2012, British artist and author of the Metamodern Manifesto (2011) Luke Turner built upon this oscillation between apathy and enthusiasm in a short article entitled 'David Foster Wallace's Hideous Men & London's Olympic Epiphany'. The article draws interesting links between Andy Holden and Raymond Conroy's 2012 theatrical adaptation of David Foster Wallace's collection of short stories, *Brief Interviews with Hideous Men* (1999), and Danny Boyle's opening ceremony for the London Olympics earlier that year – specifically regarding the inherent hope*lessness* of the former and the (back in 2012 at least, before the outcomes of the 'Olympic Legacy' were reduced to luxury tower blocks that completely priced out local residents) inherent hope*fulness* of the latter. As a novelist, David Foster Wallace has been seen as a leading figure in the New Sincerity movement – a literary shift beyond postmodern apathy and towards new forms of sincere and affective engagement whilst, simultaneously, understanding that both the contemporary author and reader cannot remove themselves wholly from a postmodern-informed reading. His most infamous text, the insurmountably long *Infinite Jest* (1996), is largely seen as an attempt by him to bring into being this New Sincerity in novel form, the aesthetics of which were originally posited by Wallace in his 1993 essay 'E Unibus Pluram: Television and U.S. Fiction':

> The next real literary 'rebels' in this country might well emerge as some weird bunch of anti-rebels, born oglers who dare somehow to back away from ironic watching, who have the childish gall actually to endorse and instantiate single-entendre principles. Who treat old untrendy human troubles and emotions in U.S. life with reverence and conviction. Who eschew self-consciousness and hip fatigue. These anti-rebels would be outdated, of course, before they even started. Dead on the page. Too sincere. Clearly repressed. Backward, quaint, naive, anachronistic. Maybe that'll be the point. Maybe that's why they'll be the next real rebels … The old postmodern insurgents risked the gasp and squeal: shock, disgust, outrage, censorship, accusations of socialism, anarchism, nihilism. Today's risks are different. The new rebels might be artists willing to risk the yawn, the rolled eyes, the cool smile, the nudged ribs, the … accusations of sentimentality, melodrama. Of overcredulity. Of softness. (Wallace 1993: 192–3)

Since Wallace's popularization of the term, New Sincerity has become one of the main characteristics connected to metamodernism (cf. Abramson 2018; den Dulk 2020; Shcherbak 2023) within wider cultural studies, and it makes sense that a theatrical adaptation of his works would trade in tendencies that reflect wider applications of the metamodern. In his article, Turner's focus is on the oscillation in the piece between contrasting styles, emotions and readings:

> We empathise with [a character's] inevitable hurt … yet at the more ridiculous junctures, we find ourselves laughing at the situation for its twisted logic. We find truth and farce in equal measure: maximum irony, maximum sincerity … Is the overall effect here intentional? Are these performances sincere, or are we in the realm of parody? Could we be experiencing both at once? (Turner 2012)

Contrasting Schuhbeck's focus on a closed stage, Turner is also interested in the metatheatrical aspects of Holden and Conroys's adaptation, with the audience continually being made aware of the play's artifice through having actors being fed their lines in a variety of ways: 'One wears an earpiece, whilst another reads off an autocue, and at one point, an offstage prompter leaps into action when it appears that an actor might have lost his place' (Turner 2012). Turner draws a link between these interventions and the multi-layered nature of Foster Wallace's writing, connecting this to the company's hope that such metatheatrical practice will 'lead the audience to experience "a kind of oscillation, or simultaneity between being absorbed in the text and being aware of how it functions"' (Turner 2012). What Turner, importantly, points out here is that Foster Wallace criticizes this tactic within a footnote to the short story collection Holden & Conroy had adapted:

> With the now-tired S.O.P. 'meta'-stuff it's more the dramatist himself coming onstage from the wings and reminding you that what's going on is artificial and that the artificer is him (the dramatist) ... that he's at least respectful enough of you as reader/audience to be honest about the fact that he's back there pulling the strings, an 'honesty' which personally you've always had the feeling is actually a highly rhetorical sham-honesty that's designed to get you to like him and approve of him ... and feel flattered that he apparently thinks you're enough of a grownup to handle being reminded that what you're in the middle of is artificial (like you didn't know that already, like you needed to be reminded of it over and over again as if you were a myopic child who couldn't see what was right in front of you) ... not interrogating you or hav[ing] any sort of interchange or even really talking to you but rather just performing in some highly self-conscious and manipulative way. (Wallace 2001: 125)

In some ways, Foster Wallace's denouncement of such metatheatrical practices, here, appears to engender appraisal of Schuhbeck's return to a closed stage. However, Wallace's own famously extended use of meta-commentary via footnotes within his fiction is antithetical to such denouncement. As an author, Foster Wallace at once criticizes and makes use of the tactics he labels manipulative, through the use of, as according to literary scholar Lucas Thompson, 'metafictional directives [that use] manipulation to dramatize the complex tension between sincerity and its antithesis' (Thompson 2016: 359).

Whilst Turner juxtaposes the 'ultimately destructive sincerity and self-loathing' (2012) of *Brief Interviews with Hideous Men* with the simultaneous hopeful sincerity experienced around the country during the 2012 London Olympics – 'as if the nation suddenly made a collective decision to go with it, to curb their cynicism and embrace the games' (Turner 2012) – he questions whether 'this newfound sincerity [will] last, or is it just a flash in the pan' (Turner 2012), conflating, through this, both contemporary theatrical practice and the wider structural feeling of British culture. In hindsight, Turner's suggestion that the country may oscillate, in the longer term, between optimism and cynicism is (and I am explicitly looking at this through my own myopic lens as a left-wing, Euro-favourable, Corbynite millennial – but this is also a relevant point of view for right-wing, Euro-sceptic Brexiteers in the years following the 2016 referendum), a decade, later, vividly pertinent.

In her 2014 article for *Notes on Metamodernism* – '"I Agree to This": Third Angel and the Price of Fame' – literary scholar Alison Gibbons makes the first claim to being able to position a theatrical production as 'distinctly metamodern' (Gibbons 2014). In her unpacking of the theatrical aesthetics of Sheffield-based theatre company Third Angel's 2014 production *The Life & Loves of a Nobody*, Gibbons explains that the piece

> might be drawing on discursive theatrical strategies that are decidedly postmodern [... when] judging the play on its first half, it would be easy to see [it] as a throw-back to the postmodern theatre of the 1990s, with its props and staging apparatus clearly visible to the audience and the absence of the main character Rachel who never appears on stage.
> (Gibbons 2014)

The piece is based around a 'normal' character called Rachel, who is presented through a combination of narration and briefly enacted scenes – meaning that, as Gibbons describes,

> the audience watches some interactions in which the narrators temporarily transform into the characters, voicing dialogue as free direct speech. Such scenes always end abruptly, so that Chambers and Walton snap back out from character to narrator and the audience ontologically moves with them – from watching Rachel's life unfold to a position in which they are acutely aware that they are a member of the audience watching Third Angel perform *The Life and Loves of a Nobody*.
> (Gibbons 2014)

Gibbons, here, is interested in this both-neither dynamic within the performer-character-story-audience relationship through Third Angel's application of the metatheatrical devices Foster Wallace was both engaging with and criticizing – in that they ask an audience to at once embrace the fact that they are being told a fictional story by the performers themselves but also to sympathetically engage with the fictional characters, being at once removed from and imbricated within the fictional narrative. It is largely the second half of *The Life & Loves of a Nobody*, though, that – for

Gibbons – shifts the piece further away from reasonably fitting solely within the framework of postmodern performance and embracing what she sees as metamodern tendencies. Whilst the first half centres around metatheatrical devices concerning the actor-character dynamic, the second half of the performance reframes the audience's involvement as being an essential part of the fictional story the performers are recounting as, in the narrative, Rachel auditions for the very show the audience are watching – 'We are now and in fact have been the whole time, the audience of the show for which Rachel auditioned' (Gibbons 2014). Building upon this, the narrative shifts to reveal that the audience – who are at once fictional and really watching the piece – are then required to vote on the final scene of the show, with their choices limited to a variety of ways in which Rachel will die. For Gibbons, the piece is 'metamodernist in its relational positioning of the audience' (Gibbons 2014), a sentiment that will be echoed in the aesthetics of metatheatre, authenticity, and engagement threaded throughout the metamodern performance discussed in this volume.

Notes on theatre: Traces of metamodernism

Alongside Schuhbeck, Turner and Gibbons's initial tracings of a theatrical shift towards metamodernism – the latter two making the first concrete steps in labelling such work metamodern – the past decade has seen a slowly increasing number of theatre-*focussed* scholars delving into the task of beginning to map out how the contemporary theatrical landscape reflects, responds to and creates the metamodern episteme. My own analysis within this book is, in part, built upon the important foundational work undertaken by these scholars. Therefore, I want to briefly lay out the main aspects of each of these to provide the foundations for such analysis. I also see this as an important act of documentation and acknowledgement – tracing the lineage of the often-disparate analysis of how metamodernism and theatre interact, undertaken by a mixture of established scholars and theatre students within the first volume dedicated to metamodern theatre, without which this volume itself would not exist.

Kemi Atanda Ilori's short volume, *The Theatre of Wole Soyinka: Metamodernism, Myth and Ritual* (2014) and following doctoral thesis 'The Theatre of Wole Soyinka: Inside the Liminal World of Myth, Ritual and Postcoloniality' (2016) apply a foundational application of metamodernism to Nigerian poet and playwright Wole Soyinka's theatre through a detailed unpacking of the keystones of metamodernism as defined, predominantly, by Robin van den Akker and Timotheus Vermeulen, which, for Illori, manifests as a 'form of cultural praxis flowing from postmodernism' (Ilori 2016: 156). Ilori's self-proclaimed 'narrow' use of the term 'theatre' – not being 'concern[ed] with any actual performance of Soyinka's plays' (Ilori 2016: 1) – limits the analysis to a literary framework and therefore shares many similarities to concurrent literary scholars' unpacking of how literature reflects, responds to and renders metamodernity, such as Antony Rowland, Seth Abramson and Alison Gibbons. Ilori's focus on liminality as a central concept within Soyinka's oeuvre, however, is particularly pertinent in regards to the wider metamodern shift across post-millennial culture (as will become clear in Chapter 3), specifically focusing on Ilori's connection of 'Soyinka's portrayal of society as a pendulum swinging precariously between hope and despair' (Ilori 2016: 165) to the central oscillation within the metamodern framework.

Whilst she never refers to metamodernism explicitly within the scope of her article published the following year, Alex Cahill's 'The Theatrical Double Reflexivity Complex: How the Spectator Creates Metatheatre' (2015) offers a reappraisal of metatheatre that builds upon historical definitions to note that the term should encompass two meanings. Through this, Cahill proffers that metatheatricality refers firstly (and historically) to the type of self-referentiality that Foster Wallace both denounces and utilizes insofar as a tool used by theatre makers to 'provide an experience of reality within the theatre that usually confronts the audience with a social or existential problem or question' (Cahill 2015: 3). Cahill then sees a secondary understanding of metatheatre emerging through an audience's metatheatrical engagement with a play. Previously, argues Cahill, metatheatrical 'self-awareness is discussed in regards to characters/actors [but] if the spectators possess self-awareness of their role in the theatre, could they also not feed into the metatheatre of the performance?' (ibid.: 12). Cahill offers two notable examples to illustrate this experience – in which a combination of active participation and spectator self-awareness allows for a space in which Cahill argues that the 'line between theatre reality and Real reality is blurred or possibly removed entirely' (ibid.: 2). Again, whilst Cahill is dealing specifically with the terminology of metatheatre – a distinction must be drawn here between this and meta*modern* theatre – I include it here because of her understanding of audience-centric metatheatricality feeding into the fascination with authenticity in works such as *Playful Acts of Rebellion* or *Love Letters at Home* and, as will become clear in Chapters 2 and 4, metamodern cultural scholars' understanding of a metamodern development of self-reflexivity.

In 2016, Nele Frieda Beinborn's thesis, *Places of Becoming: Gathering Urgency in Contemporary Political Theatre*, worked towards a metamodern understanding of contemporary political theatre that, again, moves away from Birgit Schuhbeck's earlier assessment in that Beinborn 'argue[s] for a notion of theatre not as a closed system in itself that is locked inside a theatre space' (Beinborn 2016: 6). For Beinborn, Foucault's notion of heterotopias being grounded in 'a network that connects points and intersects with its own skein' (Foucault 1986: 1) is no longer a revolutionary idea but, in our digitized, globalized, contemporary existence, now just 'stating the obvious' (Beinborn 2016: 6). She relates this demise of a linear structure of understanding, alongside a further demise in 'clear dichotomies and yes-no-decisions' (ibid.) to the 'both-neither' dynamic of metamodernism, through which she argues that certain contemporary theatrical tropes enable places of becoming – 'where the spark hits inflammable material in a metaphorical sense … triggering a motivation, a movement of mind or a way of thinking that brings along change' (ibid.: 15). As Bogart similarly states, and as I detail in Chapter 3 of this volume, Beinborn also relates to being 'raised by deconstruction' (ibid.: 9). This positionality leads her to not only critique postmodern disconnectedness, open-endedness and apathy as an impediment to progress – 'I feel that something needs to change, because somewhere something has gone completely wrong and we are the generation who has to live with decisions that are made today' (ibid.: 9) – but it also leads to a critique of the swing between apathy and enthusiasm present within the both-neither, oscillatory dynamic of metamodernism – 'the overload of possibilities … complicates the decision but at the same time making choices more meaningful' (ibid.: 13). For Beinborn, it is metamodern structures that enable 'new forms of artworks to fluctuate between sincerity and irony, employing the one while not entirely losing the other, but not focusing on either and creating a "both-neither" relationship' (ibid.: 12–13). She relates this, inherently, to Florian Malzacher's understanding of contemporary political theatre's shift beyond what can be considered postmodern practice when he describes 'a theatre that keeps the necessary self-reflexivity of the last decades but avoids the traps of pure self-referentiality' (Malzacher 2015: 20). Beinborn's 'places of becoming' share similarities with Lavender's focus on engagement within contemporary performance – understanding the liminal space of engagement between audience and performer that occurs in 'contemporary politically oriented theatre projects … fuelled by an urgency that lies in our contemporary society' (Beinborn 2016: 6). For Beinborn, metamodern performance practice takes 'forms that go beyond the blackbox and the auditorium and pushes through the borders of amusement and theatrical representation into the social-political sphere' (ibid.). Whilst I will not go into detail regarding this here, my own article published in the *Performance Philosophy Journal* in 2018, 'The Listening Theatre: A Metamodern Politics of Performance', deals with a similar understanding of politically aligned metamodern performance practice to Beinborn's in regard to theatre that 'pushes through ... into the sociopolitical sphere' (Beinborn 2016: 6). Beinborn is concerned about how she interprets metamodern oscillation between disparate polarities as an impasse to political progress – 'Having a perfect ideal in mind to be reached is per se a good thing, yet the awareness that it will never be reached is somewhat disappointing' (ibid.: 7). However, I see this 'contradictory position, one that oscillates between cynicism and hope, one that embraces hypocrisy, a conflicted movement between poles' (Drayton 2018: 174) as an essential element in how contemporary theatre – particularly that created in Britain by 'emerging', politically-minded companies – exhibits a wider metamodern shift, in that the companies explored within my previous article 'want change, but they are also inherently mindful of the limitations of theatre, working their own cynicism, that of the campaigners, and their preconceived criticism of the reception of the work', (ibid. 183) into the work itself. Building on Lavender's theatres of engagement, I proposed that a certain element of the contemporary political theatre that lends itself to a metamodern understanding is an opening up of the closed theatrical space and extending the audience engagement beyond the event itself.

Also in 2018, Nathan Sibthorpe's doctoral thesis 'The Effect of Embodied Metafiction in Contemporary Performance' situates his study within the framework of metamodernism (Sibthorpe 2018) and largely relates this to metafiction within a narrative and dramaturgical sense, over the conventional understanding of metatheatre. For Sibthorpe, the 'literariness of performance [has been] superseded by a de-hierarchisation of forms' (ibid.: 5) and a metamodern understanding of performance is based, partly, on 'metafictive traits that exist in dramaturgical logic rather than written text [and in] works that traverse a spectrum between self-conscious reality and romantic fiction' (ibid.: 5–6). In Chapters 4 and 5, I return to such metatheatrical/metafictional beyondness – building on Beinborn's, Sibthorpe's and my own previous understanding of such – as an integral aesthetic within metamodern theatre in a way that, as Sibthorpe explains, 'invite[s] an audience to indulge in the fiction from an empowered position, using self-awareness to remind them of the construction taking place and using such construction to make sense of a complex world' (ibid.: 6).

In 2020, Nina Mitova's Master's thesis at Utrecht University, 'The Beyondness of Theatre: The Twenty-First-Century Performances and Metamodernism', 'contribut[ed] to the discourse on metamodernism by moving from the concept of *between* and reflecting on another meta-dimension which is the notion of *beyond*' (Mitova 2020: 2; emphasis in original). For Mitova, similar to my understanding of engagement beyond the theatrical events mentioned earlier, 'performances that have *gone beyond* the boundaries of theatre should be considered metamodern theatre' (ibid.: 6; emphasis in original). Building on the importance of Andy Lavender's *Theatres of Engagement* to my comprehension of contemporary theatre entering a metamodern phase, I see Mitova's beyondness in metamodern theatre as an essential understanding of metamodern performance aesthetics. Mitova's focus on the beyondness of metamodernity is a welcome shift – and expansion of – metamodern cultural theory given that, prior to Mitova's publication, a majority of metamodern thinking focused on the 'betweenness' of metamodernism's oscillatory nature. As Mitova points out, for Vermuelen and van den Akker, their use of the prefix 'meta' to discern the post-postmodern structure of feeling is based on a triple-meaning – ' "with", "between" and "beyond" ' (Vermuelen and van den Akker 2010: 2) – and whilst Vermuelen and van den Akker use the three connotations in a 'similar, yet not indiscriminate fashion' (ibid.), their focus on metamodernism's oscillation, according to Mitova, 'immediately suggests that they focus more on the nature of *between* rather than *beyond*' (Mitova 2020: 5; emphasis in original). Mitova's own focus on the beyondness of metamodern theatre facilitates an understanding of how elements of contemporary performance that sit beyond the oscillatory betweenness also inhabit a metamodern landscape. To return again to The Gramophone's *Playful Acts of Rebellion* or Uninvited Guests' *Love Letters at Home* – the elements I focused on earlier in this chapter in regard to authenticity are also inherently intertwined with Mitova's focus on the beyondness of metamodernism, with both moving *beyond* the confines of the theatre space (whether in person or virtual) and into the 'real' (authentic) world.

Published the same year, Carina Westling's study on the most successful British immersive theatre company Punchdrunk, *Immersion and Participation in Punchdrunk's Theatrical Worlds* (2020), briefly references metamodernism – and reflects Mitova's beyondness – in unpacking the company's fans' continued engagement with, and expansion of, the storyworlds (which are created in Punchdrunk's immersive works) on social media. Westling focusses on online 'superfans' (Westling 2020: 33) who, through online message boards, facilitate a form of make-believe reality for each other in which the 'storyworld is positioned as a transcendent' (ibid.) experience that can be reached through pseudo-spiritual, ritualistic practice rather than – in reality – an expensive immersive theatre performance. Westling uses metamodernism, here, to understand the 'reframing of [fans'] nostalgia for the live storyworlds in a form that invokes the sublime via the possible imposition of a mystical, transcendental presence on everyday life' (ibid.: 34) whilst not actually believing in such a delusion. In an online space, the 'invocation of the sublime is a deliberate, communal, ritualistic performance that sustains the sensation of immersion' (ibid.) – enabling, through knowing make-believe, the immersive experience to prevail far beyond the limits of the performance itself.

Lastly, I have already referred to Benjamin Broadribb's 'Lockdown Shakespeare and the Metamodern Sensibility' (2022), in which he locates a sense of together-apartness which, whilst 'the pandemic ... amplified and catalysed [it, has] already defined the opening decades of the twenty-first century' (Broadribb 2022: 45). Broadribb utilizes his notion of together-apartness to unpack the paradoxical experience of viewing various virtual productions of Shakespeare produced on Zoom throughout the coronavirus lockdowns. 'Whilst creating a sense of togetherness for people worldwide,' states Broadribb (ibid.: 52), Zoom 'also serves as a persistent reminder of our enforced physical distance' – and as a result, 'offers an inherently metamodern performance space' (ibid.). Broadribb not only focuses on this paradoxical together-apartness but also notes the number of Zoom-based Shakespeare performances that utilized an 'oscillation between authenticity and artifice' (ibid.: 58) throughout the lockdowns. This is evident, for Broadribb, through the use of plastic Muppet toys as actors in a section of Julia Giolzetti's *Sofa Shakespeare* production of *Hamlet* (2021) in which the 'status and inherent humour of the Muppets gives [their] performance a sense of postmodern pastiche; but the well-worn appearance of the toys, perhaps childhood keepsakes (Kermit, playing Claudius, is missing an eye), and the low-tech charm of the puppetry lend [the] segment sincerity' (Broadribb 2022: 51). Or, in the sudden shift from such toy/puppet based disconnect to the

> unfiltered reality [of] Giolzetti herself deliver[ing] the opening lines of Hamlet's 'To be, or not to be' speech [... lying] on her bed, her heavily pregnant belly exposed, her performance one of sincere vulnerability. Hamlet's speech is famous to the point that its meaning can easily become obscured by its ubiquity; but hearing it delivered by Giolzetti in this way breathes natural life into Hamlet's words. Phrases such as 'the thousand natural shocks that flesh is air to' (3.1.61–62) take on new meaning as Giolzetti caresses her belly with one hand throughout her performance. (ibid.)

For Broadribb, such oscillatory, paradoxical positionings – together/apart, ironic/sincere – compel him to 'recognize Zoom performance in particular as inherently metamodern' (ibid.: 60). As I intend throughout this volume to connect the post-postmodern shifts within contemporary British theatre to the wider cultural understanding of a metamodern structure of feeling, Broadribb also sees the metamodernity of Zoom-based performance as reflective of a wider cultural shift that was exacerbated by the cultural and social effects of the pandemic

> oscillating between different planes of existence; simultaneously delivering new depths and losing something of ourselves; cynically questioning the events of the present whilst sincerely hoping for a brighter future; embracing new creative and connective outlets whilst yearning for the old ones to return. (Broadribb 2022: 61)

Broadribb's understanding of a general cultural and social shift beyond postmodernity that is embodied in our own individual experiences, as well as the cultural artefacts of this paradigm, underpins the analysis throughout this volume. Whilst this chapter traced the work of scholars across other cultural studies that touched on theatre and the work of theatre scholars that have touched on metamodernism in order to document the initial, often disparate, traces of metamodernism within theatre scholarship over the past decade, what becomes clear is that there is as of yet no definitive, clear claim towards a definition of – or framework for – metamodern theatre. Or, more specifically, no clarification on how contemporary theatre reflects, and develops, the wider cultural understanding of metamodernism. This volume aims to fill this gap – to define metamodern theatre. First, though, there is a question plaguing everyone's mind since they picked up this book – what, exactly, is metamodernism?

2

Metamodernism

Origins and definitions

In 2010, art critic Jerry Saltz observed what he defined as a new artistic attitude emerging: contemporary (post-postmodern) artists proclaiming that, 'I know that the art I'm creating may seem silly, even stupid, or that it might have been done before, but that doesn't mean this isn't serious' (Saltz, 2010). Timotheus Vermeulen and Robin van den Akker's following article, *Notes on Metamodernism* (2010), posited that this emerging attitude was reflective of 'new generations of artists increasingly abandon[ing] the aesthetic precepts of deconstruction, para-taxis, and pastiche in favour of aesth-ethical notions of reconstruction, myth, and metaxis' (Vermeulen and van den Akker 2010: 2) whilst *simultaneously* remaining aware of the problematics and critiques of such. The pair's proposal was built upon Linda Hutcheon's declaration of the end of postmodernism (Hutcheon 2002: 165) and her challenge to find and name the incoming post-postmodern zeitgeist. A number of theorists soon laid claim to Hutcheon's challenge and a range of other potential -ism's were born. Nicholas Bourriaud's altermodernism (2005), structured largely around globalized creolization (Bourriaud 2009), stands in opposition towards, or disregard of, contemporary political and cultural polarization. Zygmunt Bauman's liquid modernity (2000), Gilles Lipovetsky's hypermodernism (2005), Alan Kirby's digimodernism (2009) and Robert Samuels's automodernism (2010) each focus predominantly on the impact of technical advances following the turn of the millennium (cf. Vermeulen and van den Akker 2010: 3). Whilst other proposed terminologies, including transmodernism, avantpop, performativism, hypermodernism, new sincerity (cf. Bunnel 2015: 2) and Raoul Eshelman's performatism (2008), focus on what can, in hindsight, be seen as separate constituent parts of the wider framework of metamodernity. The critical reception to each of these terms limited their outreach, with Noah Bunnel stating in 2015 that despite the creativity and innovation shown through these 'proposed successors … none of them adequately describe deviations from the postmodern condition, and none have been able to gain traction in the academic community, let alone become part of mainstream usage' (Bunnell 2015: 3). The popularity of the term metamodernism, however, has shown exponential growth in both academic and mainstream spheres since van den Akker and Vermeulen's repositioning of the term in 2010 from its initial coinage by Mas'ud Zavrazadeh in 1975. Focusing his analysis exclusively on American literature throughout the 1950s to the 1970s, Zavrazadeh's original use of the term metamodernism describes, as per Ilori's understanding, 'fictions portraying reality both accurately and absurdly [with] reality as a form of certainty ha[ving] been subverted by ... randomness and uncertainty' (Ilori 2016: 155). For Vermeulen and van den Akker, Zavrazadeh's focus on tropes such as dark humour, parody and metafiction within 1970s literature mean that, with today's hindsight, Zavrazadeh's use of the term metamodernism essentially 'indicates what is today generally considered a (variant of) postmodernism' (van den Akker and Vermeulen 2017: 4). Vermeulen and van den Akker's later re-application of the term (which does, in fact, build upon the accurate/absurd juxtaposition of Zavrazedah's terminology) instead reframed metamodernism as

> a heuristic label to come to terms with a range of aesthetic and cultural predilections and as a notion to periodise these preferences [... in] an attempt to chart – in much the same way as Jameson has done for postmodernism – the dominant cultural logic of a specific stage in the development of Western capitalist societies, in all its many forms and disguises. (van den Akker and Vermeulen 2017: 4)

At the time of writing, there is a rapidly expanding number of theorists who have defined, or are defining, metamodernism as a contemporary cultural paradigm within literature (Abramson 2018; Rowland 2021), film (MacDowell 2010, 2012, 2017; Flight 2023), visual art (Turner 2015; Kovalova et al. 2022), music (van Poecke 2017; Dember 2019) and popular culture (Ceriello and Dember 2013–present; van den Akker, Gibbons and Vermeulen 2017), as well as the terminology being co-opted into political theory (Freinacht 2017) and sociology (Cooper 2017). As Smiljka Javanović reports, 'Recently, metamodernism has become recognised outside of traditional academic platforms as well; it is debated in podcasts and streaming videos and presented through popular performances and memes across social networks' (Javanović 2021: 58). For Javanović, metamodernism is understood as *the* dominant cultural logic of the [Western, capitalist] twenty-first century society (ibid.: 57), as per van den Akker and Vermeulen's claim – noting that 'other writers define and explain metamodernism by a similarly magnificent scope of etiquettes – "the mindset or sensibility or cultural code", "a post-postmodern grand meta-narrative", "a developmental stage of society" [and] "a particular lens for thinking about the self, language, culture, and meaning – really, about everything"' (Abramson 2015, quoted in Javanović 2021: 58–9). Whilst such grandiose language is somewhat unavoidable when dealing with wide-ranging concepts such as a structure of feeling, I intentionally focus throughout this volume on what certain scholars of metamodernism would – erroneously – term the 'Dutch School' (cf. Cooper 2017; Javanović 2021) of metamodernism – in which metamodernism is seen as a cultural and aesthetic turn within arts and culture largely built upon Vermeulen and van den Akker's application of the terminology, with some *inescapable* interstices with wider cultural and political understandings. This is, in part, to exclude the self-named (Freinacht 2017; Cooper 2018) 'Nordic School' or Liminal Web (Lightfoot 2021) appropriation of the terminology of metamodernism towards a predominantly political and sociological 'developmental stage' (Freinacht 2017: 15) within a Model of Hierarchical Complexity, as well as those who would go so far as to develop political movements and ideologies (Freinacht 2017; Gessen 2017) built upon this application of the term. Whilst some would argue that such strands of thought can be synthesized (Dempsey 2023), my intentionally narrow-focussed understanding of the metamodern is an attempt at limiting the scope of this analysis. Rather than a generalized attempt at periodizing culture at large, I offer a way in which to analyse and unpack specific aesthetical and methodological shifts within contemporary theatre that 'cannot be explained anymore (merely) in terms of postmodernism' (Javanović 2021: 58) and, instead, appear to mirror the understanding of metamodern attributes as documented within other contemporary cultural fields in a way that builds, specifically, from Vermeulen and van den Akker's initial application of the term.

However, as Vermeulen and van den Akker are quick to point out, I too 'do not seek to impose a predetermined system of thought on a rather particular range of cultural practices' (2010: 2) and emphasize that engaging with the concept of the metamodern – specifically within the field of theatre – 'should be read as an invitation for debate rather than an extending of a dogma' (ibid.). As the pair expand in 2017, the 'cultural ... practices we would describe as metamodern do, in our view, not offer a solution to the problematic of postmodernism (however the postmodern is perceived)' (van den Akker and Vermeulen 2017: 5). As both a heuristic and periodizing label, metamodernism within the arts and culture is 'characterised by oscillation rather than synthesis, harmony, reconciliation' (ibid.: 6), which leads to messiness, tension and a suggested impossibility of resolution. It is with this openness to disagreement and discussion in mind that I apply Vermeulen and van den Akker's term – and the expanding terminology that extends within, through and beyond this – throughout this volume.

Vermeulen and van den Akker's metamodernism is inherently tied to their understanding of the 2000s and the crises that coalesced within this period. They conceive of the 2000s not as an explicit temporal decade (2000–10) but rather as a historical period beginning towards the end of the 1990s and ending around 2011 (van den Akker and Vermeulen 2017: 11) during which the constituent elements of metamodernism began to take shape. Within this period of 'the millennial generation [coming] of age' (ibid.: 11), specific political, economic and sociological crises including 'the maturity and availability of digital technologies … the so-called fourth wave of terrorism hit[ting] Western shores … immigration policies and multicultural ideals backlash[ing] in the midst of a revival of nationalist populism … and the financial crises inaugurat[ing] yet another round of neoliberalism … emerged, converged and coagulated' (ibid.: 11–12). It is within, through and out of this 'clusterfuck of world-historical proportions' (ibid.: 17) – what others would more politely label the permacrisis (Zuleeg, Emmanouilidis and Borges de Castro 2021) – that the metamodern sensibility emerged – postmodernism no longer providing a meaningful label to the cultural and artistic responses to such a clusterfuck.

Sceptics of the perceived end of postmodernism point towards the commonly referenced idea that 9/11 put an end to the postmodern era as 'crashing two planes into the Twin Towers returned the world to the real after it's decadent dalliance with post-modernism and hyperreality' (Jeffries 2021: 290), and 'the world still had some use for [metanarratives such as] God, truth and the law, terms that they were [now] using without inverted commas' (Kunzru, 2011), as an appealing and neat theorization that is obviously too simplistic. Periodizing the 2000s as a shifting-sands stage between postmodernity and metamodernity, however, enables an acceptance of Arquilla's '(B)end of History' (2011) as a soft counter to the other commonly referenced but hotly contested flashpoint death of postmodernism – Francis Fukuyama's pronounced 'End of History' in 1989 (which Fukuyama, in fact, proposed was a little premature in a follow-up article in 2012). Rather than the end of postmodernism itself, and the birth of something entirely new, metamodernity proposes that, as van den Akker and Vermeulen state, 'the postmodern vernacular has proven increasingly inapt and inept in coming to terms with our changed social [and cultural] situation' (van den Akker and Vermeulen 2017: 2) which has led to a 'waning of a host of different postmodern impulses' (ibid.) with a *simultaneous* arrival of aesthetic phenomena that are 'characterised by an attempt to *incorporate* postmodern stylistic and formal conventions while moving beyond them [coupled with] the return of realist and modernist forms, techniques and aspirations' (p. 3; emphasis added). Rather than an entire dismissal of postmodernity, or the clean break of an instigating event that shocked us 'out' of postmodernity, it is within this period that an interest beyond postmodern aesthetics (and, indeed, a renewed interest in what came prior) starts to come to the fore in such a way that *still* incorporates those postmodern aspects – a 'both, and' nature oscillating between an entrenched postmodernity and an attempted 'other' (that some would align with modernism). Whilst some may point to the convergence of crises-like changes in societal conditions over the past few decades (including the integration of the internet, the overheating climate, increased political polarization, the pandemic and more) forcing us into a position in which 'we can no longer "afford" to be entirely glib and ironic in our arts and culture – that there is a need to fold back in the possibility of earnestness, enthusiasm and universalism that postmodernism shied away from' (Dember 2023), for Dember, the reasons for this shift is, again, centred on the individual's felt experience. Metamodernism, therefore, 'is a response in both artists and audiences to an exhaustion they feel with postmodernism's negation of the self, and sometimes modernism's atomizing of the self' (Dember 2023) and the 'essence of metamodernism is [therefore] a conscious or unconscious need to protect the solidity of felt experience against the scientific reductionism of the modernist perspective and the ironic detachment of the postmodern sensibility [*and*] to protect the sense of the interior self from the destabilizing effect of chaotic contemporary societal changes' (Dember 2023). Dember's focus on the felt experience as the central nexus of metamodern aesthetics reminds us that, whilst such a discussion inevitably leads outwards towards larger issues of culture, politics and society at large, it is through our embodied, personal and felt experience that we understand such aesthetics, strategies and *feelings*.

These feelings – as they emerge through and beyond the period of the 2000s – are 'characterised by an oscillating in-betweenness or, rather, a dialectical movement that identifies with and negates – and hence, overcomes and undermines – conflicting positions, while never being congruent to these positions' (Vermeulen and van den Akker 2010: 10), in which a new focus on an '(often guarded) hopefulness and (at times feigned) sincerity' (ibid.: 1) comes to the fore. Vermeulen, too, ties this to an individual's felt experience through and beyond postmodernity when he states that 'it's fair to say that we grew up with a particular kind of outlook on life that was of irony and deconstruction and of cynicism ... This was very much a sensibility that spoke to us, that we ... were attuned to [but in the late 2000s] something was changing [– it's no longer] about irony, but it's about post-irony, new forms of sincerity, informed naïveté' (Frieze 2014). In Chapter 3,

I build upon both Vermeulen and van den Akker's understanding of the millennial generation being raised 'on' irony and how this couples with the earlier mentioned overlapping crises converging as 'specific, internal relations, at once interlocking and in tension' (Williams 1977: 132) into specifically 'unique experiences and challenges this generation has faced' (Brown et al. 2017: 5) within our formative adult years – understanding both metamodernity and the millennials as intertwined structures of feeling, as per Raymond Williams.

In a way that reflects metamodernism's 'both, and' nature, Williams's structure of feeling being both 'as firm and definite as "structure" suggests, yet … based in the deepest and often least tangible elements of our experience' (1969: 18) refers to almost intangible, and yet experiential, modalities apparent within a particular cultural time-frame that are 'essentially related, although in practice, and in detail, this is not always easy to see' (1969: 17). In Vermeulen and van den Akker's application of Williams's framework, metamodernism is an attempt to describe a structure of feeling 'that is a sensibility that is widespread enough to be called structural … yet that cannot be reduced to one particular strategy' (Vermeulen and Van Den Akker 2015a). I detailed Williams's framework in Chapter 1, however, as this terminology will be utilized throughout both the remainder of this chapter and with regards to an understanding of the millennial generation in Chapter 3, it is important to highlight Vermeulen and van den Akker's understanding of a structure of feeling as 'a sentiment, or rather still a sensibility that everyone shares, that everyone is aware of, but which cannot easily, if at all, be pinned down. It's tenor, however, can be traced in art, which has the capability to express a common experience of a time and place' (van den Akker and Vermeulen 2017: 7). As mentioned earlier, my own narrow focus on tracing such a structure of feeling within the aesthetic and methodological shifts within contemporary British theatre limits such an analysis. The specificity regarding my particular interest in the work of British theatre makers who are, largely, working on the fringes of the theatre scene and who largely fit within the brackets of the millennial generation, further limits the overall applicability of my own understanding of metamodernity within the theatrical field. However, it is, of course, important to note that this volume is not an attempt to categorize *all* contemporary theatre as metamodern. As James MacDowell notes, Williams's terminology also takes into account that 'it is only one of many such localised "structures" at work in a particular time and place' (MacDowell 2017: 28), and a multiplicity of structures are in place at any historical moment, including the present one. My intentions in publishing this volume are – taking my cue from Daniel Schulze's use of the term metamodern – to 'spark debate [because] a clear description and even a label will prove helpful in order to refine concepts and encourage further discussion' (Schulze 2017: 54).

Oscillation

If you have heard of metamodernism before picking up this book, you will undoubtedly have heard the word oscillation quickly following in tow. If not, you will have seen it mentioned plenty in the preceding pages of this very volume. The concept of metamodernism is entwined with the concept of oscillation. The prefix 'meta' stems from Plato's metaxy, a term that Voegelin connects to the Greek *heros*, or demi-gods, highlighting an experience that contains a continual oscillation between god and man: 'order and disorder, truth and untruth, sense and senselessness of existence' (Voegelin 1989: 119– 20). In the case of the metamodern, the central aesthetic experience is one of oscillation between what Vermeulen and van den Akker 'may call – and of course cannot be reduced to – postmodern and pre-postmodern (and often modern) predilections' (van den Akker and Vermeulen 2017: 11) including sincerity and sarcasm, irony and enthusiasm, hope and hopelessness. Importantly, this oscillatory movement does not indicate a 'best of both worlds' (ibid.) approach. Instead, 'it is a pendulum swinging between 2, 3, 5, 10, innumerable poles. Each time the metamodern enthusiasm swings toward fanaticism, gravity pulls it back toward irony; the moment its irony sways toward apathy, gravity pulls it back toward enthusiasm' (Vermeulen and van den Akker 2010: 6). As Brent Cooper summarizes, 'Metamodernism is basically defined as the oscillation between modern and postmodern modes, the rapid dialectic of which creates a new synthetic discourse' (Cooper 2017). As I contend from my own felt experience watching contemporary British theatre, certain cultural aesthetics emerging in the 2000s can not *only* be ascribed to what had come to be labelled postmodern. The emergence of strategies that appeared to re-apply and/or return to certain tendencies that contradicted, or undermined, strategies and modalities that would be considered postmodern indicated a shift beyond such. These strategies include a re-application and renewed interest in historicity, affect and depth (cf. van den Akker, Gibbons and Vermeulen 2017) and an endeavour towards some form of authenticity within both artistic and personal spheres (cf. Schulze 2017), as well as what could be described as a rise in a sense of an (ironic) sincerity through a continual oscillation between disparate polarities. Importantly, though – as Dember notes – 'the oscillation in metamodernism involves a dynamic between opposing *aesthetic sensibilities*, not merely opposing beliefs, or other sorts of opposite pairs, like, say ...

chocolate and vanilla' (Dember 2023, emphasis added). In this sense, metamodernism's metaxy speaks of a movement between relevant opposing polarities, 'not a binary so much as a continuum that stretches from one to the other, not a balance but a pendulum swinging between the various extremes' (van den Akker, Gibbons and Vermeulen 2017: 11). It reconciles an acceptance and utilization of certain metanarratives, or a 'reintroduction of hope and progress' (Freinacht 2017) as self-named metamodern philosopher Hanzi Freinacht (actually a pen name for Emil Ejner Friis and Daniel Görtz) terms it, whilst also being inherently critical and aware of their frailties and falsehoods. Metamodernism does not indicate a return to the trappings of modernist metanarratives. It is not naïve. Instead, it offers what has come to be termed informed naïveté or pragmatic idealism (Turner 2015) that engages with a resurgence of the strive for authenticity, romanticism and affect whilst not 'forfeiting all that we've learnt from postmodernism' (ibid.).

How, though, does this oscillation manifest in art and cultural artefacts? For Dember, there are four kinds of oscillation occurring in what he sees as metamodern art: hermeneutic oscillation, structural oscillation, braiding and juxtaposition (Dember 2023). Hermeneutic oscillation, in this sense, is a largely subjective (and therefore difficult to quantify) oscillatory occurrence that happens in the audience's reaction to the artwork, rather than within the artwork itself: 'As the viewer swings to, say a postmodern pole in interpreting the object, the very logic of that reaction compels the viewer to swing back to a modernist pole, and then it reverses again and the cycle continues' (Dember 2023). Structural oscillation, in contrast, refers to the actual aesthetics of an artwork over audience experience, with the 'artwork itself includ[ing] pieces from both sides of a duality and it switches back and forth between them in time' (Dember 2023). Dember uses the terms braiding and juxtaposition to unpack structural oscillation a little further, referring to an artwork simultaneously containing both (in simple terms) modern and postmodern aesthetic threads and either interweaving between them (braiding) or having them exist separately within the same artwork (juxtaposition) – 'They don't cancel each other out, or form a blend, but rather they coexist separately and exist in relation to each other' (Dember 2023). In this sense, a metamodern artwork need not oscillate wholly between such polarities – it need not feel 'wholly postmodern' and then 'wholly modern', fluctuating (separately) between the two throughout its runtime – but can exhibit multiple elements of each of these polarities in tandem, whether braided together or existing in opposition to each other.

Whilst some have criticized a focus on oscillation within an understanding of metamodernism for undermining dialectical processes in that to 'oscillate between conflicting models only [is to] suspend ... commitment to any one of them [so] oscillating between beliefs is indistinguishable from believing nothing' (Ludford 2021), such critique is largely based alongside the 'Liminal Web' understanding of metamodernism as a political ideology or larger sociological movement – often referring to the metamodern epistemological 'project'. Whilst I have sympathy for such panacea-style thinking, my limited interest is on shifting aesthetics in contemporary culture – and, specifically, contemporary theatre. As such, it is not my aim in this volume to critique metamodern oscillation as a model of behaviour outside of cultural aesthetics. Rather, I am interested in the fact that such metamodern oscillation is occurring within contemporary theatre as an aesthetic and artistic choice and, consequently, what this says both about the development of theatre post-postmodernism's dénouement and about the artists that have made these choices.

Aesthetic strategies

Whilst the oscillation inherent within metamodern cultural artefacts is essential evidence of a shift beyond postmodern strategies – in that the metamodern artefact oscillates between postmodern and pre-postmodern aesthetics and therefore cannot only be described in postmodern terms – oscillation, though central, is not the *only* defining characteristic of metamodernism but one of several potential methods. In Vermeulen and van den Akker's original article, *Notes on Metamodernism* (2010), the pair propose that the aesthetics of the quirky within indie cinema (MacDowell 2010) and Raoul Eshelman's performatism (2008) can be included within their model of metamodernism as particular metamodern strategies alongside a central focus on oscillation. Following this, multiple strategies that make up the metamodern sensibility have been located by various scholars within cultural artefacts as varied as new narrative trends within contemporary blockbusters (*In Defense of the Force Awakens* 2017; Warren 2017), specific shifts in contemporary literature – including the emergence of the genres of auto-fiction, misery-lit and uplit (James 2019); the rise in empathetic and sincere modes of lyricism within certain genres of music such as freak folk and rap (van Poecke 2017; Dember 2019); the 'new golden age' of sitcoms that are 'as cynical and harsh [but have a] warmer, more humanist spirit' than their pre-2000s counterparts (Rustad 2011); and the global rise in divisive populist politics (Krumsvik and Co 2017; cf. van den Akker and Vermeulen 2017: 8). In Greg Dember's *Eleven Metamodern Methods in the Arts* (2018), he expands upon these offers by providing a list of aesthetics as a challenge to the supposition that metamodernism is rooted predominantly in the notion of oscillation and, instead, that the shift from a postmodern sensibility to a metamodern sensibility can be traced through a number of artistic methods that he observes within metamodern work. His inventory is both an expansion of and an unpacking of the metamodern sensibility as espoused by Vermeulen and van den Akker in an attempt to propose a (non-exhaustive) list of methods which cultural products that 'feel' metamodern might employ in various combinations. Later, in 2020, Simon Radchenko 'defined and tested a number of features that define a text as metamodern' (Radchenko 2020: 249) – taking what he labelled the 'main trends' (Radchenko 2019: 495) of metamodernism and developing an analytical method in which to understand and search for metamodern trends within contemporary literature (2019) and videogames (2020). In this section, I offer a brief summation of some of the main trends, methods and aesthetics that permeate metamodern cultural artefacts through Dember and Radchenko's separate models. In part, this interpretation of these features is an attempt to engender a shared language of understanding in order to define, unpack and connect such strategies within a theatrical landscape. It is not within the scope of this volume to unpack all of Dember's methods or Radchenko's aesthetics, particularly when some of these relate to wider cultural trends that have limited reach within theatre and performance – Dember's focus on the Normcore fashion trend as a metamodern aesthetic, for instance. Instead, I offer a brief, interconnected summation of a chosen number of these in the next few sections – namely those which I see as inherently connected to the central tenet of oscillation within metamodernism that, in agreement with Dember's understanding, refers to a fluctuation between 'modernist qualities and postmodern qualities, or at least between oppositional pairs of emotional or aesthetic qualities, not opposing political or intellectual positions' (Dember 2018). As will be developed throughout this volume, the following aesthetics are specifically applicable to understanding how metamodernism and contemporary theatre interact, in order to develop a shared terminology with understandings of metamodernity in other cultural fields. In Chapter 4, I offer my own inventory of metamodern methods that relate specifically to theatrical practice. For now, however, borrowing from both Dember and Radchenko's attempts, the following subsections offer a tentative inventory of aesthetic strategies that help to identify metamodern cultural aesthetics or – in a clearer sense – provide a terminology to understand why a certain artwork *feels* metamodern.

Felt experience

Dember's metamodern methods include multiple, intersecting aesthetic modalities that coalesce around a central point which is that, for Dember

(2018), 'the essence of metamodernism is a (conscious or unconscious) motivation to protect the solidity of *felt experience* against the scientific reductionism of the modernist perspective and the ironic detachment of the postmodern sensibility'. In Chapter 1, I drew on Elinor Fuchs's felt experience as an audience member witnessing the postmodern turn in theatre across New York in the 1990s as a reflection of my own embodied experience as an audience member observing the metamodern turn in theatre across Britain in the 2010s and beyond. Dember's assertion that metamodernism's central nexus is the audience's felt experience, here, is helpful in understanding how metamodern aesthetics are exhibited within theatre and performance as it enables a centring of the individual audience member's experience, and yet the 'both, and' nature of metamodernity does not, importantly, erase the inescapable multiplicity of the infinitely individual readings of each audience member that a postmodern lens enabled. Whilst the move from postmodernity to metamodernity can be viewed as a response to changing societal conditions, including a convergence of economic and political crises alongside the development of internet culture (more of this in Chapter 3), Dember remains centred on individual interiority throughout this:

> The best way to understand the rise of metamodernism is as a response in both artists and audiences to an exhaustion they feel with postmodernism's negation of the self, and sometimes modernism's atomizing of the self [and] also to protect the sense of the interior self from the destabilizing effect of chaotic contemporary societal changes.
> (Dember 2023)

To illustrate the mainstream relevance of this understanding, I want to briefly borrow from recent film criticism. Joel Mayward's review of 2021 blockbuster *The Matrix Resurrections* makes explicit reference to the original *The Matrix* (1999) being *the* exemplary postmodern film (cf. Lutzka 2006), whilst it's twenty-years-later reboot/sequel/remake *The Matrix Resurrections* reflects a metamodern sensibility through a 'blend of irony and sincerity, relativism and romanticism … as it deconstructs its own film franchise identity while also celebrating its ongoing existence … it explicitly names and critiques its own legacy in cinema history with a mixture of pride and bitterness' (Mayward 2021). Alongside this metamodern oscillation between cynicism towards and celebration of the franchise's legacy, the inherent difference between the postmodern *Matrix* at the denouement of the 1990s and the metamodern *Matrix Resurrections* at the birth of the 2020s is that the former was largely about ideas and the latter was largely about feelings. As Mayward explains, 'The narrative details aren't really what's important here [but that] what matters is how we *feel* about the film' (Mayward 2021). For Dember, whilst metamodernism's oscillation between

> the postmodern view and the modern view [... remains] important ... what we really know is what we feel and what's our interior experience. In the end, if you don't have that, there's no point. So, if your sophisticated postmodern relativism or your sophisticated modernist scientific process ends up leaving no place for the interior, you've kind of missed the boat. (The Oscillator's Stone 2023)

In 2016, Critchley (2016: 24) argued that 'art's filthy lesson is inauthenticity all the way down, a series of repetitions and reenactments: fakes that strip away the illusion of reality in which we live and confront us with the reality of illusion'. Building on this, Stuart Jeffries's *Everything, All the Time, Everywhere* (2021) simultaneously maintains that the 'waning of affect that [Frederic] Jameson took to be a characteristic of our souls under post-modernism thrives more than ever in the decades since 9/11' (2021: 294). However, at the end of his afterword to his comprehensive study on postmodernity, Jeffries reveals an intriguing desire at the centre of his own understanding of contemporary culture. He references David Foster Wallace's own longing for a post-postmodern affect, reminding us that Wallace 'yearned for something better', that 'post-modern irony became a measure of hip sophistication and literary savvy ... not liberating but enslaving ... the song of a prisoner who's come to love his cage' (Jeffries 2021: 334). Whilst Jeffries is right to state that 'the post-modern figure whom David Foster Wallace imagined alone yet connected, entranced yet immobilized before screens of various kinds – remains emblematic of how we live' (ibid.: 294) – he ends his book with a proclamation that 'we need in our culture not more irony and wit, but more thoughtfulness and kindness' (ibid.: 335). Radchenko builds on this, drawing a link between Foster Wallace's new sincerity – which Radchenko describes as 'the desire to feel and be emotional instead of being ironic' (Radchenko 2019: 249) – and metamodern affect as defined by Alison Gibbons (2017). Gibbons interprets Jameson's waning of affect (1991) as 'a human response to the history, the superficiality of postmodern representation, and the free-floating signs or intensities of a mediatised consumer bubble' (Gibbons 2017: 83). Her understanding of the metamodern (re)turn to affect relies on a post-positivistic model of identity, which 'sees both essentialism and postmodernism as unhelpful, but rather than abandon them it argues that the two exist in tension' (ibid.: 86). Gibbons therefore argues that it is now possible to speak of a 'distinctly metamodern subjectivity, to which affect is central' (ibid.) and which is built around a contemporary identity that is 'both driven by a desire for a meaningful personal emotional experience while being aware of the constructed nature of experiences' (ibid.).

Self-reflexivity

A metamodern application of self-reflexivity is particularly pertinent when we look at the development of metatheatrical performance through and beyond postmodernity. For Dember, metamodernism inherits self-reflexivity from postmodernism, within which

> the role of self-reflexivity is generally to dissolve or to call attention to boundaries – and to raise questions about the unexamined premises that such boundaries point to. Reacting against modernism's tendency to see individual pieces of art and intellectual efforts as autonomous, self-evident revelations of an objective and universal truth, postmodern work will often draw attention to the way that the author's own perspectives, flaws or belief systems may distort any meaning that might be drawn from the work, if even by simply keeping attention on the fact that there is an author. Similarly, with attention drawn to a postmodern work's own form, genre or medium, the reader is reminded that the work is, indeed, a piece of 'work' and so not to be entirely 'trusted'. (Dember 2018)

Dember ascribes a metamodern approach towards self-reflexivity as centred, again, on the affirmation of felt experience. Rather than distancing an audience from the work through drawing attention to the form, metamodern self-reflexivity draws attention to the audience's *experience* of this engagement:

> If the 'self' being referenced is the work's own form, genre or medium, the effect is that the reader is reminded that they are engaging in something that has form, genre or medium – in other words, some sort of a work, that therefore has a reader, and of course the reader is the particular one doing the reading! Again, bringing focus on the experience of the individual engaging with the work. (Dember 2018)

In a theatrical sense, such self-reflexivity echoes Cahill's (2015) reappraisal of metatheatre as both an artistic strategy employed by theatre makers *and* as an audience-centred experience that affirms active participation and spectator self-awareness, allowing for Cahill's 'line between theatre reality and Real reality [to be] blurred or possibly removed entirely' (Cahill 2015: 2). When applied to theatre, Dember's understanding of metamodern self-reflexivity is inescapably intertwined with Cahill's theories of metatheatre as both an artistic strategy and a theory of audience reception, with a central focus on the felt experience of an audience.

Dember also envelops Eshelman's performatism into his metamodern methods, as he sees Eshelman's understanding of a post-postmodern aesthetic as describing one part of metamodernism as a wider structural shift. Dember specifically focuses on the artistic strategy at the core of Eshelman's aesthetic – the double frame. Eshelman's performatism is centred around acts of wilful self-deceit, which work 'first and foremost on an aesthetic, identificatory level, to create an attitude of beautiful belief, and not a cognitive, critical one' (Eshelman 2008: 12). Performatism therefore provides a departure from postmodern ennui through a performance of belief in certain ideas even whilst understanding that they are not true through an inescapable postmodern doubt. Eshelman's double framing consists of, first, an outer frame which requires a commitment to a (performance of) belief from the audience – 'the reader is forced to make a choice to buy into all of it, if they are going to commit to engaging the work' (Dember 2018) – and an inner frame in which is the narrative that an audience can unironically engage with once they're accepting of the outer frame. If such an understanding is transposed onto the art of theatre it quickly, of course, becomes reflective of Birgit Schuhbeck's earlier suggestion that the contemporary theatre is no longer an open (postmodern) stage but is (re)closed off in order to separate fiction from reality (cf. Schuhbeck 2012). For Schuhbeck, however, such an act of closure actually enables the stage to regain itself as a critical political force – allowing for a theatre that 'reveals and deals with society's hidden power-structures, instead of simply giving up in face of an overcomplicated world' (Schuhbeck 2012). Again, I have issues here with the idea that, when put simply, the return of the 'fourth wall' within contemporary drama – whether or not an audience's engagement of such is through a performatist framing – enables a theatre that is more politically affective than one that engages with the external offstage world. However, when focussed exclusively on a theatrical framework, Eshelman's performatism is useful in it enabling an understanding of metamodern theatre's ability to embrace *both* the inherent inescapability of metatheatricality and the inherent inescapability of inauthenticity within performance, whilst also enabling an unironic commitment to the narrative/performance/work within. As a contemporary (metamodern) audience, we *know* what we are watching is not real. We are not suspending disbelief, or believing, or even – to mirror Eshelman and Dember's suppositions – *performing* belief. Instead, as audience members in a metamodern paradigm, we can engage simultaneously with the performer and the performed, the authentic and the inauthentic, the reality and the staged. This engagement can happen both ironically and sincerely. These oppositional aspects exist simultaneously, and it is not through performing belief in one that we enable belief in the other – instead, both inhabit (metamodern) performance at the same time, whether hermeneutically or structurally, whether braided together or in juxtaposition to each other. Importantly, the simultaneity of these aspects – and the fluctuation between our experiences of them – is centred around the fact that metamodern metatheatricality highlights the audience's felt experience in their viewing of the piece.

Constructive pastiche

Perhaps one of the most well-known postmodern strategies across several artistic mediums is that of pastiche. According to Ingeborg Hoesterey's analysis of postmodern pastiche as a critical aesthetic, pastiche becomes 'a central concern of aesthetic production in the postmodern arts' (Hoesterey 1995: 496). The term refers to the juxtaposing of apparently unrelated elements, which might have originated from completely disparate genres, cultures or forms, within an artistic product. For Jameson, postmodern pastiche can be seen as 'the random cannibalization of all the styles of the past, the play of random stylistic allusion' (Jameson 1991: 18). But to relegate such an aesthetic strategy to simply random cannibalization is unfair. Take 'one of the first manifestations of postmodernism' (Unframe 2021); the consumerist collages of pop-artist Richard Hamilton, which were deemed by critics in the 1970s as uncritical but were built on Hamilton's well-thought-out desire to create publicly accessible work that purposefully 'should be popular, transient, expendable, low-cost, mass-produced, young, witty, sexy, gimmicky, glamorous, and big business' (Hamilton 1957, cited in Hamilton 1983). Or take famously postmodern superstar (Jeffries 2021) David Bowie's use of William S. Burrough and Brion Gysin's 'cut up technique', in which 'words and phrases are cut from newspapers and magazines and the fragments re-arranged at random' (Jones 2015) as a compositional tool for his song writing – a process later utilized by *Joy Division*'s Ian Curtis, and, perhaps the epitome of postmodernity's cynical pinnacle, *Nirvana*'s Kurt Cobain. In 1997, Bowie stated that he utilized such a method for roughly half of his song writing, describing how he had begun to use a computer programme that enabled him to 'hit the random button and it will randomize everything' (*BBC News* [1997] 2016). However, in conjunction with such randomness was careful consideration in the curation of such results: 'If you put three or four dissociated ideas together and create awkward relationships with them, the unconscious intelligence that comes from those pairings is really quite startling sometimes, quite provocative' (*BBC News* [1997] 2016). It is a harrowing reflection when, quarter of a century later, current development in AI art generation relies on the pirated intellectual property of millions of artists, photographers, filmmakers and musicians in such a way that, rather than generating material to inspire an artist through which to then develop original work, completely bypasses the artist in order to generate imitations of pre-existing artistic products (Shaffi 2023).

In Linda Hutcheon's *Politics of Postmodernism* (1988), she critiques Jameson's assertion that the pastiche of postmodern artists (to return to the human, here) is random cannibalization, stating that to 'include irony and play is never necessarily to exclude seriousness of purpose in postmodernist art. To misunderstand this is to misunderstand the nature of much contemporary aesthetic production – even if it does make for neater theorizing' (Hutcheon 2002: 27). I do not disagree with Hutcheon's proclamation here, despite the whiff of what might later become understood as metamodern ironic sincerity (see ironesty further on) in the way that her definition reflects Saltz' observation of a silly-but-doesn't-mean-it-isn't-serious artistic attitude emerging in the 2000s and beyond (Saltz 2010). As I made clear in Chapter 1, in attempting to ascribe a lexicon to the complicated, rhizomatic, many faceted and often contradictory elements that make up metamodernity and postmodernity as interdependent cultural structures of feeling, I – and others – are acutely aware of the problematics involved regarding generalization, misrepresentation and the rewriting of history. However, there is something to be said in that Hutcheon's focus within this specific point is on postmodern *architecture*, and the intended mapping of this onto postmodern aesthetics within art, literature and theatre is somewhat problematic. Duvall's critique of Hutcheon contends that postmodern architecture is necessarily indicted far more within capitalistic structures than postmodern art, literature, and performance need be, and therefore has 'necessarily been more in tune with the desires of the ruling class [which] almost inevitably forces architecture into an identification with high culture' (Duvall 1999: 380), so the transfer of these specifics into wider – more accessible – artforms requires further unpacking. Whilst I am sympathetic towards Hutcheon's assessment that, to paraphrase, the inclusion of the silly within postmodern pastiche does not necessarily eliminate the serious (and I would also emphasize the connections this has to the general tone of metamodernism), there is a distinct difference in the pastiche employed within postmodern work and that employed within metamodern work which evidences a general shift in intentions.

Pastiche in a postmodern sense can be largely defined as dissociative – pitting 'elements against each other, with results that were usually amusingly absurd, in order to call into question the unexamined premises of each'

(Dember 2018). Bowie's postmodern use of pastiche worked to continue to develop a, somewhat unreachable, distanced legacy, ensuring that 'his songs can never truly be interpreted – not that it will keep generation after generation of intrigued listeners from trying' (Marshall 2019). The difference between this and pastiche in a metamodern sense is that the latter is potentially constructive rather than dissociative and, again, serves to foreground the inclusion of the felt experience of the audience. For Dember, this includes work that 'combines disparate elements in order to build a space inhabited by a felt experience that is not at home in either element on its own [or] allows a work of art to bring into it the kinds of cultural combinations that people experience in real life, in spite of conventional divisions between them' (Dember 2018). In this sense, metamodern pastiche builds on the self-referentiality and intertextuality of postmodern pastiche to open up a space that, again, refocuses an audience's attention to their own felt experience. For Radchencko, this reconstruction is inherently linked to a renewed need for belonging and wish to create in the metamodern individual, with the desire to 'create or reconstruct the world on a cleaned postmodern soil [an] obvious consequence of the postmodern era' (Radchenko 2019: 500). On a larger scale, Radchenko links this to a wider belief in a (re)construction of the oecumene – an overarching understanding of the known – that also takes into account the variety of systems and groups that take part in such reconstruction, arguing that this 'constructive willingness is, first of all, the answer to collapse and destruction of the previous models or their signs [and that this] desire is the basic point of post-post[modernism], the reason for these new feelings' (ibid.).

Ironesty

The final aesthetic of note at this stage (although this chapter does not provide an exhaustive list) is inherently connected to the oscillatory nature of metamodernism, as well as previous understandings of a new sincerity (Foster Wallace 1993; Thorne 2006) developing out of the irony and cynicism of postmodernism's peak. As described earlier on regarding affect's relation to the felt experience within metamodern aesthetics, several theorists and cultural commentators have observed, or even called for, a return to belief, public mindedness, and emotion (cf. Purdy 2000) as we emerged from postmodernity. New Sincerity, developed in literary studies from Foster Wallace's 'new rebels' (1993: 192), before being appropriated throughout other cultural studies, is not a complete removal of irony from cultural discourse to be 'replaced by soft, sweet sincerity' (Thorne 2006). Irony is not dead. As Lee Konstantinou reminds us, 'Postmodern irony has never disappeared [and its] imperium – as both form and content – is arguably stronger than ever' (Konstantinou 2017: 90). Instead, as according to Thorne's *Manifesto for a New Sincerity* (2006), New Sincerity is an attempt to describe the way that 'irony and sincerity [have become] combined like Voltron, to form a new movement of astonishing power'. Inevitably, such a combination becomes watered down in public discussion towards a proposal for a 'purposeful avoidance of cynicism with a deep commitment to your ideals and, most importantly, to optimism' (Marouf 2022), which, as Marouf proposes, can be used as an antithesis for the common defence of cynicism or ignorance in dealing with the permacrisis on an everyday level. Whilst Marouf insists that they 'don't ask to be rid of irony' (2022), Konstantinou problematizes such call-to-arms by pointing out that such proclamations 'either ignore the problem of irony or alleviate its torture prematurely by presuming that sincerity is what stands in opposition to irony' (2017: 89). Instead, Konstantinou proposes that post-irony is more conducive a term in which to describe this post-postmodern aesthetic as it 'doesn't decide in advance what follows the age of irony' (ibid.). Similarly, Dember problematizes the term New Sincerity in that it is bound, firstly, to a specific project or movement within literature and, secondly, bound temporally – with the word 'New' implying 'that it comes at a certain point in history' (Dember 2018). Konstantinou's post-irony comes under similar constraints in regard to a focus on *post*-ironic – a term that cannot escape its insinuation that irony is *over*, despite Konstantiou's claims to the contrary. To solve this, I turn to Dember's coinage of the term ironesty (Dember 2017a) to describe the particular threading of (modern or metamodern) sincerity or honesty *into* (a more postmodern) irony. Rather than the replacement of irony with sincerity, which would indicate a naïve return to a pre-postmodern mindset, ironesty is 'irony/sarcasm/sardonicness/snark employed in the service of making an earnest point, or expressing a heart-felt emotion' (Dember 2018) – a braiding together of irony and honesty 'in a unified aesthetic expression' (Dember 2017b). Such a braiding of seemingly opposing polarities, of course, builds upon the unpacking of metamodern oscillation above, and the metamodern cultural products that include ironic and sincere aspects simultaneously could, indeed, be folded neatly into the overarching sensibility of oscillation threaded through the cultural aesthetic. The term ironesty, however, allows for a more nuanced understanding in how, as according to Dember, metamodern artists (and the public in general) attempt to express (and hence embody, put words to and – in time, protect) the solidity of their individual felt experience 'from the destabilizing effect' (Dember 2023) of postmodern irony. To illustrate this, Dember imagines postmodern irony as a quicksand and reminds us that 'you don't escape quicksand by resisting it directly, and especially not by resisting it vertically [, instead] you have to kind of lay across the quicksand, and sort of swim your way out of it' (Dember 2017b). As such, ironesty is an attempt at being honest whilst also accepting the fact that we are still unable to wholly escape irony *without* also embracing it. Such terminology implies that it is almost impossible to be wholly honest or sincere within a contemporary artwork and, instead, ironesty enables the 'making [of] an earnest point or expressing earnest feelings, while playing nicely with sardonicness' (Dember 2017b). Whilst an *oscillation* between irony and sincerity would describe certain metamodern aesthetics, Dember's ironesty embraces the contemporary interconnectedness between the two and, rather than seeing irony and honesty as oppositional forces in contrast with one another (between which we can oscillate), the term embraces the fact that, within a metamodern understanding, irony can, ironically, be used to embrace, platform and provide honesty.

This chapter has provided a brief overview of metamodernism as an overarching cultural structure of feeling that has arisen over roughly the past two decades. This structure of feeling has largely developed through personal, felt responses to the uncertainty induced by postmodernity and precarity induced by the developing permacrisis and then expressed in artistic and cultural production. Metamodernism is an attempt at identifying interconnected artistic strategies employed within cultural products that *feel* like they do not comfortably fit wholly into what we have come to understand as postmodern aesthetics, in that they embrace a (return to) a centring of personal experience, honesty, hope and engagement whilst also being aware of the complexities of such notions and inescapabilty of (the effect of) postmodernism's dishonesty, cynicism and disconnect. I highlight the aesthetics of the felt experience, self-reflexivity, constructive pastiche and ironesty as essential examples of artistic choices that exemplify the metamodern sensibility as defined by van den Akker and Vermeulen and their contemporaries. In Chapter 4, I build on Dember and Radchenko's work to offer my own inventory of metamodern sensibilities specifically located within contemporary theatrical practice in order to develop a guide through which to locate, define and describe metamodern theatre. First, however, as Vermeulen and van den Akker similarly understand metamodernism as inherently tied to the development of the permacrisis throughout the 2000s, I argue that the metamodern shifts within contemporary British theatre are inherently connected to specific occurrences within Britain throughout the past few years – and especially the particular experiences of the generation of theatre makers who came of age during the metamodern shift: the Children of Postmodernism.

3

The children of postmodernism: Hope/lessness

I have been told that I could afford a mortgage if I simply stopped spending all my money on avocado toast and oat milk flat whites (cf. Levin 2017); been described, famously, as a lazy, self-obsessed narcissist (Stein 2013); and was, apparently, given medals simply for turning up (Blake 2014). The millennial generation, as my contemporaries and I have come to be termed, have constantly been blamed by the popular British media for wanting something other than the intergenerational inequality currently experienced throughout the country (cf. Green 2017). Our unhappiness is, apparently, simply our own fault due to having the sheer gall to desire something more. And remember, they tell us, we Baby Boomers had it much worse (O'Grady 2018) – you kids just wouldn't understand! Conversely, we millennials appear to consistently blame these Baby Boomers – the previous generation but one – for creating the structures that ensured such inequality in the first place, as well as reminding them that, as we grew up, they were the ones that promised us something more. After all, we didn't give ourselves those medals (if they even existed) – it was the Baby Boomers who handed them out. Such generational debate and delineation have become so entrenched in popular media that the meme-ification of this combat has led to the household usage of the phrase 'Okay Boomer' (Mueller and McCollum 2022). But what exactly do these generational terms denote? Are they merely media-based diatribes to enable age-based tribalism? Are they simply pop-culture appellations? Or does the concept of the 'millennial' work as a method of understanding an immutable experience of a cultural epoch? In this brief chapter, I offer an analysis of the millennial as a historically positioned generational demographic, before applying Raymond Williams's concept of structure of feeling ([1961] 1969) following Vermeulen and van den Akker's application of such to understand the 'embodied, related feelings' (Williams 1969: 18) threaded throughout the metamodern paradigm. Through this, I similarly position the millennial as a structure of feeling – a series of embodied, related feelings that a number of people born in the roughly defined age range experience(d), which, possibly in part due to the media fixation on the millennial generation and the following amplification of such narratives through social media and online meme culture, becomes a pervasive appellation. As van den Akker and Vermeulen inherently connect the development of metamodernism to the concurrent 'clusterfuck' (van den Akker and Vermeulen 2017: 17) – or permacrisis – that spread, largely, from the mid-2000s onwards, I am specifically interested in how the development of metamodern theatre is affected by the generational experience of these 'emerging' companies – particularly how their economic, cultural, educational, political and sociological experience as millennials in Britain over the past two decades has influenced both the development of the theatre they (are able to) create and also limited who is able to create any theatre in the first place. As such, I then return to the experience of being a millennial theatre undergraduate in the 2000s, laying a foundational understanding of the environments the millennial-led companies throughout this volume are creating work within. Such analysis does not seek to equate the millennial with the metamodern, or argue that only millennial theatre makers or artists are the ones that are creating metamodern theatre or art. This is clearly not the case. Instead, as the permacrisis is inherently interconnected with the development of metamodernity out of postmodernism, so, too, is the millennial structure of feeling inherently connected to both the permacrisis and the metamodern, with the three – as I see it – symbiotically linked. Theatre is inherently affected by the political and economic structures of the time, and the contemporary theatre detailed in this book is therefore fundamentally connected to the generational experience of these theatre makers as they emerged through and beyond the age of postmodernism into the age of metamodernity.

The millennial (as a) generational demographic

The idea of analysing generations as separate and often disparate entities can be traced back to Karl Mannheim's 1928 essay, 'Das Problem der Generationen', in which he analysed generational differences within a socio-historical context (Pilcher 1994: 482). Through this, Mannheim located 'certain definite modes of behaviour, feeling and thought' (Mannheim 1952: 291) affected by such factors as geographical location, political and cultural participation, and the generation's 'differing responses to a particular situation' (Pilcher 1994: 483) that produced a form of 'distinctive consciousness' (ibid.) within a specific cohort, dependent on 'the tempo of social change' (ibid.). As Ng and Johnson summarize in their analysis of millennial-focused research, the generational concept built from Mannheim's work theorizes that 'the environment in which Millennials grew up during their formation years [their teenage to young adult period] impacts their values, attitudes, and behaviors' (Ng and Johnson 2015: 3). In general terms, therefore, my generation's values, attitudes and behaviours have been affected by, as according to Mannheim's theory, being 'raised during the boom times and relative peace of the 1990s' (Williams 2015), only to emerge, as Rebecca Huntley proclaims, 'into an adult world where only one rule exists – the certainty of uncertainty' (Huntley 2006: 15).

When it comes to specifics in terms of age, the sheer range of definitions of 'millennial' from a variety of sources seems to prohibit straightforward standardization. The popular and media-ascribed terminology, too, has blurred the boundaries between the specific traits of the millennials of the United States and those of the United Kingdom. In my effort to establish a definition for the purposes of this book, I intentionally make use of work focused on both US and UK millennials, not through a conflation of the two but in order to utilize the wealth of research and insight generated through US-based study as a theoretical model in order to better understand the specifics of the UK-based generation. It is also important to note that a number of generation-shaping, historical reference points are shared across the two in regard to the relative prosperity in the 1990s–2000s and the following global financial crash of 2008, the rise in divisive nationalist and populist political discourse, the propagation of continuous online access and social media, and cross-cultural popular media consumption (we watched *Friends* across the pond, too). The term itself – millennial – also originates from American historians Neil Howe and William Strauss's 1991 book *Generations: The History of America's Future, 1584 to 2069* to describe the group of children that would start to come of age at the turn of the millennium.

Howe and Strauss originally defined the millennials as those 'born in or after 1982' (Howe and Strauss 2000: 4). The UK House of Commons, meanwhile, specifies that the age bracket falls between 1983 and 1992 (Brown et al. 2017: 3), whilst The Resolution Foundation's Intergenerational Commission suggests a larger dater range of 1981 to 2000 (Shrimpton, Skinner and Hall 2017: 7) and the Pew Research centre, which 'stud[ied] the Millennial generation for more than a decade' (Dimock 2019), suggests that the generation began in 1981 and the 'cutoff point' (ibid.) is 1996, whilst, rather paradoxically, simultaneously noting that such 'generational cutoff points aren't an exact science' (ibid.). Whilst age is an obvious determiner in locating the millennial generation, the boundaries of the specific age range remain debatable and, as agreed by the UK Parliament, 'not formally defined' (Brown et al. 2017: 5). I locate the millennials as having been born between roughly the early 1980s through to the mid-1990s but, in keeping with the spirit of Vermeulen and van den Akker's periodizing on the 2000s in a way that allows for porous boundaries, rather than focusing on defined age-brackets as the specific determiner, I follow the judgement of Brown et al. (2017) in emphasizing the importance of 'the unique experiences and challenges this generation has faced' (ibid.: 5) in shaping and therefore defining our shared generational experience.

To unpack this generational experience, it is important to position the demographic within a rough timeline. The most commonly accepted version (cf. Brown et al. 2017: 5) of this in a British sense begins with the Lost Generation, who would have fought, and died, in the First World War, quickly followed by the 'Greatest' Generation, who would have fought, and died, in the Second. They were followed by the Silent Generation; those who were too young to join the forces but, in turn, were too old to participate in the upcoming Summer of Love. These were then followed by the Baby Boomers, born during the post-war economic upturn, who's formative years saw participation in the civil rights movement and rock 'n' roll. The Boomers then gave rise to Generation X, who grew up in one of the 'most passionate eras of social and cultural upheaval … with often painful consequences for political, economic, family and educational institutions' (Howe and Strauss 2000: 48). Generation X's formative early adult years saw the rise of a popular culture that was intrinsically self-aware and ironic. In 1999, Rob Owen's analysis of Gen X televisual culture cited a number of societal issues, ranging from crime rates, to the increasing availability of news footage, to their parents leaving 'them at home with TVs in order to pursue their own career goals or simply to work to make ends meet' (Owen 1999: 55) that led to a prevailing sense of anger in their humour and popular culture, stating that 'out of this anger, [came] cynicism, sarcasm and irony' (ibid.). The millennials, who would have been children during the denouement of the postmodern era, grew up exposed to the cynicism and ironic detachment of Generation X, whilst also becoming instilled with the 'optimism and idealism of their Boomer parents' (Huntley 2006: 14) that had been prompted by the end of the Cold War and the 'turbo-charged economic upswing and fantastic social unravelling' (Howe and Strauss 2000: 99) of the 1990s. Hence, from an early age, millennials – the children of postmodernism – inhabited a paradoxical, oscillatory social and cultural climate.

The millennial (as a) structure of feeling

Generational research is, at best, inherently flawed and, at worst, exclusionary. And yet, due to generational terminology and discourse around generational difference becoming pervasive throughout popular culture, mainstream media and online discourse, appropriating such terminology in order to understand an emergent structure of feeling – as detailed in this subchapter – among a particular demographic can be useful, whilst *still* being aware and critical of the flaws of such. John Higgs counters such initial reticence when he describes that 'at the heart of the post-Millennial's metamodern culture is a shift in the way we view things that are flawed' (Higgs 2019: 158). Higgs does not suggest that 'post-millennials' (his moniker for millennials and Gen Z) cannot or refuse to see the flaws in various concepts, but that we continue to see value in ideas *even though* they are flawed. For Higgs, the post-millennials

> arrived after postmodernism, so they were not raised to expect absolutes in this world [but] raised in a culture where every position was understood as being limited or flawed in some way. When no position is the great unarguable truth, then the fact that all things are flawed now becomes unimportant. … The ideological approach to truth starts to give way to a practical approach. Forget what's ideologically pure – what matters is whether or not something is useful in the here and now. (Higgs 2019: 159–60)

As such, I apply generational research through Higgs's 'flawed-but-useful' approach in understanding the millennial generation and propose that – in a similar vein to Vermeulen and van den Akker's use of the term in order to unpack metamodernity as a shared sentiment that is felt, that people are aware of, but 'which cannot easily, if at all, be pinned down' (van den Akker and Vermeulen 2017: 7) – we turn towards Raymond William's structure of feeling in an appreciation of generational terminology. As James MacDowell notes, 'A structure of feeling will not be "possessed in the same way by many members of the community"' (MacDowell 2017: 28, citing Williams 1965: 65). Rather, Williams's term attempts to put to words a 'practical consciousness of a present kind, in a living and interrelating continuity' (Williams 1977: 132) – an embodied structure of 'specific, internal relations, at once interlocking and in tension' (ibid.). My attempt to discern the millennial through Williams's framework is built upon a locating of these interlocking tensions – the 'unique experiences and challenges' (Brown et al. 2017: 5) – of members of my generation and an attempt, through this, at understanding how these have affected the embodied, related feelings of this demographic. Of course, the 'millennial' as a concept is not all-encompassing, nor relevant to every person born from the early-1980s 'up to and (sometimes) after the millennium' (Brown et al. 2017: 3) – and yet there is a certain 'experience of the present' (Williams 1977: 128) that can be expressed through Williams's term.

Katie Beswick's work on unpacking the complications around demarcations and measurements of class within Britain, particularly in relation to cultural access, similarly leads her to understand class as a shifting structure of feeling, pointing towards the 'disjuncture between the measurements social scientists use to determine class position ... and the "felt" experiences of those "identifying" as working class' (Beswick 2020: 265), reminding us that more so than race, sex and generational bracket the demographic demarcation of class is 'not fixed but fluid' (ibid.: 266). Reflective of the central thread of embodied, felt experience as a main driver of the theoretical exploration throughout this book, Beswick proposes to 'take seriously *felt* class identity [as] *class feeling*' (ibid.: 267; emphasis in original) through both Williams's terminology and Diane Reay's 'psychic landscape of social class' (Reay 2005: 911). Building on Beswick's acknowledgement that the 'means by which people come to know themselves as working-class are often vague and emergent' (Beswick 2020: 269), there is similar vagueness and emergence in how members of the millennial generation would 'come to know' themselves as such, with the caveat that the generational demographics come with predetermined (albeit slightly porous) age demarcations. When reading the millennial as a structure of feeling, therefore, the emergent 'feel' – or, dare I use the 'post-millennial' (cf. Higgs 2019) re-appropriated slang term, *vibe* – of the millennial experience is allowed to come to the fore.

Primarily, I suggest that the millennial structure of feeling is built upon a dichotomic fluctuation between cynicism and hope. This was instilled in the generation from an early age through such coalescence of previous generational influences – an oscillation between the optimism of our Boomer parents and the cynicism and ironic detachment that has arisen from both childhood exposure to Generation X culture and the economic and political crises of our formative adult years. It is this oscillation between optimism and cynicism that defines the metamodern millennial. Such fluctuation, however, is not only affected by the millennials' exposure to conflicting generational mentalities within our childhoods. It is compounded by the crises affecting our formative years as we emerged from the relative prosperity of the 1990s and early 2000s into a precarity 'inextricably connected to the conditions of cultural capitalism ... now felt by a wider network of people' (Fragkou 2018: 5) that permeates our politics, economics, career prospects and ecology. The following outlines some of the unique experiences that have affected millennials at such critical moments.

First, my moniker – the Children of Postmodernism – not only refers to our being born into the postmodern episteme but to the much-discussed extended childhood and adolescence that we have experienced both culturally and economically. John Higgs argues that a reticence towards abandoning childhood has extended over the past century, noting that millennials' shift beyond the 'irony, nihilism and cynicism' (ibid.: 124) of Gen X comes hand in hand with an adoption of the extended *adolescence* that started with the Baby Boomers (as the first teenagers) and developed through Gen X's *MTV* into a form of extended *childhood* that Higgs defines as a counterpoint to the irony of the previous generation. To illustrate this, Higgs notes that the childhood interests of previous generations would 'have been dropped in embarrassment when drink and dating entered the picture' (ibid.: 125) but it is the millennials' continual enjoyment of such that has meant that the most successful films of the past decade have been Disney-branded superhero ventures. For Higgs, millennials see nothing wrong with having 'adult' jobs – and even our own children – and discussing our thoughts about the latest Captain America adventure, whilst, to 'Baby Boomers or Generation Xers this can seem embarrassing or disappointing, [but the] Millennials feel no shame about it' (ibid.). Whilst Higgs describes this as a 'non-ironic sincerity' (ibid.), I would argue that – whether in my own enjoyment in unpacking the directions of the Marvel Cinematic Universe with friends over the past decade, or in other millennial parents I know taking their children to Disneyland more for their own enjoyment of the Disney franchise than their children's – we are *aware* of the irony of such enjoyment of 'childish' material and yet *also* are completely sincere in our enjoyment of such. It is a fluctuation between, and braiding of, irony and sincerity – not simply ironic *or* sincere engagement.

This extension of childhood is exacerbated by the fact that, whilst our childhood fell alongside the relative prosperity and peace throughout Britain following the end of the Cold War and the removal of Thatcher, the economic precarity, political crises and technological accelerationism converging within our formative adult years has made belief in a secure and stable future feel unimaginable, with millennials stuck in a specific state of precarity which our childhood and adolescent experiences did not prepare us for. Katheryn Owens and Chris Green's work on performing millennial precarity makes explicit links between the specific precariousness of the millennial rental market – and the even more precarious nature of shared housing – and a state of extended adolescence (Owens and Green 2020: 46). Basing their understanding on both data and personal experience, the pair understand millennial precarity as 'particularly felt in regards to housing, where a relative lack of regulation over the private rental sector, high deposits for mortgages that renders buying property unattainable for many, and the decimation of social housing models means that renting is often insecure and expensive' (ibid.: 44, referencing Corlett and Judge 2017). Such is the impossibility of house ownership for a large portion of millennials that we have been relabelled 'generation rent' (Timperley 2020) – which is not surprising considering that 'the average house in the UK currently costs around nine-times average earnings, based on data as at 30 November 2022 [and] the last time house prices were this expensive relative to average earnings was in the year 1876, nearly 150 years ago' (Lamont 2023). As such, in 2018, as more millennials slipped into their thirties, the Resolution Foundation found that 40 per cent of the generation were renting into our fourth decade, which was twice as much as the preceding Generation X at the same point in their lives (Ahmed 2018). Owens and Green call attention to the high number of our generation renting rooms in Houses of Multiple Occupation (HMOs) – where a private landlord charges per room for multiple people to live in the same household – and relate this to a liminal experience of domestic anxiety, in which tenants are indefinitely 'stuck' somewhere between the historic experience of HMOs as student and graduate digs and the (now-seemingly-impossible) rent or ownership of their own property. They also point out that such arrangements also include sharing a house with cohabiting couples, as shared income between partners is no longer a guaranteed route to being able to afford to rent your own flat, or save towards a mortgage deposit, particularly in larger cities. In fact, the situation has led to an increase of adult children (a person aged over eighteen years who is living with their parent(s) and does not have a spouse, partner or child living with them) continuing to live at their parent's/s' home. The 2021 census revealed that almost 5 million adults across England and Wales still lived with their parents (ONS 2023), and although there is a possibility that some of these might be attributed to issues surrounding Covid-19 at the time of the survey, the ONS suggests that this is part of a longer trend. In 2021, most Gen Z's in their early twenties were living with their parents (ibid.) and more than one in ten millennials aged between thirty and thirty-four were too. Therefore, if we are to talk about an extended adolescence in the Children of Postmodernism, or even – as Higgs terms it – an extended *child*hood, it would be remiss to suggest that this was centrally a cultural (or creative) shift (cf. Higgs 2019). Instead, this is a reaction born out of the financial situation imposed on my generation, and those below us, through a particular and extended precarity.

The effects of this precarity upon my generation's mental health are becoming increasingly measurable. Curan and Hill reiterate that the 'neoliberal governance in the United States, Canada and the United Kingdom has emphasized competitive individualism' (2017: 410) since the 1980s. They describe millennials as experiencing 'multidimensional perfectionism' (ibid.): the pressure to achieve ever increasingly higher standards, whilst the reality of the economic situation we find ourselves in is antithetical to such an aspiration. As such, the effect of this discordance is, in turn, exacerbated by the relative ease of online image crafting via social media and imposed by the neoliberal market that places, as the pair maintain, a 'heavier burden on recent generations of young people to strive against one another under the auspices of meritocracy' (ibid.). The integration of multiple social media networks into millennials' everyday lives, whilst crafting positive connection and a possible increase in in-person empathy, has also been intrinsically linked to a higher risk of depression and anxiety (Primack et al. 2017) through feelings of inadequacy and Fear Of Missing Out (Fathadhika, Hafiza and Rahmita Nanda 2019). This is coupled with an epidemic of loneliness within young adults, with recent studies indicating that one in five millennials feel like they don't have a single friend (Chan 2022). This is also inherently connected to the precarious employment system: with work-life becoming transactional, insecure and commodified, millennials move from job to job at a much higher rate than previous generations and, increasingly, work remotely – meaning that the traditional social connections built between work colleagues is a thing of the past (ibid.). Such a loneliness epidemic naturally leads to increased mental health issues (Matthews et al. 2018), particularly when coupled with the base level of inadequacy felt by the generation.

This felt inadequacy, implemented by a system that 'misinformed' (Newport 2012) us (see the next section), is multiplied through the act of comparing our own lives to that of our cohorts through continual updates on social media. Even back in 2014 (when the algorithms of Instagram and Twitter were still in their infancy, Snapchat had just been released, the idea of Tiktok was non-existent and people below the age of forty still used Facebook) the *Social Comparison, Social Media, and Self-Esteem* study found a distinct pattern in participants feeling worse when looking at someone else's profile if it exhibited 'upward comparison information' and feeling better when they saw someone else's profile that showed 'downward comparison information' (Vogel et al. 2014). In short, seeing someone else you know doing expressly better than you on social media can categorically make you feel worse. In 2013, Tim Urban employed a metaphorical equation to tender a hypothesis regarding what he saw developing as millennial discontent: 'happiness = reality – expectations' (Urban 2013). For Urban, social media manufactures an experience for millennials in which 'A) what everyone else is doing is very out in the open, B) most people present an inflated version of their own existence, and C) the people who chime in the most about their careers are usually those whose careers (or relationships) are going the best' (Urban 2013). Although millennials are highly aware of the unreality of their peers' posts on social media in that they only represent a 'snapshot of a second in time that doesn't share the pain, the compromise, the sacrifice, their hard work, their insecurities, their anything' (Raphael 2019), there is still a seemingly inevitable social comparison that occurs between our own lives and the curated extracts when we view them online. This paradoxical reaction is reflective of the 'as if' modality of the metamodern in the fact that we are contradictorily believing in something – or negatively affected by something – that we understand to be untrue. It is also reflective of the stance of the millennial generation in general; we continue to use social media whilst also feeling 'that it is depriving [us] of deeper personal relationships' (Huntley 2006: 10); we decree that we are victims of the gig economy but are also the most 'enthusiastic users of gig-economy apps and services' (Parkinson 2017). We occupy a contradictory position, one that embraces hypocrisy. Through a conflicted movement between poles, we are a 'Paradoxical Generation' (Huntley 2006: 10).

When framed as a structure of feeling, the specific generational experience of the millennials – of coming out of a period of reasonable stability into a sustained period of neoliberal precarity in our formative adult years, which we as a generation were ill-prepared for – has led to a deflation of expectations within the cohort, exacerbated, in part, by the permeating dominance of social media. Of course, in more recent years, the negative economic impacts of Brexit, the as-yet-unknown social, economic and psychological impact of the pandemic, and the continual economic and political uncertainty imposed upon the United Kingdom through over a decade of increasingly chaotic Conservative governments has increased the levels of precarity and uncertainty across members of all generations in the UK. The generations below mine, Generations Z and Alpha, have a distinctly different relationship with such precarity than the millennials in that they were born into it. There is much discussion about Gen Z – the first iPad kids (Purchase 2022) – being the primary generation to grow up as children with the internet as a part of their daily lives, and the following Generation Alpha have never known a time without such digital integration. However, both younger generations have also never yet known a period of stability within Britain, with the eldest Gen Z's being roughly ten years old at the time of the global financial crash of 2008 and Generation Alpha currently only ever experiencing a Conservative government. My focus in this book is on my own generation and, in part, on my own situated and embodied understanding of being a member of this cohort and the interconnectedness of the structure of feeling throughout. As such, I do not go into detail – and do not care to speculate – on the experiences of the generations following my own. Suffice to say that I fully expect that Generations Z and Alpha will have it considerably worse than I or my millennial counterparts across a number of measures. Whilst I focus on the fact that millennials graduated university and 'entered Britain's labour market amid the 2008 financial crisis [and] are still "scarred" by its impact on their employment and earnings potential' (Taylor 2019), at least our educational experience was not entirely disrupted by consecutive (yet necessary) lockdowns and strike actions. At the time of writing, for example, the graduates of 2023 have not experienced a single year of 'normal' higher education (HE) and are set to enter the workforce at a 'perilous moment' in terms of economics (Murray 2023), employment, housing and, of course, the climate. The precarities experienced by the millennial generation – without a major upheaval in British politics – will continue to be exacerbated for the generations below me. However, I am particularly interested in how the experience of the millennials is defined in the dichotomy between our childhood and adulthood in regard to our childhood falling within a relatively peaceful, prosperous, postmodern and post-Cold War Britain and our becoming adults alongside the upending of these conditions towards metamodernism and the permacrisis.

In Chapter 1, I discussed both Andy Lavender's observation that the 'real' has returned to theatre (Lavender 2016: 19) and his contention that a 'new fascination with authenticity' (ibid.: 23) is integral to understanding this paradigm shift, and Daniel Schulze's linking of a resurgence in an interest in the authentic within theatre to the wider metamodern paradigm as a direct response to an existence within the postmodern condition. This strive for the authentic, however, is not a direct retraction from the postmodern, but situates itself both *through* and *beyond* it. As Schulze remarks, it is only once 'mankind comes to terms with the fact that the subject, the world, the languages we speak ... are constructed and in themselves meaningless – that a new history can begin' (ibid.) – a phrase that is, again, a far cry from Fukayama's proclaimed end of history. Schulze points to Wolfgang Funk's assertion that authenticity re-emerges during crucial moments in time (Funk 2015: 38). That, in periods of great disruption and change, a strive towards authenticity, sincerity and veracity (ibid.: 15) resurfaces as a counterpoint. As Schulze summarizes, 'It is no exaggeration to say that authenticity, or rather the longing for it, always goes hand in hand with a profound feeling of having lost something' (15). Schulze refers to the Greek derivation of the term authentic – *authentikós* – as meaning 'self-consummating' (Kalisch 2000: 32, in Schulze 2017: 15) – something that is 'whole or complete' (Schulze 2017: 15), not 'in individual terms but rather in finding one's predestined place in society and the cosmic order' (ibid.: 16). He posits that this concept of spiritual self-fulfilment is fragmented via the dawning of modern science and the 'deconstruction of theories of divine order' (ibid.), leading to a re-emergence of a 'tentatively tested out' (ibid.: 17) authenticity within the Renaissance era as a counterpoint to the further deconstruction of an anthropocentric and religious worldview. Schulze argues that this is mirrored in contemporary responses to the postmodern paradigm, which has driven humankind to feel 'far-removed and isolated from nature and its own origins, sentenced to live in a world which is perceived as fake and superficial [and feeling] a sense of loss in a complex world' (ibid.: 26), with a rising interest in authenticity surfacing as a natural counterpoint to such. As Schulze summarizes, throughout history, the rise of 'authenticity is the counter movement to these profound feelings of uncertainty and instability' (ibid.: 23). Congruent to Schulze's 'sense of loss' (ibid.: 26), Mark Fisher's concept of 'lost futures' (2014), developed from Derrida's notion of hauntology (1994), speaks to his interconnected observance of contemporary, specifically British, culture being oppressed by an awareness of a loss of possible futures and futurity, through a 'slow cancellation of the future [that] has been accompanied by a deflation of expectations' (Fisher 2014: 8). Rather than such a cancellation slowly dripping in through inactivity, such lost futures are the outcome of what Fisher describes as a 'time of massive, traumatic change' (ibid.), citing neoliberalism, post-Fordism and increasing digitization as catalysts for such, leading to a sense of culture that has 'lost its ability to grasp and articulate the present' (ibid.: 9). For millennials existing in such a web of insecurity, it is no wonder that we are searching for an authentic response within ourselves, our society, our art, and our consumer trends, with Gerosa arguing that authenticity has become the 'fundamental value orienting consumers' tastes in late modern capitalism' (Gerosa 2024). This search for authenticity also manifests in a variety of movements engaged in by millennials: from a generational increase in access to therapy services across the NHS (Landis 2020) as well as the mental-health app and teletherapy industries (Santos 2020), to a developed commitment to self-improvement programmes (Field Agent 2015), the expansion of the wellness industry and the experience economy (Usborne 2017), to more insidious movements such as the interconnected alt-right, incel (self-named involuntary celibates) and manosphere communities, who – through figures such as Andrew Tate and Jordan Peterson – offer 'an antidote to chaos' (Peterson 2018) through an espoused belief in the existence of a naturalized gender and sexual order. On the other hand, it also encapsulates the millennial-led support for Labour's Momentum campaign in the run up to the 2019 election (Ipsos Mori 2017; Higgs 2019: 350), alongside the millennials' engagement with the development of contemporary protests from the Occupy movement at the start of the previous decade to the Extinction Rebellion disruptions at the end of it. These patterns across multiple aspects of millennial behaviour are reflexive of either an internal or external struggle to *improve* or to *find the truth*. As Vermeulen describes, 'Everything's at stake, and you don't know how to change it; that's the kind of double bind of the Metamodern individual' (Gorynski 2018). Returning to Vermeulen and van den Akker's observance of the re-emergence of the figure of utopia 'as a trope, individual desire or collective fantasy' (Vermeulen and van den Akker 2015b: 57) as part of the 'the passage from postmodernism [to] metamodernism' (57), there is a clear interconnectivity between the return of historicity, affect and depth (van den Akker, Gibbons and Vermeulen 2017) as part of the development of the metamodern paradigm and the emergence of a desire for change within the millennials, whilst simultaneously exhibiting a scepticism and 'sense of sadness' (Freinacht 2017: 6) due to being haunted by futures that failed to happen (Fisher 2014). Whilst British millennials are bucking the trend of getting more right-wing as they age and continuing to remain largely left-leaning politically (Mahdawi 2023), 'for every person on the political left in the UK under the age of 30, one thing is constant: we have never celebrated winning a general election that we voted in' (West-Knights 2019). Whilst it's not unusual for political parties to endure long years in opposition, West-Knights argues that the particular experience of the left in the UK feels generational: 'Perhaps', she wrote on the eve of the upcoming defeat of Corbyn's Labour movement in the 2019 General Election, 'all these past defeats mean that we're particularly idealistic: we haven't yet had the chance to become disillusioned by getting what we wished for and seeing it fail to live up to our expectations' (ibid.).

Through an examination of the interconnected issues surrounding and permeating the millennial generation, a desire for 'sincere and constructive progression and expression' (Turner 2015) becomes a panoptic sensibility within the millennial structure of feeling. This desire, however, is manifest in a 'pragmatic idealism' (Turner 2015) that engages with revival of the strive for authenticity and progression, whilst not 'forfeiting all that we've learnt from postmodernism' (Turner 2015). Through an oscillation between a sense of optimism and cynicism, between hope and hopelessness, this mode of informed naïveté describes a suitably paradoxical 'climate in which a yearning for utopias, *despite their futile nature*, has come to the fore,' (Turner 2015, emphasis added). This yearning for forms of utopia, for 'sincere and constructive progression' (Turner 2015), is set alongside a pervasive sense of a mourning for futures that could have been (cf. Fisher 2014). The structure of feeling of the millennials is also affected by an extended childhood as both a financial and cultural experience imposed upon the generation through sustained periods of economic precarity and uncertainty that is antithetical to the focus on unending prosperity within our upbringings and educational experiences. Through this, millennials have become interested in ideas of (self)betterment and authenticity despite the impossibility of such, manifested in factors as varied as the increase in online therapy and the rise of Andrew Tate. Mirroring the oscillation between irony and sincerity that has permeated our generational experience from the Boomer/Gen X dichotomy of our childhoods and sustained precarity of our formative adult years – there is a distinct fluctuation throughout the structure of feeling of the millennials, therefore, between something akin to hope and something akin to hopelessness. This hope/lessness dynamic is a dominant aesthetic across the performances recounted throughout this volume and will be further unpacked in the relevant chapters. Suffice to say that this paradoxical positioning of the millennials being a major ideology within the theatre made by millennials is also inherently connected to the particular generational experience of the millennial theatre makers.

'Follow your passion': New Labour's impact on the British theatre scene

For the past decade, certain news media has consistently portrayed millennials as entitled snowflakes who have never had it so good (cf. Collins 2019). James Cairn's *The Myth of the Age of Entitlement* (2017) describes the perpetuation of this myth throughout popular discourse being due to the fact that, like all myths, the claim of millennials' 'expected' entitlement is 'malleable [and] able to fit the needs of the storyteller' (Cairns 2017: 2). But, as Cal Newport (2012) explains, 'The problem is not that we're intrinsically selfish or entitled. It's that we've been misinformed', or as millennial author Emma Gannon summarizes: 'We were sold a career ladder that doesn't exist anymore' (Thompson 2018).

Newport's *Solving Gen Y's Passion Problem* (2012) is built around the fact that we were 'raised when "follow your passion" became pervasive career advice' (Newport 2012), with Google Ngram data revealing that between roughly 1998 and 2008 the phrases 'fulfilling career' and 'follow your passion' experienced a significant upsurge in usage throughout both print and web media whilst the phrase 'secure career' was used significantly less (ibid.). Newport's issue regarding this is that the danger of the phrase 'follow your passion' is that it implies not that you should aim for a fulfilling work life but that 'the verb "follow" implies that you start by identifying a passion and then match this pre-existing calling to a job' (ibid.). There is an interesting correlation in Britain, at this time, with the reign of Blair's New Labour government (1997–2010) who, at turn of the millennium, set a precedent that 'by the end of the decade half or more of young people would be entering higher education' (BBC News 1999). At the time of

Blair's pronouncement, 39 per cent of seventeen to thirty-year olds were estimated to be entering HE for the first time, and by 2016, 'Blair's target of half of young people going into higher education had almost been achieved' (Economic Affairs Committee 2018) with the amount of young people 'following' their passion and enrolling on their first university degree increasing to 49 per cent. Whilst just over two hundred and fifty thousand first degrees were awarded in 2000, this increased to just over four hundred thousand in 2017 (ibid.). Additionally, data collected by the Higher Education Statistics Agency (HESA) reveals that in the decade between 2002 and 2012, the number of students enrolling per year on undergraduate 'Design, and Creative and Performing Arts' courses rose from 104,600 at the start of the decade to 149,610 at the end of it – an increase of almost fifty thousand students beginning courses in the creative arts each new year (HESA 2019a, 2019b). Whilst their data doesn't delineate further than this general subject area, it is safe to assume that the number of undergraduate enrolments across drama and theatre studies courses in UK universities also increased at a similar, if not equivalent, rate. Speaking strictly to my own experience of school and college throughout the noughties, it always felt like there was a definite, planned trajectory that ended with as many of us as possible at university. There was no discussion from teachers or support staff of any other options – as if university was simply one more step in the ladder of education that was compulsory to climb. Of course, the reality is more nuanced than my position of privilege, with intersectional factors of educational inequalities throughout a student's educational experience – family income, local authority, gender, ethnicity – being important 'differences in educational attainment [that] emerge early in childhood and develop throughout an individual's lifetime' (Farquharson, McNally and Tahir 2022) to continue to interrupt such a ladder climb. That being said, the overall guidance throughout our educational experience surrounding the 'follow your passion' trope alongside Blair's target was nevertheless revealed to be incompatible with the economic situation we later found ourselves in upon graduation. Blair's 'arbitrary target [of] no ifs, no buts' (Independent Voices 2015) doubled the number of graduates in the working-age populous from that of two decades before (Wright 2013). Writing with hindsight from 2021, David Goodhart argues that Britain's lack of a German-style apprenticeship system for those who don't go to university alongside this increase led to social division that ultimately 'exacerbated regional inequality' (Goodhart 2021) and that the lack of equal graduate opportunities to the number of graduates led to a 'new generation of dissatisfied graduates, one third of whom are not in graduate employment five to 10 years after graduating' (ibid.). By the end of the 2000s, the 'problem facing Britain's university leavers [was] simply stated: too many graduates, too few graduate jobs' (Independent Voices 2015).

I am aware of the possibility of coming across as anti-HE here. Or, even worse, of gatekeeping the educational experience. Neither are my intention. As Goodheart rightly points out, 'Many young people want to go to university, even though they are not academically inclined, because it is three potentially exciting years away from parents and small town or suburban life' (Goodhart 2021). He proposes that a system be set up so that non-academically inclined students should 'be able to leave home to do an apprenticeship or a sub-degree course of some kind' (ibid.) as an alternative to the university-years. Additionally, as HE degrees, particularly within the humanities, offer students often the first dedicated chance to develop the critical thinking skills necessary 'in order to adapt to unfamiliar situations and to prevent the spread of misinformation, as the pace of change continues to accelerate and the complexity of work and the world around us intensifies' (Bellaera et al. 2021), critical thinking should become an expected outcome earlier in the educational experience of UK pupils when developing such alternative HE-level pathways. Whilst I do not wish to speculate on the direction of travel of such developments, what I wish to illustrate at this point is that the educational experience of my millennial peers and I was underpinned by the upsurge of advice regarding following a *passion* into a university degree and then into a career, built on the stability and increasing prosperity of our 1990s childhoods. Whilst this offered inherent positives in terms of social mobility for first-generation graduates, the 'motivation for New Labour's wish for continued growth in HE [was] essentially economic' (Ryan 2005: 89), but there is little evidence, now, that it had any positive economic impact (Goodhart 2021).

Around the same time as this shift, the teaching of theatre in a British HE context largely started to move from that of theatre studies or drama studies to *performance* studies, following Richard Schechner's proposal in the early 1990s that, following the aesthetic shifts from modern to postmodern and dramatic to postdramatic, 'the new paradigm is "performance", not theatre [and therefore] Theatre departments should become "performance departments"' (Schechner 1992: 9). Whilst this was initially met with mixed responses (Auslander 1997: 2), Phillip Auslander's later unpacking of such a postmodern transition allowed for an understanding, for both theorists and students, that 'theatre is a much larger category than I had originally conceived it to be, and that it is, in turn, a subset of a still larger category reasonably called performance' (ibid.). Part of this shift, of course, included the work of postdramatic performance companies becoming an important part of undergraduate curriculums. My own undergraduate cohort was introduced not only to Forced Entertainment but to companies such as Gob Squad, Stan's Café and Punchdrunk as examples of those developing cutting-edge performance practice within Britain in the late 2000s. The impact of these companies across both the field of professional contemporary performance and performance studies cannot be denied, and it was obvious to us at the time that such companies had made a success across both: having been making their own forms of work for several decades and having their innovative practices detailed within academia. Whether or not we were completely enamoured with their performances, we looked up to these companies who were able to create such an oeuvre. And the best thing? Each of these companies started out of university! Forced Entertainment began as a group of Exeter University graduates in 1984. Stan's Café formed in 1991 from Lancaster University. Gob Squad – a combination of Nottingham Trent University and Gießen Universität students in 1994. Even Punchdrunk was formed by another round of Exeter University graduates in 2000. For performance studies students at the time, these companies were the blueprint. As we formed small production groups for assessments, and theatre companies alongside or immediately following our degrees, we aimed to follow in the steps of these greats – as if we were spotty teenage bandmates badly rehearsing rock music in our parents' garage and these were the bands displayed on the posters on the damp walls; we were determined to follow our passion and become the next graduate theatre company success stories. However, the economic reality facing this increased number of theatre students upon graduating since 2007 was antithetical to such aspirations.

Although the number of unemployed millennials in Britain is now lower than it was before the 2008 financial crash (Statista 2022), the current epidemic of precarious, or atypical, labour plays an intrinsic role in this seemingly positive statistic, with many millennials 'piecing together survival wages through a patchwork of low-paid, part time work' (Cairns 2017: 97). Cairns pinpoints the rise of 'entrepreneurial education' (ibid.) as another factor perpetuating the myth of millennial entitlement. He argues that the reorienting of post-secondary education has 'encourage[d] students to approach working life as an unstable, fierce competition in which success comes through the capacity to constantly sell oneself as being a flexible, self-motivated and resilient hustler in the face of continuous hardship' (ibid.). As Oli Mould explains, there has been a 'fundamental shift in how labour is conceptualized in contemporary capitalism' (ibid.: 30) and the current neoliberal system that 'tells us we must be "creative" to progress' (ibid.: 3) – that 'champions flexibility, agility and dynamism over institutions [and] social formations' (ibid.: 31) – actually inhibits creativity that does not support the capitalist narrative and, consequently, leads to increasing precariousness. Alongside this, the rise in prevalence of the 'gig economy', which, as Prassl points out, 'evokes the artists life' (Prassl 2018: 2), offers work as a 'one-off task or transaction, without further commitments on either side' (2). This 'increasing casualisation of labour' (Mould 2018: 33) emphasizes (creative) flexibility but causes precarity.

Between this precarious labour market that has seen a decline in real wages over the past decade and increasingly high rental costs in larger cities, where a majority of millennials (and theatres) are concentrated (Chapman 2019), millennials have been forced to choose between an insecure labour model in order to cover city-based rent costs and to stay in smaller towns and risk 'stunting' their pay and career prospects (Snaith 2019). Together with a 'skewed' (Gardner 2019) arts funding system that bears the risk on those at the beginning of their careers, the structural set up in which millennials can create theatre led Lyn Gardner, in her 2019 investigation into millennial-led Damsel Production's staging of a London Fringe performance, to proclaim that she was 'astonished that anything ever gets made at all – and it wouldn't if not for the … self-exploitation of all those involved' (Gardner 2019). Although forging a creative career has never been an easy endeavour, the specific precarity of the millennials' situation, to borrow from sociologists Shaun Wilson and Norbert Ebert, 'translates into social precarity' (2013: 264). Whilst the emerging British theatre makers of previous decades may have been able to make use of funds such as the 1983 Enterprise Allowance Scheme in order to supplement their work, the precarity of the labour model available to millennials alongside a skewed funding system, the complexities of which graduates are little prepared for upon graduation, 'raises questions around who can afford to make theatre and who is excluded by the financial constraints' (Gardner 2019). Such an aspiration, therefore, is not only limited by age – of course – but often only to those that have financial, mental and physical support systems in place to subsidize and support such work. Obviously, this did not stop, and has not stopped, graduates from theatre and performance degrees becoming an integral part of the British fringe theatre scene. Often propped up on a profit-share agreement between company members, and a whole lot of passion-following, such 'smaller-scale companies are an essential part of the theatre ecology, but they are also one of the industry's most vulnerable groups, with often no core funding and little security' (Gardner 2021). The majority of this book is focussed on such small-scale companies, several of which did begin life during or immediately after their university degrees – Eager Spark started as Write By Numbers at Goldsmiths in 2009, YESYESNONO at Birkbeck in 2018, Poltergeist at Oxford in 2017 – and of course some of the millennial-graduate-formed-companies from the past few years seem destined to have the success garnered by those we originally studied in the previous decades – Sh!t Theatre, for example, who began life as students at Queen Mary University of London in 2010. But the sheer number of 'emerging' companies formed by the increased number of theatre and performance studies graduates between roughly the mid-2000s and the mid-2010s should have, if following the same trajectory of graduate companies in previous decades, produced more companies running for longer periods of time. The reality of the situation, however, is that financial pressure takes precedence for those without separate support systems and that the number of companies and projects formed outweighs the funding available from a continually squeezed arts system. The juxtaposition of the increase in British theatre students alongside the realistic impacts of the 2008 financial crash upon such an increased amount of graduates is important in that it had a significant effect not only on the ability of those newly formed theatre companies to make, and continue to make, essential and innovative performance work but also on the type of work such companies make and the themes and aesthetics within this work. As illustrated later in this book, it is no wonder that such companies develop work that mimics the inherent sensibility of the metamodern millennial – a sensibility that wraps around ideas of impossible utopias, a longing for connection and the hauntology of lost futures – that of hope/lessness.

4

Metamodern theatre: A spotter's guide

This chapter begins to develop a heuristic system in which to unpack and contextualize certain strategies within current theatre practice as part of the wider metamodern structure of feeling. In this sense, the following is an inventory of the constituent elements of metamodern theatre to – at long last – answer the question troubling everyone who initially picked up this book: just what *is* metamodern theatre? I have subtitled this chapter 'A spotter's guide' to contextualize how I envision this chapter can be used as a model through which to determine noticeable strategies to pinpoint *why* a particular production *feels* metamodern. However, as Dember reiterates regarding his own catalogue of metamodern strategies in popular culture – *Eleven Metamodern Methods in the Arts* – this 'should be thought of as a proposal, a theory in progress' (Dember 2018), and I offer the following as a proposition for further development, debate and dialogue around just what constitutes metamodern theatre practice. As Radchenko rightly questions, 'How can we study something that has not been completely described yet?' (Radchenko 2019: 495). It is with this paradoxical positioning in mind that I attempt this analysis.

In Radchenko's application of metamodernism as a hermeneutic tool used to understand the aesthetic and narrative shifts seen in contemporary literature and videogames, he suggests that 'the important part of studying the contemporary novel (or any other genre) is to employ the instruments that will reveal its core ideas' (Radchenko 2019: 496). When focusing on the post-postmodern turn, Radchenko implores that

> searching for the right code requires a number of attempts before the more or less complete scheme of the new structures is created. For now, the concept of metamodernism is probably one of the most complex ideas that integrates a variety of tools allowing us to draw some conclusions. (ibid.)

Radchenko admits that that the 'use of the features of metamodernism in literary research demands careful adoption of them for this purpose, defining the basics of their principles and meanings' (Radchenko 2019: 497), and this chapter intends to follow such careful adoption in my application of metamodernism towards theatrical practice. Whilst Dember's Metamodern Methods are purposefully broadly applicable across a range of cultural mediums, this chapter follows Radchenko's provision of artform-specific catalogues of metamodern attributes by providing one tailored to the field of theatre and performance.

Theatre, of course, is an inherently multifaceted medium. Even at its barest – a performer, an audience and an empty space – the intersections of these various elements are numerous. As such, rather than simplifying this chapter to a list of individual attributes which would mean that, on the surface, such elements may seem equally weighted in their positioning within the theatrical metamodern structure of feeling, I have divided the following guide into three interconnected sections to, in part, delineate between the form and the content of such practices. The first section, 'Overarching Sensibilities', describes certain sensibilities that are essential to the wider understanding of metamodernism and that, I proffer, are found infused throughout all metamodern theatre practice. The second section, 'Aesthetic Strategies', then begins to define the theatrical aesthetics and forms of performance that are used within such practices that mark a break from previous/postmodern work and emulate metamodern aesthetics as defined within other cultural practices, and therefore serve to create, develop or strengthen the overarching sensibilities. Finally, 'Themes' addresses both the narrative and intertextual topics and ideas that are explored through these strategies. As the experience of theatre is a complex interplay between form and content, between staging and text, this chapter offers an example of how both aspects can be considered in assessing why certain contemporary theatre and performance projects *feel* metamodern. As described throughout the previous chapters, when experiencing a production as an audience member, my initial understanding in regard to it being metamodern or not is a *feeling* – an embodied awareness that what I am experiencing *feels* different/new/post-postmodern/metamodern. The following is an attempt at isolating and defining the particular aspects within contemporary theatrical practice that induce, lead to or support such feelings.

Overarching sensibilities

By overarching sensibilities, I refer to certain modalities that are ingrained throughout both the form and content of metamodern theatre. These modalities permeate a production in such a way that the aesthetic strategies and themes utilized within the performance serve to deliver or enhance these overarching sensibilities. Whilst examples of metamodern theatre don't need to exhibit all of the following aesthetic strategies or themes – some may exhibit two or three, some may exhibit them all and some may exhibit strategies that are not covered in this list – I proffer that these overarching sensibilities will be present throughout. In this sense, the following sensibilities are the predominant and initial points in sensing that a piece exhibits a metamodern quality, in part because they reflect two of the main modalities that are associated with metamodernism at large: oscillation and new sincerity/felt experience.

Oscillation

As covered in detail in Chapter 2, the concept of oscillation is so ingrained within the general understanding of metamodernism that the terms are often synonymous. The oscillatory sensibility within metamodern theatre reflects an inherent dynamic 'between a modern enthusiasm and a postmodern irony' as defined by Vermeulen and van den Akker (2010), within which reside subordinate oscillations between intersecting modalities, some of which are detailed by the pair as oscillating 'between hope and melancholy, between naïveté and knowingness, empathy and apathy, unity and plurality, totality and fragmentation, purity and ambiguity' (ibid.). It is important to remember that this oscillatory movement indicates a continual fluctuation between such polarities whilst refusing to remain congruent to either. As mentioned earlier, as one of two overarching sensibilities within metamodern theatre, this oscillation is made possible through several of the aesthetic strategies discussed further on, as well as evident throughout several intertextual themes. In the previous chapters, such oscillation is palpable in the together-apartness of Uninvited Guests' *Love Letters at Home*, or the continual switch between the performed and the authentic in The Gramophones' *Playful Acts of Rebellion*.

To return to Dember's modes of oscillation as detailed in Chapter 2, oscillation in metamodern theatre is both structural and hermeneutic. If oscillation is evident in both the form and/or content of a piece, it is therefore a structural feature of such work. Whether this is evident through juxtaposing, braiding or within reconstructive pastiche, structural oscillation refers to when 'the artwork itself includes pieces from both sides of a duality and it switches back and forth between them in time' (Dember 2023). In the analyses throughout the following chapters, my attention regarding oscillation will be largely focused on that which is structural, as the aesthetic strategies within the following pieces, and the archival material available to others, are concrete articles through which such oscillation can be observed. However, it would be remiss to then eliminate Dember's hermeneutic understanding of oscillation, which is based within the audience's experiencing of such performances. Rather than structural oscillation between polarities throughout the performance itself, hermeneutic oscillation occurs throughout the audience's experience of such – in that their response to a piece fluctuates between disparate polarities. As Dember explains, 'As the viewer swings to, say a postmodern pole in interpreting the object, the very logic of that reaction compels the viewer to swing back to a modernist pole, and then it reverses again and the cycle continues' (Dember 2023). Whilst there might not be a clear oscillatory movement within the structure of the piece itself, it is the audience that are doing the oscillating within their response. Of course, Kirsty Sedgman's audience-centric research (Sedgman 2018) reminds us that there is 'not really any such thing as "the audience" at all' (Bakk 2016), and when discussing 'the audience's experience' we are negating the fact that an audience is necessarily made up of various individuals with various modes of interpretation and individual experiences of the same production. In keeping with my approach to centring on my own embodied experience throughout this volume, when referring to hermeneutic oscillation in the experience of viewing or participating in a particular performance, I only refer to my *own* embodied experience of such. Of course, such an understanding of oscillation can only *be* a personal, embodied experience. I cannot claim to speak to what you, reader, or any other audience members *felt* during a performance, or how you/they interpreted it throughout. Neither can I claim to assert whether that feeling oscillated between an ironic and a sincere, or an empathetic and an apathetic state, for instance. Instead, in reference to Fuchs's *The Death of Character* (1996), I remain centred on my own embodied experience of hermeneutic oscillation, continuing to centre feelings – and protecting the solidity of felt experience – within this understanding of metamodern theatre.

Felt experience

My approach to understanding metamodern theatre being feelings driven first and foremost is – in part – because, as Dember asserts, 'the essence of metamodernism is a (conscious or unconscious) motivation to protect the solidity of *felt experience* against the scientific reductionism of the modernist perspective and the ironic detachment of the postmodern sensibility' (Dember 2018; emphasis in original.). In this respect, I see felt experience as part of the second overarching sensibility that permeates metamodern theatre. This is, to some extent, because both sensibilities are integrally intertwined – with the oscillatory movement enabling the centring of the felt experience. Structural oscillation, according to Dember, 'allows for the expression of the fullness of the [artist's] interiority, not being limited by the doctrine imposed by either one of [the polarities] alone' (Dember 2023). Whilst metamodernism and oscillation are inherently interwoven, a structural *juxtaposing* of tones could, of course, be evident in a postmodern production. However, in 'a postmodern version, the [polarities'] opposition might cancel each other out, each undermining the emotional reality of the other, but in this metamodern [oscillatory] version they add together' (Dember 2023). This paradoxical positioning, in which the work oscillates between sensibilities *and* 'adds together', constructs a liminal space in which both polarities are accessible, expressed and essential to the space's construction. This space is also where the audience/writer/performers' felt experience can then be centred. To clarify this, Dember (Dember 2022; The Oscillator's Stone 2023) offers a visual metaphor of a postmodern 'pole' and a modern 'pole' leaning against each other in a two-sided tent formation. Both poles are required to support each other, and yet are working against each other – the pressure of each pole's desire to succumb to gravity, push the other pole down and fall to the ground, in effect, propping up the other pole. This support-through-opposition tension effectively creates a new space between these two poles which would not be able to exist within a postmodern work, and in which, Dember suggests, the solidity of the felt experience can exist (see Figure 4.1). As Dember explains, the 'aesthetic benefit of leaning two or more tones against each other, like tent poles in tension, is to prop all of them up, thus creating a "safe" space for the fullness of a person's felt experience' (Dember 2022). Such an understanding of the aesthetic effect of oscillation within a tent-pole structure reflects Alison Gibbons's focus on a (re)turn towards affect within metamodernism. Such affect is based on essentialism and postmodernism being seen as inherently unhelpful when separate but now existing in tension with one another. In this respect, the tent space created by such tension is where a 'distinctly metamodern subjectivity, to which affect is central ... both driven by a desire for a meaningful personal emotional experience while being aware of the constructed nature of experiences' (Gibbons 2017: 86), can exist. Where my use of felt experience differs from Dember's in this respect is that I, following Radchenko's (2019, 2020) analysis, see it as inherently connected to both Gibbons's understanding of metamodern affect as a desire for meaningful emotional experience whilst understanding the artificiality of the cultural constructs that engender and enable such, and Foster Wallace's new sincerity as 'the desire to feel and be emotional instead of being ironic' (Radchenko 2020: 249) whilst remaining inside, and part of, ironic sensibilities. Through

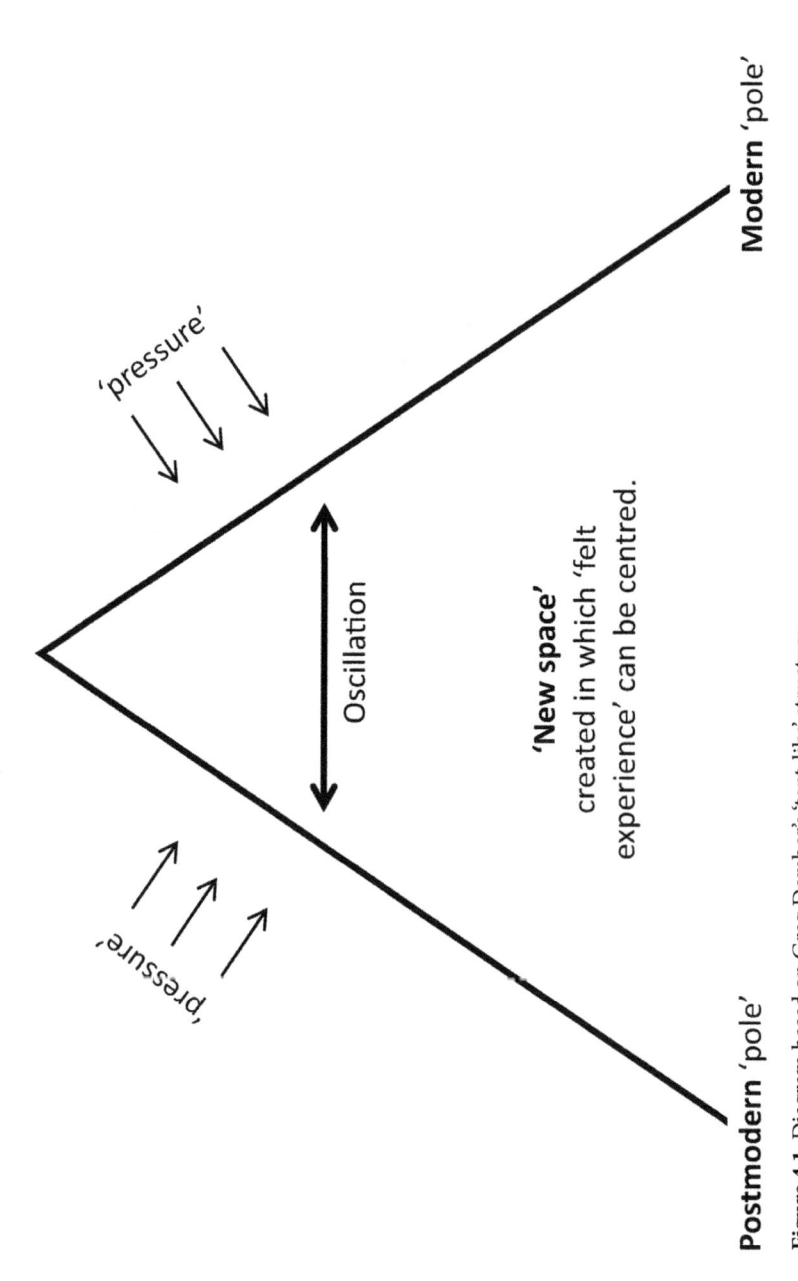

94 Metamodernism in Contemporary British Theatre

Figure 4.1 Diagram based on Greg Dember's 'tent-like' structure

Source: Produced by the author with kind permission from Greg Dember.

this, I inherently connect the focus on felt experience (within the audience member's response to metamodern theatre) to Foster Wallace's new sincerity. This second overarching sensibility is therefore, in part, a space that is constructed for emotions to be felt throughout the experience of a production. However, it is important to note that this space is only constructed through the tension between a modern engagement and a postmodern detachment. It is not wholly sincere but aware of the insincerity and artificiality of the constructed nature of such sincerity, at the same time as *trying* to be sincere. It is a felt sincerity, or a *feeling* of sincere feelings that are at once in tension with, and admitting the existence of, the artificiality of the mechanisms that led to such feelings. In this sense, my use of the term felt *experience* in naming this second overarching sensibility could also be labelled felt *sincerity* to encompasses both the space created through oscillation in which the felt experience of an audience is centred, strengthened and protected (cf. Dember 2018) and the awareness of the fact that these feelings are centred, strengthened and protected through artificial mechanisms. To return to Jerry Saltz's original observation of the post-postmodern artists' mentality being that 'I know that the art I'm creating may seem silly ... but that doesn't mean this isn't serious' (2010) – as an overarching sensibility within metamodern theatre, felt sincerity states that 'I know the theatre is fake, but that doesn't mean that these feelings don't feel real'. It points to works that embrace this paradoxical dichotomy, that are open about the surreal nature of the in/authenticity of theatrical performance, that ask the audience to *sincerely* feel again whilst also knowing that we, and performance as an artistic method, remain inescapably inauthentic. It is centred, too, on our embodied, felt, experience throughout this. For, as Dember reminds us, whilst we attempt to develop an understanding of performance in a post-postmodern paradigm, we are building upon the facts that postmodernism dealt us: that truth is individual, that responses to a text are multiple – possibly infinite. But that 'what we really *know* is what we feel and what's our interior experience. In the end, if you don't have that, there's no point' (The Oscillator's Stone 2023).

Aesthetic strategies

As overarching strategies, both oscillation and felt experience permeate metamodern theatre and are the first touchpoints with which an audience member might notice – or feel – that a performance exhibits metamodern tendencies. You might observe a continual fluctuation between the fictitious and the factual, or the performer and the performed, for instance. Or you may notice that the work – despite being open about the fact that it is inherently an inauthentic medium – is concerned with authenticity and eliciting surprisingly authentic emotions from you *at the same time* as being transparent about the construction of these emotions. As oscillation functions to support a space in which the felt experience or – slightly ironest – felt sincerity can be expressed, the following aesthetic strategies are examples of particular aspects within metamodern theatre that serve to create and develop these overarching sensibilities. As an attempt at forming a definition of metamodern theatre, I offer an initial definition of six aesthetic strategies in this section, through which we can examine metamodern theatrical tendencies. Some of these strategies are interconnected, and the definitions of some bleed into each other, in part because such strategies are examined in the wake of a performance and are, essentially, attempts at unpicking interconnected modalities from the perspective of a critically reflective audience member. They are not, it has to be said, intended to be seen as definite and discrete building blocks through which to create metamodern performance. As Dember rightly warns us, 'Those of us who discuss metamodernism do not have the job of bringing it into being, nor (to a large extent) the capacity to do so' (Dember 2018), and it would be remiss of me not to, again, emphasize that theatre makers do not go into the creative process with a toolbox of aesthetic strategies through which to intentionally develop metamodern theatre. These aesthetic strategies are defined after the fact and are an attempt to unpack what the specific elements are within contemporary theatre that indicate a break from previous modern and postmodern practice. In this sense, these are the markers of metamodern theatre and will be employed throughout the remainder of the volume as methods through which to unpack how metamodernism is both reflected in and developed through the work of contemporary British theatre companies.

Authenticity

I have spent enough of this volume already discussing the metamodern (and millennial) interest in the (strive towards the) authentic whilst accepting that authenticity is, perhaps, an impossible goal. Regarding its position as an aesthetic strategy within metamodern theatre, my use of authenticity, here, similarly refers to an attempt at working *towards* something authentic within a performance, or evidence of an interest in 'the authentic' throughout a performance alongside a simultaneous, or oscillatory, acceptance of the complexity, messiness and ultimate un-achievability of this preoccupation. By referring to the authentic within performance, I do *not* mean to indicate that this is a return to the modern dramatic attempt to authentically represent 'real-life' onstage as per the naturalistic, representational drama of modernist playwrights and directors. This is not a return to fourth-wall dramatics, or – indeed – an acceptance of the naturalistic actor's ideal of producing an 'authentic performance' (whatever that actually means). Such a metamodern interest in authenticity is balanced against the fact that it is impossible to be 'authentic' within a performance, as performance itself is inherently an 'act'. Daniel Schulze's (2017) focus on how the resurgence of an interest in authenticity throughout contemporary forms of theatre is essential to understanding post-postmodern practice is also not concerned with a modernist dramatic version of authentic representation, but it leads him to concentrate on contemporary trends concerning an 'authentic experience' for the audience through intimate forms of theatre, immersive theatre and the forms of authenticity within documentary theatre and verbatim practices. Whilst all such forms are exemplary of the resurgence of interest in the authentic and an 'authentic experience' within contemporary theatre practice, my own understanding of a metamodern drive towards authenticity within theatre is that such a desire to be authentic, to offer an 'authentic experience' (whatever this means) or to portray something 'authentically' (whatever *that* means), is always met with, or fluctuates/oscillates towards (and then back away from), the fact that the succeeding of this desire is an inescapable impossibility. As will become clear in Chapter 5, the forms of authenticity evident within this metamodern theatre practice exist as an interjection of an authentic acceptance about the reality of the construct of the performance or an interjection of the audience/performer/writer's (dare I use the term) 'real life' into the performance itself. Such an aesthetic is inherently connected to the use of metatheatre (see further on) as well as specifically enhancing the overarching sensibility of felt experience, in that the *authentic* can both be manifest as an acceptance of the disconnected nature of performance and an attempt towards authentic connection between performer-audience or between participants. Rather than a belief in the power of performance to achieve authentic representation (which, of course, can never actually escape the inherent inauthenticity of the medium itself), authenticity as an aesthetic strategy within metamodern theatre is manifest as an interest in how the authentic can be approached and utilized within a performance in a way that serves to at once remind an audience about the disconnected (and inauthentic) nature of performance whilst also striving *towards* authentic connection – centring the paradoxical felt sincerity of such a performance – which, in itself, is at once both authentic and inauthentic.

Metatheatre

In referring to metatheatre, I am, of course, talking about theatrical work that comments in some way on its own form and/or construction. In the barest sense, metatheatre is theatre that is open about the fact that it is theatre. Throughout performance studies, the definitions of the term are numerous, being 'variously understood as theatricality, reflexivity, auto-referentiality, forms of theatrical illusion, or what is called play-within-the-play' (Paillard and Milanezi 2021: 1). Of course, metatheatre is not a distinctly metamodern aesthetic. In fact, as William Eggington rightly points out, 'There can be no theater that is not already a metatheater, in that in the instant a distinction is recognized between a real space and another, imaginary one that mirrors it, that very distinction becomes an element to be incorporated as another distinction in the imaginary space's work of mimesis' (Eggington 2003: 74). It is also not a distinctly contemporary movement. Paillard and Milanezi proffer that 'while in the past some have considered metatheatre to consist in the breaking of the theatrical illusion or the crossing of the fourth wall, others have argued that such a phenomenon does not apply to the ancient theatre' (Paillard and Milanezi 2021: 1–2) as modernism's fourth wall had not yet been constructed; therefore elements of what we would now label metatheatre are observable within the theatre of ancient Greece. Whilst metamodern elements can be found throughout cultural artefacts from various eras (with some metamodern scholars referring to such as proto-metamodern), my own precept regarding metamodernism as a structure of feeling is that it is distinctly post-postmodern and must be understood as part of the epistemological chronology as defined in Chapter 1. Whilst elements that we might consider part of the metamodern structure of feeling now may, indeed, be seen in traditional, modern and postmodern works, metamodernism as a collection of aesthetics or strategies is only viably understood when historically situated against that which came before. Just as the rejection of the fourth wall in postdramatic theatre is only possible through the construction of the fourth wall within the modernism that preceded it, metatheatrical elements in postmodernist work differ from metatheatrical elements in Shakespearean drama *because* of the modernism that directly preceded postmodernism, as does the metatheatricality within metamodern theatre subsequently. Building on Paillard and Milanezi's cataloguing of metatheatrical elements (2021: 1) and Richard Hornby's understanding of five devices of metatheatre – the play within the play, self-reference, the ceremony within the play, role-playing within the role and literary and real-life reference (Hornby 1986: 32) – I proffer that a metamodern use of metatheatrical elements is based on three specific modalities: self-reflexivity, performatism and beyondness.

In the first instance, metamodern metatheatre absorbs Dember's notion of metamodern (or hyper-) self-reflexivity, which was defined in detail in Chapter 2. In brief, postmodern reflexivity draws attention to the work being a piece of work to highlight that it is therefore not to be trusted (Dember 2018), whilst metamodern self-reflexivity draws attention to the fact that the work was created and is being experienced in order to centre the felt experience of the creator(s) and/or audience/participants, respectively. This can occur through a more human-centric self-reflexivity that focuses on the writer, performer, company or individual audience members (see sections on The Gramophones, Poltergeist or YESYESNONO in Chapter 5) or one that focuses on the act of performance or the piece itself (see sections Arinzé Kene or Middle Child in Chapter 5). Either enables a centring of the felt experience of the piece – whether in highlighting the humanity behind the creative team or in highlighting the realities of the construct of the performance. In this sense, a metamodern, self-reflexive metatheatricality serves to highlight, support or develop the experience of the overarching sensibility of felt experience.

Secondly, a metamodern metatheatricality absorbs Raoul Eshelman's notion of performatism through Dember's understanding of this as one of many methods within metamodernism rather than, as Eshelman originally proposed, an overarching cultural structure of feeling. Whilst the ostension (the act of demonstrating and not just describing a fictional world) of theatre reveals its duplexity (cf. Eversmann 2004: 141), because 'theatre is simultaneously produced and received, it contains two frames: that of the fictional and that of the actual' (Krüger 2016: 244), a metamodern performatist framing works to, in some ways, reveal several 'fictional' levels working in tandem. Savyna translates the artistic technique of placing a smaller copy of an image within itself – the *mise en abyme* or 'placement in abyss' – to a performance context through her analysis of Tim Crouch's *The Author* (2009), in that the actual play that the audience experience in Crouch's production is about 'the process of creating [a fictional] play and its further reception by the audience' (Savyna 2021: 71). She labels this initial, outer level the 'semantic frame of the play' (ibid.) and the fictional play within the play – the *mise en abyme* – as 'its "heart", the narrative on which all the thematic layers are strung' (ibid.). This reflects the double framing within Eshelman's performatism which consists initially of an outer (sometimes fantastical) frame requiring a commitment to a (performance of) belief from the audience. In *The Author*, this outer – or semantic – frame is that of the audience engaging with 'Tim' – played by Crouch – as the author of a *fictional* play. As Dember explains, this outer frame forces the audience 'to make a choice to buy into all of it, if they are going to commit to engaging the work' (Dember 2018) within the second, central frame – its 'heart', as according to Savyna – inside which is a narrative that an audience can unironically engage with after accepting the logic of the initial outer frame.

Nathan Sibthorpe presents a similar understanding of metatheatrical levels within contemporary theatre in his analysis of Charlie Kaufman's play *Hope Leaves the Theater* (2005). Intentionally emulating the act of recording a radio drama, the piece sees the cast sat on stools, delivering their lines into microphones accompanied by live sound effects performed by an onstage foley artist. For Sibthorpe, the levels of (metatheatrical) narrative in this production can be understood as a series of three concentric circles, starting with the outer level A, inside of which sits Level B, inside of which sits Level C (Sibthorpe 2018: 24) (see Figure 4.2). The innermost Level, C, represents the 'play within the play' of Kaufman's production – 'a whimsical narrative about a man and a woman meeting in an elevator, performed by Meryl Streep and Peter Dinklage' (ibid.). This level of narrative is continuously interrupted by Level B, in which 'Streep and Dinklage play scripted renderings of themselves and Hope Davis plays Louise, a member of the audience' (ibid.). Level A, in this sense, indicates the 'real' audience experiencing the 'real' production, the felt experience of which is heightened by the narrative construction of the continually interwoven Levels of B and C. As Sibthorpe explains, *Hope Leaves the Theatre* focuses an audience's engagement on their own experience of watching/listening to the piece by engaging them in a story of an audience member 'who struggles to encounter a theatre work' (ibid.: 25). Sibthorpe argues that this 'gives dramaturgical relevance to the world of A, which represents the actual reality of our given circumstances as an audience and the nature of the real performance encounter. Where A is a real event, B is a dramatization of that event. The relationship between B and C [then] becomes an allegory for the relationship between A and B' (ibid.). Additionally, by placing the character of Louise (Level B), played by Hope (Level A) in the actual audience (also Level A), Sibthorpe argues that the audience then occupies a position of impossible fictionality – 'a paradoxical state of being [in which] we become hyper-aware of the activity we are engaged in, and must intellectually assert our presence as a genuine receiver of the work' (ibid.). In Chapter 5, we will see how companies such as Poltergeist exhibit this form of metamodern metatheatricality in ways that – in contrast to the bleakness of Crouch's attempt to remind an audience that 'we have lost a thread of responsibility for what we choose to look at' (Crouch 2009) through a harrowing inner-frame story about child abuse – attempt to centre the elements of joyful connection within the felt

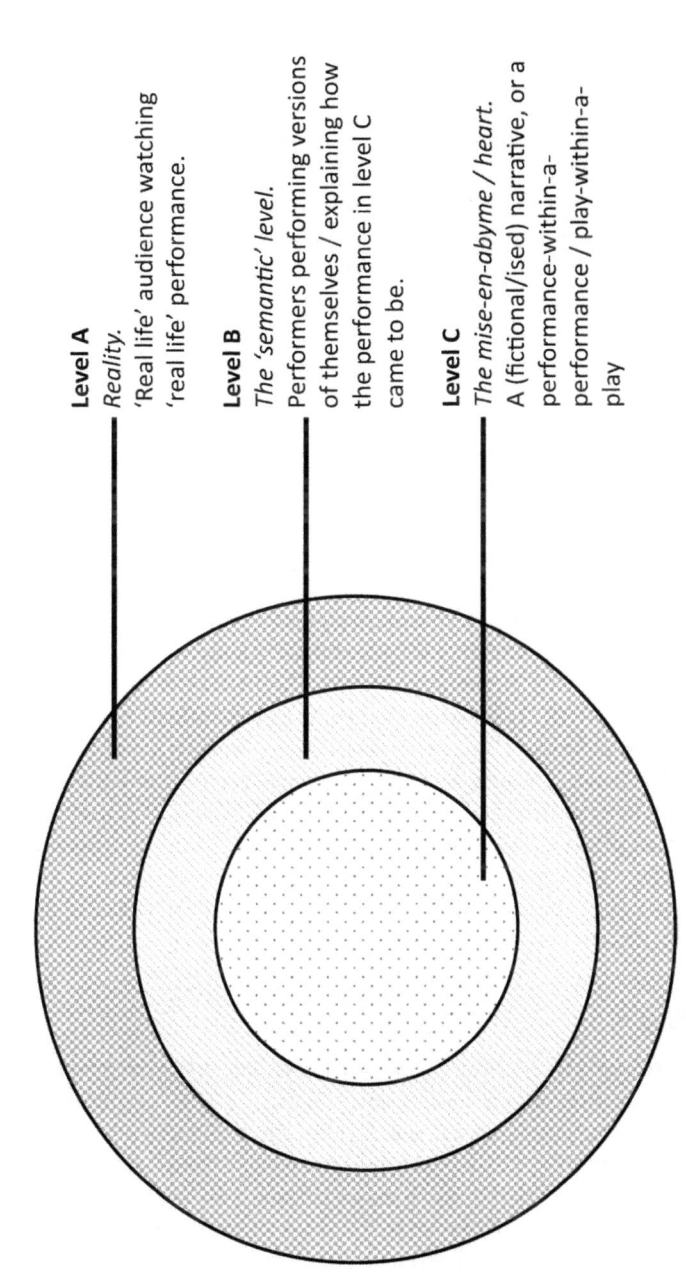

Level A
Reality.
'Real life' audience watching 'real life' performance.

Level B
The 'semantic' level.
Performers performing versions of themselves / explaining how the performance in level C came to be.

Level C
The mise-en-abyme / heart.
A (fictional/ised) narrative, or a performance-within-a-performance / play-within-a-play

Figure 4.2 Diagram illustrating levels of metatheatricality in metamodern theatre, Combining elements of Eshelman's Performatism (2008), Sibthorpe's levels of narrative (2018) and Savyna's metatheatricality (2021)

Source: Produced by the author with kind permission from Nathan Sibthorpe.

experience of both the audience and that of a company's attempt to develop such a self-reflexive piece. This is not, however, to say that such shows are purely altruistic, joyful or hopeful in comparison to Crouch's *The Author*, although some will trade in the creation and manipulation of such feelings at points through their application of metatheatre – as will become clear.

Finally, in reference to metamodernism's prefix 'meta' referring to being between, betwixt and beyond, Nina Mitova offers a forward movement in metamodern theatre studies from the inbetweenness afforded by oscillation and contends that 'performances that have *gone beyond* their boundaries in terms of materiality and physicality and have changed their structure with regards to the time, space and agency of theatre [should] be considered metamodern' (Mitova 2020: 2; emphasis in original). For Mitova, this is particularly acute in the use of technology as both a tool to extend the traditional stage space into the virtual sphere and in productions staged entirely outside of the boundary of a theatre space or the boundary of a physical space – with such theatre '*going beyond* the physical dimension of the "here and now", as the "here" becomes a virtual location and the physical presence of the audience is not the same place as it would be in a theatre setting' (ibid.: 36; emphasis in original). I appropriate aspects of Mitova's focus on the beyondness of theatre within this second aesthetic strategy – metatheatre – in that I propose that a metamodern approach to metatheatrical elements can reach 'beyond' the boundaries of a performance without necessarily leaving the boundaries of the performance space whether physically or virtually. As Mitova contends, 'Paradoxically, bypassing the boundaries can actually enhance the awareness of the boundary itself' (ibid.: 2) – hence, by extending an audience's focus outside of the boundaries of the performance or performance space through a metatheatrical awareness of the construction of the performance, the focus also reflects back towards the limitations of the performance itself.

Storytelling

Anne Bogart's (2014) observance of a return to an interest in the power of stories and narrative within contemporary theatre, and the championing of a participatory, individualistic and political form of such, reflects the third aesthetic strategy of metamodern theatre detailed here – storytelling. Importantly, I want to clarify that I am specifically referring to the act of story*telling* and the use of *stories* within a performance, which is not synonymous with an interest in narrative drama or a return to centrality of dramatic narrative. As detailed in previous chapters, metamodern theatre does not remove itself from the postdramatic or return, naïvely, to modernist or dramatic drama. Instead, what I am observing across contemporary theatre practice reflects Bogart's own observation of an interest in the efficacy of storytelling within a performance framework. This is a postdramatic-adjacent appreciation of stories in that a narrative need not be the central drive of a performance but, in contrast to the 'traditional' postdramatic 'levelling out' of theatrical aesthetics in which story or narrative either becomes one of many equally valid semiotic-driven foci or, in some cases, is removed entirely, storytelling (and a critique of storytelling) is a central tool in the metamodern theatre maker's arsenal. As we will see in Chapter 5, this may manifest in such a way that characters within a piece tell stories to each other or the audience but most prominently manifests as performers directly addressing the audience as (seemingly) themselves to tell them a story. Often these stories serve as a constituent part of the metatheatrical element – with works such as The Gramophones' *End to End* (2012) or Poltergeist's *Lights Over Tesco Car Park* (2018), for example, being built around the conceit that the company members of each show are telling the story of the development of that show to the audience throughout the show itself. Other times, this focus on storytelling relates to Bogart's own reflection on the power of stories and the act of storytelling in regard to the communication and communion that storytelling enables, despite an inherent awareness of the limitations of the storytelling medium and the complexities that come from the relationship between storyteller, story and audience that postmodernism revealed to us, as evident, for example, in Eager Spark's *Beneath the Albion Sky* (2013). In this sense, the use of storytelling in metamodern theatre embraces (a return to) the power of storytelling whilst also remaining critical about the act itself.

Reconstructive pastiche

As previously explored in Chapter 2, pastiche generally refers to cultural products that apply elements from different, possibly conflicting, genres. In a postmodern sense, these genres may be pitted in conflict to deconstruct or poke fun at each other (Le Cunff 2019) whilst metamodern, constructive pastiche follows Dember's tent-like structure, in which the separate elements lean against each other like tent-poles, 'holding up a structure that allows a kind of feeling that wouldn't otherwise be expressible' (ibid.). The use of reconstructive pastiche in metamodern theatre arises from the groundwork laid by Fuchs's death of character and Lehmann's 'theatre of states' (Lehmann 2006: 68) built from a 'deconstructive project from within the theatre [concluding in the fact that the] stage is no longer a site of mimetic transcription of action and dialogue; therefore, signification is not the be-all and end-all of performance [and] text and stage are set free from one another' (Defraeye 2007: 214). Through postmodern deconstruction, theatre was broken down into constituent elements which could then be juxtaposed against each other in new and surprising ways but remain largely dissociative – with elements remaining in tension or opposition to each other. Reconstructive pastiche, in contrast, combines the constituent elements revealed through postmodern deconstruction in ways that enable a new space in which these otherwise inexpressible feelings would not be able to exist. Of course, reconstructive pastiche is essentially connected to the oscillation between modern and postmodern polarities within metamodern theatre and, in some ways, is a focussed subcategory of such an overarching sensibility. In Chapter 5, we will see how reconstructive pastiche is evident in works such as Middle Child's *All We Ever Wanted Was Everything* (2017).

(Post-immersive) dialogical engagement

I was reticent, here, to introduce another 'post-' prefix this late into the game, as it were. However, in discerning the following aesthetic strategy evident within the framework of metamodern theatre, it becomes clear that the term post-immersive, as defined by Jorge Lopes Ramos, Joseph Dunne-Howrie, Persis Jadé Maravala and Simon Bart in their *Post-Immersive Manifesto* (2020), best encapsulates the developments in the performer-participant relationship evident within metamodern theatre practice. The authors argue that the term immersive has become 'one of the most overused terms to describe theatre productions that aim to involve audiences in unconventional ways' (Lopes Ramos et al. 2020: 196). Whilst immersive theatre began life as an experimental form that disrupted both traditional theatrical boundaries and expected behaviours between audience and performers, it has 'become detached from its radical origins [and its] appropriation by advertisers, events promoters and PR consultants has rendered it a shorthand for selling tickets to elaborate and expensive fancy dress parties' (ibid.: 197). As an antithesis to this corporate appropriation, Lopes Ramos et al.'s *Post-Immersive Manifesto* seeks to address the fact that 'the term immersive was not enough' (ibid.: 199) to describe the efforts of companies creating work outside of this corporate appropriation of immersion, as the term is now synonymous with 'irresponsible and poorly conceived practice, and in fact was risking alienating audiences from theatre for life' (ibid.). The authors propose that new forms of immersive practices are being developed that move beyond the neoliberal takeover of immersive work and are therefore *post*-immersive. These practices 'validate intimacy, tenderness, empathy and care over immersive spectacles' (Lopes Ramos et al. 2020: 196), valuing the act of connection and communion between participants or performer and participants over spectacle. At their core is 'human social interaction and the constitution of a kind of performance collective, a temporary community' (ibid.: 204) that should be open to the crucial role that diversity and inclusivity of audiences should play in the creation of these communities – a contrast to the privileged few able to afford tickets to an immersive production staged by the popular, if expensive, companies such as Secret Cinema or Punchdrunk.

The concept of the post-immersive builds on Grant Kester's dialogical art as 'collaborative, and potentially emancipatory, forms of dialogue and conversation' (Kester 2005: 154) within an artistic product. Essentially, whilst dealing with forms of immersion and embodiment, Lopes Ramos et al.'s post-immersion is concerned with the immersive quality of dialogical interaction between participants and performers. As such, Kester's understanding of an aesthetic that is 'based on the possibility of a dialogical relationship that breaks down the conventional distinction between artist, art work and audience' (Kester 2009), the boundaries and definitions of which might be 'relatively intuitive or unconscious' (Kester 2009), reflects the core of the post-immersive drive. Kester references Mikhail Bakhtin's (1982) theories surrounding dialogical interchange being an open system that is less combative and more open to facilitating cooperation than a more dominant dialectical (closed) exchange (Sennet 2012). Dialogical art aims to categorize what Kester observed as an 'emergence of a body of contemporary art practice concerned with collaborative, and potentially emancipatory, forms of dialogue and conversation' (Kester 2005: 2). He describes the emergence of this shift as occurring within the mid-1990s, highlighting particular works that 'solicit participation and involvement so openly' (ibid.). Marissia Fragkou suggests that such an '"affective turn" towards relations of intimacy and relationality' (Fragkou 2018: 184) within British theatre is inherently connected to the precarity of contemporary neoliberal structures. The proliferation, she indicates, of 'notions of responsibility, solidarity and care for Others' (ibid.) in such theatre is reactive to the 'neo-liberal narratives of "responsibilization"' (ibid.), indicating that such performance offers alternative narratives of responsibility and social solidarity in the public sphere. Grant Kester's use of Habermas's concept of the public sphere in his defining of dialogical art is reflective of such alternatives, in that he contends that such art works to curate a discursive space free of the 'coercion and inequality that constrain human communication in normal daily life' (Kester 2005: 4). In this way, Kester encapsulates Habermas's communicative action in which the 'very act of participating in these exchanges makes us better able to engage in discursive encounters and decision-making processes in the future' (ibid.). As Fragkou surmises, such theatres of 'intimacy and relationality' may offer methods of 'transforming the shape of contemporary subjectivities' (Fragkou 2018: 185).

As an aesthetic strategy throughout metamodern theatre, dialogical engagement that reflects the post-immersive drive is evident in a levelling out of the performer-audience/participant hierarchy, with a drive towards co-creation and communal solidarity through an immersion in the dialogical act. Reflecting the paradoxical positioning of other aesthetics, this drive is inherently altruistic whilst also being aware of the limitations of the construction or medium that the engagement sits within. Such engagement is post-immersive, as it develops alongside and beyond the corporate appropriation of immersive theatre's radical origins and, through this, looks in towards the felt experience and felt sincerity of the participants involved. In Chapter 5, such an aesthetic is clearly seen in Hidden Track's *Drawing the Line* (2019) or Nathan Ellis's *work.txt* (2022), with the main precept of this dialogical engagement not only reflecting a focus on the felt experience of communion and communication through post-immersive participatory structures but also reflecting Freinacht's claim that we will 'come closer to the truth if we create better dialogues' (Freinacht 2017: 4).

The quirky

Borrowing predominantly from film scholarship, I appropriate the term quirky in order to attempt to describe an aesthetic throughout metamodern theatre that shares certain similarities to the use of the term within contemporary film theory – chiefly by film scholar James MacDowell – to discern a metamodern structure of feeling that reflects an ironest sensibility within the visual and narrative structure of a film. MacDowell's use of the term quirky refers to 'a contemporary comedic sensibility that is intimately bound up with the tonal combination of "irony" and "sincerity"' (MacDowell 2012: 21). In response to what he sees as the lazy use of the word within film criticism (MacDowell 2010: 1), MacDowell has defined 'such a seemingly intangible thing' (ibid.: 2) via Susan Sontag's understanding of a sensibility (such as camp) being 'almost, but not quite, ineffable' (Sontag 1969: 267), through Raymond Williams's understanding of a structure of feeling and, inevitably, as a constituent part of the wider frame of metamodernism (MacDowell 2017). In film marketing, the use of the term quirky suggests that the film being advertized is something other than the 'norm' but 'not *so* unique as to discourage those who might be repelled by descriptions such as "strange" or "avant-garde"' (MacDowell 2010: 1; emphasis in original). MacDowell's developed use of the term, however, draws on how films labelled as quirky – including those by Wes Anderson, Greta Gerwig, Noah

Baumbach, Charlie Kaufman and Spike Jonze – combine various forms of comedy – including deadpan delivery, the comedy of embarrassment and an intermittent use of slapstick – with 'moments that come closer to melodrama [in such a way as to] form a comic address that invites us to remain removed from *and* emotionally engaged with the fiction, [to] view the fictional world as both artificial *and* believable' (MacDowell 2012: 8). In reference to Wes Anderson's distinct aesthetics, MacDowell describes a quirky landscape of 'static, flat looking, medium-long or long shots that feel nearly geometrically even, depicting isolated or carefully arranged characters, sometimes facing directly towards us, who are made to look faintly ridiculous or out-of-place by virtue of the compositions rigidity' (MacDowell 2010: 6). MacDowell draws distinct connections between the quirky as an aesthetic sensibility and the metamodern through a tension between the flatness of these aesthetics and the depth of emotions portrayed, arguing that

> the common mixture of comic registers means we can simultaneously regard a film's fictional world as partly unbelievable, laugh at its flat treatment of melodramatic situations and still be invited to be moved by characters' misadventures. Its aesthetic can both seem self-conscious and promote an appreciation of naïveté. Evoking innocence allows many films to both recapture some of the enthusiasm that comes with childhood and simultaneously remind us that it must finally remain forever out of reach. Together these elements help create a tone that exists on a knife-edge of comic detachment and emotional engagement – or, put in another, blunter, way: a conflicted tone dealing in tensions between 'irony' and 'sincerity'. (MacDowell 2012: 10)

As I define metamodern theatre in relation to the postmodern theatre that came before (and continues to exist alongside) it, MacDowell defines the quirky's particular application of sincerity by drawing a distinction 'between these movies and another strain of 1990s and 2000s indie film regularly discussed in terms of its irony and cynicism' (MacDowell 2012: 11). He refers to the work of directors such as Todd Solondz and Quentin Tarantino in regard to this, using the popular term for such work – 'smart cinema' – to define 'one cinematic manifestation of the postmodern as one especially prevalent late twentieth-century structure of feeling … a central characteristic of which is the ironic tone' (MacDowell 2012: 12). In contrasting quirky films to those of the 'smart cinema' sensibility, MacDowell inescapably links the aesthetics of the quirky to the ironic-sincere oscillation of metamodernity in contrast to 'smart' cinema's singular focus on (postmodern) irony. In a theatrical sense, the filmic aesthetics of the quirky don't necessarily translate altogether to the stage. The aesthetic language of film and the language of the stage contain inherently different methods of visual storytelling, for instance. Importantly, I am not suggesting that all metamodern theatre looks like a Wes Anderson film – although a stage production that emulated the quirkiness of Anderson's ironic-sincere aesthetics would, of course, most likely feel metamodern, and examples of Anderson-style theatrical productions (*Rushmore* 1998; *Moonrise Kingdom* 2012) and theatrical aesthetics (*The Wonderful Story of Henry Sugar* 2023) are littered throughout his films. Rather, I see elements of the aesthetics utilized in the metamodern projects in this volume reflecting, or working in tandem with, the quirky as a sensibility predominantly defined within film theory. Alexander Legget is perhaps the only scholar to have applied the term quirky in a dramaturgical context. However, Legget's application specifically relates to access and inclusion within approaches to dramaturgy – proposing a form of 'quirky dramaturgy [that can be] utilized alongside access policies to make more effective and holistic legislation for autistic people' (Leggett 2023: 3), and his application of the term has little relation to the term as defined by MacDowell. I apply quirky towards the theatre in a different way to Leggett, therefore – as an attempt to describe some of the comedic and aesthetic choices utilized by companies creating metamodern theatre in ways that reflect MacDowell's understanding of quirky as both a visual aesthetic and comedic choice, which enhances an ironic sincerity by somehow augmenting the audience's felt experience in connecting with characters and performers *through* a distancing or dampening effect created *by* the quirky elements. I see this as inherently tied to the generational identity of the millennial theatre makers developing this work. Not only is millennial humour steeped in ironic-sincerity, which can be visualized and staged through an application of the quirky, in that such a sensibility allows us to be both silly and serious – as per Saltz (2010) – at the same time. But, as explained in Chapter 3, a number of the productions and millennial companies that I am concerned with throughout this volume are working with very limited or precarious budgets. This lack of budget, and the requirements of fringe productions to be able to either set up and strike within a small black-box space at speed straight after the previous show and before the incoming one, or to be able to be packed away into a tour van (if you're lucky) or carshare/bus/train (if you're not), means that a lo-fi, minimalist aesthetic becomes the go-to design for such companies. Whilst, of course, the companies in this volume are not interested in a modernist authentic re-creation of real-life onstage, such budgetary and practical limitations also lead to inventive, minimalist approaches to staging which, often, then lead to a silly-but-serious staging that is analogous to MacDowell's understanding of the quirky in cinema – as a constituent element of metamodernism.

As will become clear in Chapter 5, The Gramophones' *End to End* (2012) and *Wanderlust* (2014), Feat.Theatre's *The Welcome Revolution* (2018) and Poltergeist's *Lights Over Tesco Car Park* (2018) all make use of the quirky as an aesthetic in ways that echo MacDowell's understanding of the sensibility's ability to enable an 'overarching tone of defiant affirmation, commitment and sincere engagement in the face of an implicitly acknowledged potential for despair, disillusionment or ironic detachment' (MacDowell 2017: 39) through an aesthetic oscillation between the silly and the serious.

Themes

So far, this chapter has focused on how the structure of performances, rather than content, exhibit metamodern elements. Specifically, it has concentrated on the overall aesthetic sensibility evidenced throughout the form of such pieces and the constituent structural elements that coalesce together to construct such sensibilities. The aesthetic strategies are, however, not strictly limited to being evident only within the staging, form or structure of such performances. An oscillation between irony and sincerity, for instance, can also be evident in a metamodern performance's text. Whilst a shift from a postmodern to a metamodern theatre is predominantly a shift in terms of aesthetic and methodological approaches to the theatrical form, there are certain intertextual topics or narrative themes that connect several of the productions exhibiting this metamodern trend. Such themes may not be explicit within the arrangement of a metamodern performance but, instead, are revealed in the content of such. The following is not a comprehensive list of all the themes addressed within the broad umbrella of metamodern theatre, and it is important to note that a performance could still feel metamodern even if it didn't address any of the following themes. However, the inherent connection of such thematic interests to the wider structures of feeling of metamodernism and the millennial mean that the inclusion of such themes throughout the text of a performance reinforces the inherent association between such performances and the metamodern as a wider cultural structure of feeling.

The as if

As Luke Turner states, the metamodern structure of feeling includes a certain pragmatic idealism, or informed naïveté (Turner 2015), which Seth Abramson expresses as '*knowing* your optimism is naive — but plowing on anyway' (Abramson 2018; emphasis in original). Within the metamodern paradigm,

Abramson contends, we understand that our metanarratives are 'insufficient, they're fragile, they're false – but they help us' (Owls at Dawn 2017) and that, now that we have moved beyond the deconstruction of metanarratives through postmodernism, the metamodern paradigm is 'very much about living *as if* something were true' (Owls at Dawn 2017). Vermeulen and van den Akker appropriate Immanuel Kant's 'negative' idealism (Vermeulen and van den Akker 2010: 5) towards their understanding of the metamodern structure of feeling regarding this paradoxical 'as if' (performance of) belief, summarizing his philosophy of history as 'as if' thinking – in that 'each ... people, as if following some guiding thread, go toward a natural but to each of them unknown goal' (Kant 1963: 12).

A further application of Kant, specifically transcendental aesthetics, allows for deeper understanding of the levels of belief in unreality, or in structures that we know to be false (or at least frail) as an observable trend within post-postmodern culture. Such thinking is reflective of certain, contemporary political trends that Vermeulen (Krumsvik & Co. 2017) and Turner (2015), amongst others, have ascribed to metamodern modes of thought, in their application of the concept of a form of truth that is somehow, as yet, unobtainable. In this respect, Kantian aesthetics can be used as a lens to comprehend particular, metamodern shifts within contemporary politics, including the rise of agonistic, populist discourse. In *The Critique of Pure Reason* (1781), Kant posited that we can never understand or experience *true* reality due to the limitations of our biological senses:

> All our intuition is nothing but the representation of phenomena; the things that we see are not by themselves what we see ... It remains completely unknown to us what objects may be by themselves and apart from the receptivity of our senses. (Kant 1934: 151)

According to Kant, the structures we perceive to exist, therefore, are mediated through how our own understanding and senses have developed over time. 'When the mind looks at the world, it has no choice but to view it with ideas that are built into the mind' (Blumenau 2001), such as spatial and temporal distance. Kant termed this act of perceiving *Anschauungen*, literally translated as views or opinions, but a more appropriate interpretation would be tools of understanding. Whatever we are truly viewing, however, cannot be experienced outside of the *Anschauungen* as the act of viewing dictates that the 'view' is mediated through the 'tools'. Bertrand Russell (1998: 624) uses an analogy that encapsulates Kant's *Ding an sich* by imagining a world in which everybody wore blue tinted glasses. In such a world, the layman would posit that the universe was blue, but the philosopher, upon realizing that they wore blue glasses, would posit that they could not know whether or not the world *was* blue, as the experience was always mediated through the spectacles. In Radchenko's cataloguing of metamodern aesthetics, he draws distinct links between the 'as if' and Foster Wallace's new sincerity:

> Besides the wish to have feelings and act according to them, the 'new sincerity' leads to the belief (mostly blind) in the existence of the transcendent and unreachable truth somewhere beyond the horizon of the known. This belief is the motivator for acting and searching, *as if* it were possible to find the truth. It motivates the metamodernist despite the postmodern understanding that the search is fruitless, so the metamodernist is *ready to believe*. This determines the naïveté of the metamodernist – faith in spite of reason. (Radchenko 2019: 498; emphases in original)

Such endeavouring towards a seemingly unreachable goal is inherently reflective of certain tendencies within the metamodern structure of feeling. If each of us proceed through life 'as if' there is a purpose despite knowing – whether at face value or deep down – that 'there is no purpose in history or nature' (Vermeulen and van den Akker 2010: 14), we are, in essence, believing in structures that we know not to be true – a key component in how the metamodern structure of feeling differs from the postmodern. Kant's concept of the unreachable truth, then, aids us in understanding specifically contemporary *political* endeavours occurring as part of a post-postmodern paradigm in their reapplication of specific metanarratives as part of what Luke Turner describes as a 'climate [of] yearning for utopias, despite their futile nature' (Turner 2015). This unexpected 'figure of utopia' has reappeared 'across the arts in the past few years, often alongside a renewed sense of empathy, reinvigorated constructive engagement, a reappreciation of narrative and a return to craftswo/manship' (Vermeulen and van den Akker 2015b: 55). This (re)emergence of utopia and concerns surrounding the notions of authenticity and truth are inherently connected to the political mindset of the millennials

> [who] know too much of today's exploits, inequalities and injustices to take any meaningful decision, let alone position themselves on a convenient subject position, yet they appear – from the political left to the political right – to be united around the feeling that today's deal is not the deal they signed up for during the postmodern years. (Vermeulen and van den Akker 2015b: 58)

This 'sense of ... hope' (van den Akker and Vermeulen 2017: 8) is present in a range of contexts and phenomena alongside the political, 'without being reducible to any of them in particular' (ibid.). Such utopic rhetoric is seen within both ends of the political, and populist, spectrum; in the United States, Trump offered to 'make America great again', whilst, in the UK, Brexit was a similarly symbolic offer of a 'return' to a false-nostalgic (cf. Campanella and Dassù: 2019) fake narrative of Britain's own 'former glory'. Metastasizing throughout the Covid-19 pandemic, and continuing to build beyond it, we also see the popularization of a range of conspiracy theories feeding, in part, on the public's desire for clarity and culpability in the face of chaos and multiplicity – with conspiracies such as QAnon permeating populist discourse and political parties across the Global North, and Lewis et al. (2018) noting the transferal of populism from the fringes of the political debate to the mainstream as inherently connected to the period of the 2000s, alongside the shift from the post- to the metamodern. Brexit, Momentum, Occupy, Trump and Corbyn are all exemplary of a politics of *it can be different* (cf. Krumsvik & Co: 2017) manifest in populist rhetoric focused on a strive for forms of utopia outside of the current construction. These politics, and other displays of these impossible (and often nostalgic) utopic ideologies across popular culture, such as the development of the literary genre of solar punk, or the contemporary relevance of magical realism (van den Akker 2017: 22), are 'as diverse in their aims as they are similar in their libidinal investments, modes of organization and, indeed, utopian longings' (Vermeulen and van den Akker 2015b: 58).

As an intertextual theme, a fascination with the 'as if' is threaded throughout several of the works in this volume, whether this is evident in work that deals with the complexity of (im)possible utopias such as Hidden Track's *Drawing the Line* (2019), or utilizes magical realism within a performatist framing such as Eager Spark's *Beneath the Albion Sky* (2013), or politically charged work that strives for change through the power of theatre *as if* it has the ability to effect meaningful societal impact despite being aware of the limited possibilities of such effects such as Feat.Theatre's *The Welcome Revolution* (2018).

Lost futures

Mark Fisher's concept of lost futures (2014), as discussed in Chapter 3, builds upon Jacques Derrida's hauntology (1994), though which Derrida initially refers to the paradoxical positioning of (conceptual) ghosts existing at once both within the past and the present. Derrida bases this understanding partially through a theatrical lens, linking the expectant tension in the opening of Karl Marx and Friedrich Engels's opening of *The Communist Manifesto* – 'Ein

Gespenst geht um in Europa – das Gespenst des Kommunismus' (Marx and Engels 1848: 1) – 'a ghost is haunting Europe – the ghost of Communism' – to the similarly ghost-focused, expectant tension at the opening of *Hamlet*. As Derrida explains, in two similarly 'rotten State[s], everything begins by the apparition of a spectre' (Derrida 1994: 2), whether manifest as Hamlet's father's ghost or the ghost of a failed Communism. This similarity persists through the act of

> waiting for this apparition [or these apparitions]. The anticipation is at once impatient, anxious, and fascinated: this, the thing ('this thing') will end up coming. The *revenant* is going to come. It won't be long. But how long it is taking. Still more precisely, everything begins in the imminence of a *re*-apparition, but a re-apparition of the spectre as apparition for the *first time in the play*. (ibid., emphasis in original)

Derrida builds on this interconnection by referring explicitly to the Prince of Denmark's proclamation that 'time is out of joint' (Hamlet I.v.189) and neologizes the word hauntology in his problematizing of Francis Fukuyama's proclamation of the end of history (Fukuyama 1989) – the declaration that asserted the dominance of Western Capitalism and, therefore, the death of ideology. Whilst, as Magnus and Cullenberg describe in their editors' introduction to the 2006 edition of Derrida's text, in 'the wake of the orgy of self-congratulations which followed the 1989 crumbling of the Berlin Wall [and] the subsequent dissolution of the Soviet Union [… the] contagious optimism was best exemplified by the confidence and popularity of Francis Fukuyama's claim' (Derrida 1994: vii). But, the pair assert, at 'the same time many of us felt a vague sense of foreboding, a haunted sense that international changes of such magnitude were as likely to result, at least initially, and perhaps for a long time to come, in transformations as malign as they are benign' (ibid.). Whilst I have touched on Jameson's understanding of a waning of affect (1991) through postmodernity regarding the subsequent return of (a strive towards) affect within metamodernity (Gibbons 2017), Jameson also connects, as Mark Fisher describes, the 'postmodern "waning of historicity" with the "cultural logical of late capitalism"' (Fisher 2014: 13). Fisher draws an inherent connection between Fukuyama's end of history, Derrida's hauntology and Jameson's waning of historicity when he describes a 'dyschronia' in reference to a feeling that culture has failed to progress and a system of simultaneous nostalgia and longing for unformed, and now seemingly impossible, futures as a kind of dominant sensibility – or structure of feeling – throughout, roughly, the first decade of the twenty-first century. 'This dyschronia', writes Fisher, or temporal disjuncture, ought to feel uncanny, yet the predominance of what [Simon] Reynolds calls 'retro-mania' means that it has lost any *unheimlich* charge: anachronism is now taken for granted. Jameson's postmodernism – with the tendencies towards retrospection and pastiche – has been naturalised. (Fisher 2014: 14)

Fisher describes this cultural stagnation throughout the turn of the millennium as a 'slow cancellation of the future [that] has been accompanied by a deflation of expectations' (ibid.: 8). The chronological complexity of Derrida's hauntology and Fisher's lost futures, in that the ghosts that are haunting contemporary culture are not simply based in past events but in events that did not – and now *cannot* – come to be, differentiates hauntology from pure nostalgia. The definitively British hauntological framework initially developed by Fisher, and taken forward by his contemporaries such as Alex Niven (2019), Andy Sharp (2020) and Matt Colquhoun (2020), shifts Derrida's hauntology towards a specifically British mindset based largely in the haunting of mid-to-late twentieth-century pop-culture sensibilities throughout the current period – due to, in part, the inability of contemporary (2000s–mid-2010s) popular culture to, according to Fisher, offer any meaningful progress: 'What has vanished', states Fisher, 'is … a virtual trajectory' (2014: 22) at a time in which culture has even 'lost its ability to grasp and articulate the present' (ibid.: 9).

In Chapter 3, I detailed how the millennial structure of feeling is moulded by this mourning for futures that can no longer come to be. Whilst Fisher's framework is largely based in the culture of his own Gen X contemporaries, the concept of lost futures is just as applicable to the general experience of the millennial generation in regard to our own specific issues of generational grief, nostalgia and hope/lessness, as well as the connection between an inescapable 'nostalgia for modernism' (Fisher 2014: 133) (albeit alongside an inherent postmodern scepticism) within metamodernism. The issue here, however, is the disjunct between Fisher's observation of a stagnation of cultural development and Vermeulen, van den Akker and their contemporaries' contention that the advent of the metamodern is evidence of a culture that is transcending beyond cyclical hauntology. Fisher argued that perhaps the inability for Britain's cultural output to move forward and offer new forms was because, despite 'all its rhetoric of novelty and innovation, neoliberal capitalism has gradually but systemically deprived artists of the resources to produce the new' (Fisher 2014: 15), acknowledging that the

> postwar welfare state and higher education maintenance grants constituted an indirect source of funding for most of the experiments

in popular culture between the 1960s and the 80s [and the] subsequent ideological and practical attack on public services meant that one of the spaces where artists could be sheltered from the pressure to produce something that was immediately successful was severely circumscribed. (ibid.)

This relates explicitly to the lost futurity of the artists of the millennial generation as their coming of age convened with the permacrisis. Fisher contrasts this contemporary precarity to how the cultural progression in London across the 1970s and early 1980s in the punk and postpunk scenes 'coincided with the availability of squatted and cheap property ... since then, the decline of social housing, the attacks on squatting, and the delirious rise in property process have meant that the amount of time and energy available for cultural production has massively diminished' (ibid.: 15–16). Such analysis also holds true when applied directly to the UK theatre scene, as detailed in Chapter 3 in regard to UK theatre graduates working in an increasingly precarious economic situation. In contrast to Fisher's stagnation, however, the companies addressed in this volume offer evidence of work that moves beyond the postmodern practice of the late twentieth century – whilst continuing in some ways to engage with it – and also to make us of a melancholic nostalgia for modernist tendencies, too, paving the way for new forms that, simultaneously, embrace the old.

In the context of this volume, the theme of lost futures refers to Fisher's application of Derrida's hauntology within a British context but shifts this from Fisher's Gen X cultural melancholia to the generational scarring (Brown et al. 2017) of the millennials. We see this theme manifest in works that explicitly address this generation's being haunted by futures that did not come to be, such as Middle Child's *All We Ever Wanted Was Everything* (2017), or in works that address im/possible futures, such as YESYESNONO's *we were promised honey!* (2022). It is an inherently metamodern preoccupation, dealing, as it does, in a liminal space between, betwixt and beyond the past, present, and future in a desire for / belief in / mourning for things that have not (yet) come to pass. Whilst a positivistic desire for utopia, and for hopeful betterment, may be more advantageous in the face of the overwhelming convergence of contemporary crises – the rise of far-right populism and global heating, for instance – it seems a particularly paradoxical, and inherently millennial and metamodern, position to also face such utopic desire with a matching conviction in the inescapability of it all – remaining trapped within an oscillating hope/lessness in a reflection of Fisher's nod towards Wendy Brown's (1999) critique of a melancholic left that 'makes a virtue of its incapacity to act' (Fisher 2014: 24).

The desire for belonging

The final theme addressed in this guide (which of course is by no means an exhaustive list) is appropriated from Radchenko's cataloguing of metamodern narrative trends within contemporary literature and will become evident in the following analysis of Eager Spark's *Beneath the Albion Sky* (2013), Poltergeist's *Lights Over Tesco Car Park* (2018) and Arinzé Kene's *Misty* (2018). For Radchenko, several of the narrative themes that he associates with metamodernism – 'sincerity, the willingness to connect with another human being and to transmit feelings' (Radchenko 2019: 499) – all stem from the same desire 'to be a part of something more, to be bound with something' (ibid.). He refers to Nicoline Timmer's understanding of a post-postmodern syndrome as a contemporary, 'structural need for a "we" (a desire for connectivity and sociality)' (Timmer 2010: 359). Whilst Dember (2023) asserts that metamodern aesthetic strategies stem from an overarching need to protect the solidity of (inner) felt experience, Radchenko, whilst not negating such an internal focus, also looks outwards. A metamodern 'contrast to the postmodern individuality and the wish to be remarkable [works to] avoid the chaos of postmodern deconstruction', states Radchenko, 'In the search for the unreachable truth ... the metamodern character looks for sociality and for the possibility of belonging to any kind of system' (2019: 499). He refers to Hanzi Freinacht's assertion that metamodernism 'reintroduces hierarchies as a unit of analysis, as a reaction against the postmodern relativistic attitude stating that all hierarchies are bad' (Freinacht 2015). However, rather than espousing a (return to) highly problematic (and frankly dangerous) hierarchies – or the appropriation of the language of metamodernity onto the theoretical framework of stage theories or models of hierarchical complexity, as has been done by scholars building from Freinacht's theories – I understand this desire to belong as an individualistic attempt at finding or creating an identity, a strengthening of individual felt experience in relation to others. Whilst a rough postmodern understanding of such a challenge to find an identity may be crafted around the importance of individuality and 'sticking out from the crowd', a metamodern understanding of such a desire envelops the developments in online socialization over the past decade, in that it has become easier than ever to find and engage with like-minded people in a way that is no longer limited by geographical location, only by the ability to access the internet, through which both an individual and group identity can be forged. Therefore, Radchenko's assertion that the 'metamodern character needs the feeling of belonging' (Radchenko 2019: 500) is not in opposition to the postmodern ideology of individualism but enables a forging of identity both within and between these two spectrums. Whilst a teenager might be able to carve out an individualistic identity within their school year through their niche interests, for instance, or even feel unfairly subjugated due to differences they can't control such as gender identity or sexuality, Web 2.0 now enables easy access to and engagement with like or like-minded individuals across the planet – enabling an existence at once individual in one area and part of a tribe in another. Of course, the ability for young members of the LGBTQ+ community currently living in traditionally conservative areas, for instance, to be able to have online access to groups of similar and supportive individuals is an important positive aspect of such a metamodern drive, but the far-right radicalization of young men through figures such as Andrew Tate and the interconnected incel movement, or the increasing number of millennials drawn deeper into the QAnon conspiracy theory through the 'in-on-a-secret' group mentality of Q-focussed online forums (Djupe 2021), is the other side of the same coin. Such is a healthy reminder that, whilst I am clearly advocating for the use of the term metamodernism and the terminology surrounding this, and in opposition to the appropriation of metamodernity towards a political ideology by Freinacht and their contemporaries, not everything 'metamodern' is inherently positive. It is simply metamodern.

Throughout this chapter, I have attempted to provide a preliminary guide to the main 'markers' of the way in which I understand how the framework of metamodernism as a cultural structure of feeling – as initially crafted by Vermeulen and van den Akker and then developed through the subsequent elaboration of this framework by cultural scholars across fields other than theatre – can *also* be observed within contemporary theatre practices. By breaking this down into three separate areas, I have endeavoured to provide a streamlined guide to several metamodern elements as they relate both to theatre and their wider cultural context. The *overarching sensibilities* of oscillation and felt experience are the initial touchpoints in this – sensibilities that permeate the totality of a metamodern performance. The secondary *aesthetic strategies* are the elements that come together to create and strengthen the two overarching sensibilities; authenticity, storytelling, metatheatre, reconstructive pastiche, post-immersive dialogical engagement and the quirky being examples of how the contemporary theatre practices that make use of such strategies exemplify, are situated in and develop the metamodern. Finally, the three narrative *themes*, whilst obviously not requirements within metamodern theatre, offer examples of how the metamodern-adjacent preoccupations within the content of a piece also add to its overall situatedness within a metamodern framework. This 'spotters guide', as I have at once both somewhat optimistically and sarcastically labelled this section, is used as a framework in the following chapter in order to unpack how the works of certain British millennial theatre companies over the past decade exemplify not only a generalized post-postmodern progression within contemporary theatre practice but are evidence that shifts in theatrical trends are also following a similar route as to that of other cultural products and practices which have already been understood as part of this particular structure of feeling – metamodernism. At this juncture, however, I turn to Dember's important reminder that, whilst I offer this 'spotter's guide' in some attempt to catalogue, combine and demarcate elements of contemporary theatre practice that can be understood to be part of the same general shift, 'not everybody who has an opinion even agrees on exactly how to define metamodernism in the first place' (Dember 2018). However, I feel that this act of attempting to discern this interconnectivity is important, despite the possible impossibility of or flaws inherent in such an attempt as, in Dember's words, 'there is something happening out there — art and film and music and culture [and theatre!] are being produced that share a certain sensibility [which] would exist regardless of what name we gave it, and regardless of whether or not we even named it at all' (Dember 2018).

5

Metamodernism in contemporary British theatre

This chapter details ten productions from nine different companies that explicitly exhibit metamodern theatrical practices. These performances are drawn from a pool of work by British theatre companies spanning across a decade (2012–22), predominantly from artists working within the fringe theatre circuit, and created or led by writers, directors or performers within the millennial generational bracket. I have chosen these specific productions to present a range of approaches to performance forms, company demographics, and of topics and themes addressed, as well as to capitalize on the opportunity to detail the practice of companies that are creating important, innovative work but who have not been, in most cases, majorly documented within academia. I contend that it is in the experimental, genre-defying work of these 'emerging' companies that real innovation – and the metamodern theatrical form – is found.

The following analysis refers to the methodological frameworks defined in Chapter 4, with reference to theories discussed throughout Chapters 2 and 3. It is understandable that readers might have turned to this chapter first. As such, the following text aims to be accessible enough to those approaching this topic for the first time in such a way that hopes to engender further interest in the detailed aspects of metamodern theatre as defined earlier in this volume. However, the following benefits highly from previous engagement with the comprehensive analysis of the overarching sensibilities, theatrical aesthetics and narrative themes throughout this chapter, as well as the aesthetics, theories and methodologies that are defined and analysed in the previous sections of this book.

Treading the line between fact and fiction: Eager Spark's *Beneath the Albion Sky* and The Gramophones' *End to End* and *Wanderlust*

The house lights dim and we jump straight into it. 'I got up, packed my bag and left', Paul tells us as he steps into the stage. 'I was on the 8.24. I had to change at London, and it got me to Penzance at 15:11 ... I was knackered, and I knew the next day was going to be the hardest, as first days always are' (Furness and Whitworth 2013: 1). We are – again – in the brick-walled basement of the now-sadly-closed Bike Shed Theatre in Exeter. It's 2013, and Paul is telling us a story of his unbelievable walk up the length of Britain. 'There's lots of things I'm going to tell you, and I don't expect you understand them all', he warns us. A pause. 'In fact', he confesses, 'I'm not sure I understand them all' (ibid.).

Beneath the Albion Sky (2013) by Eager Spark – who rebranded themselves from Write by Numbers in 2018 – was co-writers Corinne Furness and Charlie Whitworth's experiment in how to tell a story about a walk. The one-man, hour-long show was initially created as a twenty-minute performance as part of Battersea Arts Centre's partnership with Latitude Festival in 2012, before being redeveloped for the 2013 *Exeter Ignite* festival at The Bike Shed, Exeter. From there, *Beneath the Albion Sky* toured the UK throughout the next five years, visiting traditional theatre spaces as well as village halls, community centres and churches, and receiving development support from a suitably geographically varied assortment of theatres such as The Yard in East London and The Wardrobe Theatre in Bristol along the way. The piece's final outing was in 2018 as one of the last shows to play at The Bike Shed before the building's closure later that year.

The piece is the 'story of one man's walk along the St. Michael's Ley Line over a period of several summer months' (Hasted 2014). From the very beginning, we are constantly reminded by Paul, who completed the walk, that he is telling us the story of this journey. 'It might be suitable at this point in time for me to answer a few questions that may have popped into your head' (Furness and Whitworth 2013: 20), he offers about halfway through his tale, before explaining the practicalities of such a long journey on foot – 'Cleanliness and Hygiene? I did not shower once' (ibid.: 21). The tale begins with the finding of a map in his recently departed father's belongings that traces a line from St Michael's Mount in Cornwall to the Suffolk coast. Paul's recollection then takes us to the start of his walk in Land's End, through the variety of UK towns he passes through, and the people – and creatures – he meets along the way, revealing some of the reasons behind him making the decision to embark on this journey, and, of course, ending with the completion of the walk in the summer of 2012. Throughout the telling of this journey, Paul – 'an unlikely hero … with his sturdy boots, waterproof watch and neat nylon anorak' (Hasted 2014) – continuously frames the walk as a narrative, with himself as both the protagonist and storyteller, journeying from Cornwall to Suffolk, from beginning to end. Paul's inherent self-reflexivity, however, continuously undercuts this idea of the journey as 'successful' narrative when he reveals that both the journey and his own felt experience are not living up to the ideals of what this narrative should be: 'I'm not someone who holds particularly romantic notions about these sort of things,' Paul tells us as he recounts the start of his trek at the southernmost tip of the UK, 'but if somewhere, deep down, I'd been wanting some significance to the beginning, Land's End would have quickly dispelled it' (Furness and Whitworth 2013: 2). The hordes of tourists and pirate-themed ghost rides apparently prohibit any opportunity for him to be *in the moment* at the beginning of his hero's journey. 'If this were a proper story' (Furness and Whitworth 2013: 28) is a phrase that constantly echoes throughout Paul's telling. The piece appears to follow a similar narrative path to that of the tradition of popular, autobiographical, walk-based travelogues (Fermor 1977; Strayed 2012; Winn 2018), in that Paul is recounting the story of his own pilgrimage following a recent trauma. He is unflinchingly honest about the complicated feelings and memories that have surfaced following the recent death of his father. He tells us about his first time hiking with his dad when he was nine years old and how his own complaints about blisters and the cold led to his dad cutting the trip short; 'as he closed the car door and prepared to take me home two days earlier than planned', Paul tells us, 'I saw his face just before he turned and I knew then – just as much as I know now – that in some tiny but important way I had disappointed him. I, Paul, was not exactly as he hoped. And, instead, we were both trapped trying to pretend otherwise' (Furness and Whitworth 2013: 20). Following his father's passing, Paul decides to follow a line traced on his dad's map – St Michael's Ley Line. The concept of Ley Lines – although now largely seen as 'essentially a failed amateur archaeological concept' (Jankovic 2013) – was first posited by Alfred Watkins in *The Old Straight Track* (1925), based on the notion that certain ancient sites and monuments across the British Isles 'appear to be in alignment more often than chance would predict' (Williamson and Bellamy 1983: 51). Alongside the resurgence of popular interest in these lines in the 1960s, John Michell posited that these 'alignments mark lines of power, along which passed "earth energy"' (ibid.: 53). Since Michell's thesis, so-called Ley Hunters have also identified connections between these alignments and 'a variety of paranormal phenomena, all of which appear to occur regularly on (or above) the alignments' (ibid.). Whilst the entire concept of Ley Lines is disputed, 'often by sound logic: in the UK alone the number of appropriate sites is so great it would be difficult not to draw a straight line across half a dozen of them at any time' (Jankovic 2013), Jankovic describes in her review of *Beneath the Albion Sky* for *Exuent* magazine that 'the magical powers enforced onto a suspiciously empty concept are just what Paul, the sole character in the show, is after' (ibid.). For, when travelling along the longest Ley Line in Britain, Paul really does encounter what can only be described as magic – as the piece begins to embrace the concept of Ley Lines *as if* they were true whilst concurrently scrutinizing such belief.

After relaying the practicalities of the first stage of his walk, Paul describes reaching Glastonbury Tor. 'And then', he very casually, declares, 'I heard it. The breath, the heavy footsteps, the slithering, skulking powerful prodding footing putting towards me from the other side of the Tor. A Dragon' (Furness and Whitworth 2019: 9). In complete contrast to the realistic nature of the piece so far, Paul now describes a harrowing fight with this dragon, in which he assumes the role of fairy-tale knight, wielding a sword in which to vanquish the beast. However, he also intercuts this with decidedly contemporary references – moving in slow motion 'like I was Neo in the Matrix' (ibid.) or running up the tower 'in a way a character in a Chinese martial art film could only dream of' (ibid.). His telling is at once an exhilarating tale straight out of a book of ancient myths and incredibly nonchalant and matter of fact – 'I accepted that I would come across a Dragon at some point', he tells us. 'The Chinese call ley lines Dragon Lines after all' (ibid.). Eventually, the Dragon is slain, and Paul rather casually continues the story of his walk; 'I didn't stay in Glastonbury that night. I walked on until I was outside Shepton Mallet. Even though it was really dark, I got the tent up in no time and I slept long and deep into the next day' (ibid.: 10). A little further on, about three weeks into his journey, Paul recounts a recognizable and awkward situation, in which a fellow walker wants to make conversation, but Paul would rather be left alone: 'There's a bit of quiet as I frantically think of a way to get away from him – without it being really, really rude. Failing that, I start to contemplate just making a run for it' (ibid.: 12). Paul tells us how, after a while, it became clear that the conversation he was having with this stranger – Mike – was different to a usual day to day discussion: 'He doesn't tell me about world affairs. We don't talk about politics. There isn't a mention of sport. He talks about his life, and I talk about some of the things I've seen on my walk' (ibid.: 13). For Paul, it starts to fit into place: 'Here I am, talking to a friendly, sage like, elderly gentleman on St. Michael's ley line, who's also walking along the line, and he's introduced himself as "Mike" ... I know who he is' (ibid.). Later, Paul recounts how he helped a man at a campsite who was struggling to put up his tent wearing what Paul only describes as a damaged fancy dress costume but who, in the retelling of their conversation, Paul casually reveals to us is called Lancelot. Later, a dance with a woman outside Bury St Edmunds is revealed to be an encounter with Boadicea, who then 'turns and runs and her hair flies out behind her, and I stand and watch as if I am a statue forced to watch her run forever' (ibid.: 24).

Throughout Paul's retelling of his journey, these encounters with mythical figures are given no more significance than that of a chance encounter with a friend along the trail, or the repetitive act of putting up his tent. The delivery is designed in such a way that echoes Dember's appropriation of Eshelman's performatism, in that *Beneath the Albion Sky* is 'imbued with enough fantasy elements that the reader is forced to make a choice to buy into all of it, if they are going to commit to engaging [with] the work' (Dember 2018). Paul's mythical encounters are an essential part of his story, and they are introduced in such a way that the audience is already invested in the human story of Paul – who is setting off on a journey to 'find himself' after the trauma of his father's death – before he casually drops in these fantastical elements without any admission that these are unbelievable. As such, if the audience is to continue to engage in Paul's tale, they are forced to accept that these fantastical encounters are also part of this story *as if* these elements were true, despite their obvious unreality. Paul's story oscillates between the seemingly real and the seemingly fantastical, giving no preferential precedence to either. Instead, it asks the audience to accept such aspects equally. However, the piece is not naïve to the difficulties in asking a post-postmodern audience to engage in such a way, and as Jankovic (2013) explains, 'If it wasn't for the considerable finesse writers Corinne Furness and Charlie Whitworth show in their shaping of Paul, he would quickly become a completely deluded and one-dimensional character' to empathize with. It is through Paul's continual oscillation between the fantastical mythological encounters and his being 'disappointed by how mundane his trip is' (ibid.) in not living up to the 'standards' of a mythic quest or pilgrimage that turns Paul into 'an image of complexity – he's [also] cynical' (ibid.). Paul is not a traditional hero but reflects the concerns of members of the millennial generation of the time about life not measuring up to expectations. Perhaps, as Jankovic posits, his disappointment in the mundanity of the trip 'is the turning point of exaggerating silly encounters into fantasy, or perhaps just in a state of rediscovering his imagination after years of grinding and boring existence' (ibid.). In Michael Hasted's review of the piece at the Everyman Theatre in Cheltenham in 2014, he describes the show as Paul recalling 'his experiences, both real and imagined' (Hasted 2014) and reveals that, whilst 'you would think that you were watching the man himself and that the story was his story ... Paul was played by an actor, Andy Kelly, reciting the words of Corinne Furness and Charlie Whitworth' (ibid.). Such is Kelly's nuanced portrayal of Paul (Jankovic 2013) that another layer in the complex interstice between the real and the fictitious is added. This story is not autobiographical, or even autofictional, but a wholly fictitious tale. There is no more reality to Paul's revealing of his innermost thoughts to the audience than there is to his encounter with a dragon on Glastonbury Tor. Both are equally mythical.

Beneath the Albion Sky oscillates between the realistic and the fantastic whilst necessitating that the audience accept both as equally 'true'. Through Kelly's performance of Paul, the piece is framed as though it were a recounting of an authentic experience, with Kelly telling us the story of his own walk, and Furness' and Whitworth's insistence on oscillating between – and therefore blurring – the lines between the real and unreal, leads to a point in which whether any of this is true or not doesn't really matter. Rather than focus on truth, the piece offers a metamodern centrality of storytelling – manifest as a return to an interest in the act of storytelling and the power of stories, in three specific ways. Firstly, Whitworth's direction of the piece 'resists the temptation of casually inserting projections, sounds and other easy-way-out props just for the sake of it' (Jankovic 2013), and so the theatrics of the piece itself are focussed solely on 'Paul' telling us his story. Paul takes us, as an audience, through a retelling of a journey that he has undertaken – framing himself as the protagonist, and the hike across the United Kingdom as the narrative journey. Secondly, the telling of this story blends realism and fantasy in two respects – in the obvious oscillation between the realistic retelling of a trek and the impossibly fantastic encounters with mythical creatures, and in the framing of the piece as Paul telling his story to the audience when, in fact, Paul is a fictional character portrayed by an actor. In its focus on storytelling, *Beneath the Albion Sky* – even in its titular use of the ancient name Albion over the modern Britain – also returns to an older form of storytelling, using the Ley Line as a guide through which to utilize British myths in such a way that embraces the epic and fantastic in order to focus on – and tell the story of – Paul's own inner, human experience following the death of a parent. All three storytelling aspects, here, serve to highlight and centre the 'felt experience' of Paul's grief. Both the character and the writers are not naïve in their metamodern asking of the audience to embrace the oscillation between the fantastical and the ordinary, the fictive and the real, but are fully aware of the inauthenticity of this – how the mechanics of storytelling are inherently inauthentic and are not reflected in our actual lived experiences, which are more complex than a traditional hero's journey narrative. As Paul describes on reaching Hopton-on-Sea towards the end of the piece,

If this were a proper story, this would be the most important part of it. Not because of anything particularly dramatic or thrilling – you don't get giants or dragons or knights of the round table in Hopton-on-Sea, it's not that sort of place

But because I would stand looking out to the sea, having done this walk, and though everything might not be okay, I would know something.

I'd have defeated the dragon, resisted temptation, found the grail.
And in some tiny way, things would be better.
I would be better.
But it's not like that at all.

It's just a Thursday afternoon in July in a tiny seaside town on the east coast and I'm a man standing on a beach and there isn't a fanfare or even a marker at the end of the line and my Dad is still dead [… even] though I've walked all this way. (Furness and Whitworth 2013: 28–9)

At the end of his story, Paul comments on the fact that – as his lived experience does not (cannot) neatly reflect that of a written narrative (even though it is) – both the piece and the journey itself do not have tidy endings with a neat moral. 'When I'd finished it [the walk]', he states, 'I was looking for something – some sort of understanding' (Furness and Whitworth 2013: 30) but that revelation, that sense of an ending, does not come. Instead, Paul returns to the act of storytelling, remembering his dad telling him that, as a child, Paul 'liked the story of the walk more than the walk itself. And he was right. … And that is why I'm telling my story now' (ibid.). Perhaps it doesn't matter what the reality of a story is, but it is the act of telling that story that is important.

Eager Spark's championing of the act of storytelling both as a theatrical device within the structure of *Beneath the Albion Sky* and as a method of dealing with grief within the narrative itself reflects Anne Bogart's observation – at a similar time – of a rejuvenated interest in the act and power of storytelling within theatre and throughout our own lives (Bogart 2014), as well as my own understanding of the act of storytelling being a central aesthetic strategy in metamodern theatre. Additionally, the piece's utilization of an oscillation between the fantastic and the realistic asks an audience to engage in a performatist framework (as per Eshelman 2008) – embracing the fantastical nature of the magical-realism in order to fully appreciate the inner-narrative of Paul and his grief – viewing both the story Paul is telling and the performance of Kelly performing Paul *as if* both were true, even if we know they are not. As such, these aspects serve to protect the solidity of the felt experience of Paul as the fictional writer of this tale. *Beneath the Albion*

Sky, therefore, utilizes the aesthetic strategies of authenticity and storytelling in both its form and narrative, and reconstructive pastiche in its application of myths and legends, oscillating between the real and the fictive in such a way that enables an in/authentic structure through which the felt experience of 'Paul' is centred and strengthened. Back in 2013, as I experienced the piece in the Bike Shed Theatre, I felt like this piece was something *different*. The complex interplay between the seemingly authentic and the surely impossible, alongside the company's commitment to the strength in the act of storytelling whilst also being critical and questioning of the structure of stories themselves, felt – though dealing with old forms of storytelling and ancient myths – somehow – *new*. Whilst, at first glance, *Beneath the Albion Sky* can be seen as an example of unassuming folk theatre, the piece offers distinctly metamodern performance practice.

At the same time that Eager Spark were developing the narrative of Paul's fictional walk, three members of The Gramophones – Hannah Stone, Ria Ashcroft and Kristy Guest – were making a very real journey. Beginning at the same point as the fictitious Paul – Land's End – and aiming to end at the northernmost tip of the United Kingdom – John O'Groats – the company undertook an eighteen-day long, '874 mile journey using as many forms of transport as possible, … a minimal amount of cash [budgeting £1 per mile] and relying largely on the kindness of strangers' (Ellis 2012). The impetus for such a journey came from what the female company felt was a need to artistically 'respond to the expectation that as women in their 20s and 30s they ought to be settling down and starting families' (ibid.). In opposition to this, the group decided to take 'advantage of their freedom at a stage in their lives when so many of their friends had decided to settle' (Eltringham 2013) and, instead, 'go on an adventure and show the advantage of being "without ties" and free to set off across the country on a whim' (Ellis 2012), relying on the kindness of strangers to help them achieve their goal. Later that year, the story of this female-focussed reclamation of a sense for adventure was retold by the company members in their show *End to End* (2012). Directed by Tilly Branson and presented as part of PBH's Free Fringe at the Edinburgh Festival Fringe that year, *End to End* later gained funding from Arts Council England to enable a tour of the UK in 2013, 'retracing their steps and performing the piece in 22 venues [including community halls, sixth forms, arts centres and more traditional theatres] en route' (Eltringham 2013).

The three performers greet us as we enter the theatre space, asking us to fill in postcards with our idea of 'home'. One performer invites us to mark our heights on a signpost on stage, 'Not only do you see yours,' Co-artistic Director Hannah Stone told me in 2016, 'you see the previous audience's [as well] and then it comes out later in the show that we did that at someone's house, and it makes a mark on that place from that journey' (Stone 2016). What follows is an energetic retelling of the group's expedition, the encounters along the way and the stories of others' journeys and ideas of 'home' that they collected from people throughout the trek and from the previous performances of the show itself. Similar to *Beneath the Albion Sky*, *End to End* re-centres storytelling as the central theatrical act but does so to relate an actual authentic experience to the audience. What shifts this portrayal into the sphere of metamodernism, here, is the Gramophones attempt to portray their experience in such a way that focuses on the company's almost impossible task of portraying such events authentically through the inherently inauthentic medium of theatre. The form of *End to End* is built around metatheatrical storytelling of the work carried out by the company in order to develop the material to generate the show. The performance, therefore, is about the events undertaken to make the performance. The show *End to End* would not exist without the journey originally undertaken, but that journey would not exist without the later promise of it being performed. In this sense, the authenticity of the autobiographical nature of *End to End* is central, and whilst the act of storytelling as the principal force throughout this production does not – as in *Beneath the Albion Sky* – mean that the piece is bare-staged (in fact, The Gramophone's work has, as Ellis (2012) states, 'a strong visual and kinaesthetic aspect'), the company make an effort not to embellish the stories recounted or 'perform' the people met along the journey. 'If we've collected a story from someone', Stone told me, the company always consider 'how would we feel if that person is then in the audience, will it mean a lot to them, or will they hate what we'd done with it?' (Stone 2016). As Ellis explains in her review, sometimes the 'characters were described with affection, and sometimes we would hear them speak or see a photograph, but they were never caricatured [… with the company deciding that] if they couldn't portray a person to their face, i.e. during a show, then they shouldn't do it at all' (Ellis 2012). This sense of authenticity and responsibility permeates the entire production, with Cunningham's review stating that 'the striking thing is just how honest it is [… it's] very, very sincere; when they speak about how the journey affected them, they do it seriously' (Cunningham 2012). Ellis reflects a similar surprise at the authenticity inherent throughout; 'the performers gave a refreshingly candid account of the emotional ups and downs of their trip which felt very real as they were recounted. The bond between them was evident in their frequent smiles and glances at each other remembering characters that they had met' (Ellis 2012).

Alongside the sense of authenticity that permeates the group's retelling of their journey is a sense of optimism and joy in adventure, friendship and the kindness of strangers. Co-artistic Director Ria Ashcroft believes that theatre should be seen as 'a space for risk-taking, gift-giving and trust [and that, whilst it was] a form of escapism for me over the years ... now it's my way of embracing the world, sharing stories with others and inviting them to join us on our adventures' (Left Lion 2015). This ethos is also evident in the group's approach to the journey itself. By approaching the trip with a somewhat radical sense of openness – opposing both the pressure on the group of women to settle down and the innate sense of danger in the act of women asking strangers for a lift, even whilst in a group – Ria describes the journey as 'the most incredible thing I've ever done ... the kindness we received from strangers was overwhelming. It made me feel genuinely good about the world' (Left Lion 2014), with the group finding 'that people wanted to help us complete the challenge and really connected with us' (Left Lion 2015). As such, this sense of optimism in humanity saturates both the story and the way that The Gramophones tell it. Such a positive outlook is coupled with the group's original focus on clowning and slapstick, leading to a heavily kinaesthetic, energetic and 'colourful' (Ashcroft 2016) form of 'dynamic' (Ellis 2012) storytelling – in which 'every prop was used at some point: maps with pins, a stool which becomes both a bike and a screen for the hand-held projector, clothes racks with coat hangers for costume changes [... the group's] background in circus performance [is] evident' (ibid.) in the physicality of the show. Over the coming years, such aesthetics became synonymous with The Gramophones' performances, leading to descriptions of the company often featuring words such as 'wacky', 'quirky', 'colourful' and even 'twee'. 'Some people', Ashcroft told me when discussing *End to End*, 'might be like, "Oh shut up", and "You're too twee, I'm not interested in that. I want the dark, raw side of life!"' (Ashcroft 2016). However, Stone and Ashcroft describe an apparent appetite for a show that embraced optimism and positivity – for a message that reminded them 'don't forget to actually live. That kind of thing – don't walk around with your eyes shut, like actually have a look around at the world and see how beautiful it is. And how horrible it is, too. Just all of it' (ibid.). At a time in which the trope of the 'quirky millennial woman' was fast coming under scrutiny within cultural criticism and academia through its inherent connection to the problematic 'Manic Pixie Dream Girl stereotype' (Vázquez Rodríguez 2017), the Gramophones actively utilize this quirkiness in a way that, as Antony McIntyre similarly details in regards to the artistic output of actress/songwriter Zooey Deschanel at that time, employs 'a form of cuteness [in a way] that obfuscates contemporary cultural exhaustion' (McIntyre 2015: 436). The Gramophones offer what feels like a radical reclaiming of an inherently female-driven joy in their work. In this sense, whilst *End to End* doesn't oscillate between hope/lessness, its focus on offering a bright and hopeful performance of female adventure and friendship, as Cunningham (2012) describes, 'offered an injection of optimism' at the Edinburgh Festival Fringe that year. In this sense, there is a post-postmodern aesthetic to the group's ideology of positivity over pessimism. The group's focus on truthful representation of the journey itself and the people who helped them on the way rather than presenting a caricatured performance also imbues the piece with a sense of an unachievable and paradoxical goal – of performing a story authentically whilst embracing the inauthentic nature of performance. The group's physical-comedy background, too, alongside the backdrop of the 'quirky girl' in popular culture at the turn of the 2010s, lends an inherent sense of the quirky to the aesthetics of the piece in the sense of MacDowell's (2010) understanding of the term within film scholarship. Both metamodern elements serve to focus on the group's attempt to centre their own felt experience of the original walk; the optimistic outlook is threaded throughout the retelling because that's how the group experienced the trip. However, such retelling is not solipsistic. Instead, the Gramophones are acutely concerned with the audience's felt experience throughout this sharing, too, which becomes further evident in the development of a subsequent production – 2014s *Wanderlust*.

In an attempt at inspiring the audience to take their own journeys following the performance of *End to End*, the group gave each audience member a seed and a postcard at the end of each show, asking them to 'go on an adventure. Plant a seed. Then write to us and tell us about your journey' (Stone 2016). This meant that, in addition to the postcards the group had amassed from the people that had helped them in their original Land's End to John O'Groats expedition, and those collected at the start of each performance in relation to audience members' ideas of home, the group began receiving postcards from audience members long after the show had finished touring. 'We still get them now!' Ashcroft told me in 2016, with Stone explaining that they contain messages such as 'Oh, I kept your seed for you, and I've just been to Norfolk, and I planted it' (Stone 2016). Eventually, the group realized that the stories they had collected from audience members during and after performances were so interesting that a whole new show could be created from this material. Commissioned by Creative Arts East Live and supported by Create Theatre, the group travelled to rural and mobile libraries in Norfolk, Suffolk and Nottinghamshire – armed with the postcards they had been sent – in order to collect further input from people outside of the bubble of theatregoers. In a shift away from *End to End*'s concern with an authentic recreation of an actual event, *Wanderlust* instead became built upon the themes that recurred throughout the material collected by the group. Focusing on the idea of stories and storytelling itself, rather than using storytelling to relay their own experience, *Wanderlust* makes use of traditional Norfolk folk tales as impetus for the main character – Wanderlust – to travel through stories in a perpetual search to find *something* that she feels is missing from her life. Armed with a similarly kinaesthetic set to *End to End*, a live accordionist and a handheld projector, *Wanderlust* embraces the group's (by this stage well-developed) aesthetics of the quirky. The upstage area is taken over by an array of shelves bursting with glass jars, inside of which are various objects – a flower, a Lego figurine, sand, a scrap of a map. Attached to some of these jars are handwritten labels and notes, explaining the significance of these objects in relation to journeys undertaken by their respective owners. At the end of each performance of *Wanderlust*, the audience is invited to come onto the stage and explore – to open things, read things, touch things and to add their own jar (Stone 2016). Stone and Ashcroft described the process of audience engagement within *Wanderlust* as beginning as soon as a ticket was purchase:; 'We'd ask them ... to bring something in a jar that represented some memory, or something that was important to them' (Ashcroft 2016) which they would then add to the set – continually developing a physical archive of the journeys and stories of people met throughout the initial *End to End* journey, the tour of *End to End*, the postcards sent to the group following that tour, the visits to rural libraries and the audience members of *Wanderlust* (see Figure 5.1). Ashcroft (2016) remembers 'a huge amount of people who really did want to talk', with some presenting very personal stories and objects as part of the post-show opportunities for discussion. In this sense, the audience engagement throughout *End to End* and *Wanderlust* extends far beyond the performances themselves – existing both prior to and following the time in theatre space. The group's focus on theatre as an opportunity to share stories and invite the audience with them on their adventures (Left Lion 2015) leads to an extended form of engagement that 'does feel like it stretches further than the moment and further than that night. It stretches beyond that, before the show, leading up to it, and after. Even years after' (Stone 2016). For the Gramophones, theatre is part of a wider conversation with a community of audience members that reflects Nina Mitova's understanding of 'performances that have *gone beyond* the boundaries of theatre [and] should be considered metamodern' (Mitova 2020: 6; emphasis in original). Whilst the Gramophones' pieces aren't participatory in the sense of the work that Lopes Ramos et al. locate as post-immersive, the fact that the group aim to engage in an extended dialogue with the audience is exemplary of a dialogical engagement that extends far beyond the theatrical form – evident even several years after the performance itself. Whilst Jen Harvie rightly critiques participatory performance that appears to 'offer social bonds which are, in fact, thin' (2013: 59), through The Gramophones' continual

Figure 5.1 Ria Ashcroft (centre) with audience members onstage at the end of The Gramophone's *Wanderlust* (devised by the company, 2014). The jars provided by the audience can be seen in the background to the right

Source: Ralph Barklam. Reproduced with kind permission from © The Gramophones.

engagement with their audience, it is clear that there is an impassioned endeavour to curate a durational connection between artist and audience in order to further facilitate some form of 'authentic' dialogue, one that is not simply constrained to the time and spatial limitations of the performance, even if this is impossible, 'thin' or feigned.

Whilst Eager Spark's *Beneath the Albion Sky* and The Gramophones' *End to End* and *Wanderlust* vary in how they approach their telling of the stories of their respective journeys across the United Kingdom, they share a focus on a re-application and re-appreciation of the power of storytelling, a concern with authenticity within the inherently inauthentic medium of performance and an essential focus on an attempt to centre and protect the solidity of the felt experience of the people undertaking the journey and/or the audience's experience throughout the telling of these stories. In the early 2010s, each show offered an optimistic appreciation of the power of sharing adventure, stories and myths that appeared at odds to synchronous postmodern practices which eschewed narrative and storytelling in favour of simulation, fragmentation and an 'incredulity towards metanarratives' (Lyotard 1984). Whilst the companies remain critical and questioning of how stories are told – with Eager Spark's reconstructive pastiche of mythical British history adding a sense of magical-realism to an otherwise believable story, and the Gramophone's concern with the ethics of performing other people – each show embraces the communal potential of storytelling, of the magic of following a ley line, of the kindness of strangers, of the power of adventure, all imbued with a sense of what can only be described as authenticity and 'genuine empathy' (Ellis 2012).

The sound of lost futures: Middle Child's *All We Ever Wanted Was Everything*

We stand huddled together – clutching cans of lager or plastic cups of vodka and coke – in the middle of The Welly, a nightclub in Hull, surrounded by scaffolding platforms filled with a mix of actors and bandmates. Deafening bass thumps from the speakers as the lights flash sporadically through the smoky haze and onto the sticky floor. The MC, played by Marc Graham, emerges from within the crowd and starts to climb some of the scaffolding. 'Now, everyone', he shouts above the bass into a handheld microphone,

> Get your phones out – get your phones out. Go on – get 'em all out. Don't worry! No-ones gonna tap you on the shoulder and say 'Excuse me! You're breaking the rules of theatre! How could the actors possibly concentrate if you've got your phone out?' We're not in another building tonight. Get your phone out! We're going live! Instagram! Facebook Live! Periscope – if that still exists – I dunno if it does. Are you ready for this? LET'S DO THIS!. (*All We Ever Wanted Was Everything* 2017)

The volume of the bass rises, the band kicks in and Act Three begins. 'We're fucking immortal', the company sing, no – shout, 'And we're not going anywhere' (Barnes 2017: 45). Commissioned as part of Hulls' year as UK City of Culture, local company Middle Child's *All We Ever Wanted Was Everything* (2017), written by Luke Barnes with music by James Frewer and directed by Paul Smith, 'drew its creative team ... from the UK's lively yet often undersung fringe theatre ecology' (Nicholas 2019) as one of many artistic projects that were commissioned to 'speak of the city, its people, their creativity and energy' (Hull City of Culture 2017, 2018) during the year-long celebration. Barnes' *All We Ever Wanted Was Everything* uses the backdrop of Hull's decline 'from being a hub of the shipping and fishing industries to one of the most deprived cities in the UK' (Nicholas 2019) to focus on interpersonal and intrapersonal conflicts, concentrating specifically on the experience of the millennial generation within Hull throughout the past three decades. In contrast to several of the commissions throughout Hull's time as City of Culture – including new work by the Royal Shakespeare Company – Middle Child's work centres the working-class experience and prioritizes working-class access to theatre, taking, as Tom Nicholas explains, 'inspiration from the theory and practice of John McGrath, who sought to foreground elements of popular, working-class culture within his performance texts' (ibid.). During McGrath's tenure of Scottish political theatre company 7:84 throughout the 1970s, such a foregrounding of popular working-class culture manifested, for example, in the inclusion of ceilidhs in their performances staged in pubs and working-men's clubs. For twenty-first-century theatre company Middle Child's work, however, this foregrounding of the working-class experience in a theatrical framework is manifest in the integration of nightclub and gig culture aesthetics.

Gig theatre was becoming an increasingly common label amongst critics and a self-identified practice among theatre makers by the time *All We Ever Wanted Was Everything* premiered in Hull (Williams 2017), with Camden People's Theatre even producing a festival dedicated to the form the year prior (Cearns 2016). The term refers to a style of performance that Thomas Andrewes defines as 'theatrical pieces that double as real musical performances, in which the real performance situation of the gig synchronizes with the theatrical logic of the show' (Andrewes 2020: 124). In essence, gig theatre makes use of the mechanics and aesthetics of a gig as the framework for which the narrative is to be told. As Nicholas explains regarding *All We Ever Wanted Was Everything*, 'The music is a constant presence throughout the production … indie-inspired songs which elevate pivotal moments within the show are consistent with a somewhat do-it-yourself aesthetic. Audience members are free to roam the performance space during the show —with frequent opportunity to visit the bar' (Nicholas 2019). As the popularity of gig theatre continued to grow throughout the 2010s, Middle Child's sole focus on this medium as their go-to aesthetic is based on their becoming aware of an increasing 'cultural dissonance between theatre and the popular world' (Barnes 2018). As playwright Luke Barnes describes,

> A lot of people from outside of the theatre fandom, feel that theatre is too long, overpriced, boring, irrelevant, dull, over-intellectual, and happens in buildings that communities don't feel is theirs. We wanted to make the opposite of that. We wanted to find a form of theatre for our generation that speaks to us beyond intellect and can happen in spaces already occupied by the general public. (ibid.)

The use of the mechanics of gig theatre in *All We Ever Wanted Was Everything* is metamodern in the sense of the mechanics existing beyond the boundaries of the traditional theatrical dichotomy between actors and audience, manifesting in what would be labelled as an immersive experience for the audience. As Slobodian describes in her review of the piece at Reading Fringe Festival in 2017, the 'action weaves through the crowd, performers speak lines pointedly to individuals, sit atop the bar and occasionally co-opt audience members for silent bit parts' (Slobodian 2017), with the audience always included in the atmosphere of the gig. The MC asking the audience to livestream the show from their phones – in blatant disregard of, or even in direct opposition to, mainstream theatrical etiquette – is just one example of the many ways in which Middle Child include the audience in their storytelling. Take a conversation between the two respective parents in the show, Brian and Kimberly, which Smith stages in such a way that each character is positioned at a separate end of the nightclub – with the entire audience between the two of them (in metatheatrical Level A – see 'Metatheatre' section in Chapter 3). However, in the universe of the play (metatheatrical Level C), the characters are mere feet from each other, beside a shelf in Hull's Virgin Megastore in 1997, attempting to buy the first Harry Potter book for their respective children. As they talk, the MC underscores their conversation with a whispered-into-the-mic-demand that someone in the audience take the book from Brian's hand and pass it down through the crowd – like some sort of book-focussed-crowd-surfing – to Kimberly, in order to portray the action of Brian handing her the book: 'Someone get the book. Get the book! Pass it on! Pass it down, pass it down', he instructs, before a pause – 'Try not to undermine the scene!' (*All We Ever Wanted Was Everything* 2017). Later, one performer forgets their handheld microphone at the other side of the club and has to go back and get it. Marc Graham's MC turns this blunder into an in-joke with the audience – 'Oh, he's got to go get back and get it! Oooooh!' (ibid.). The crowd joins the 'Ooooh' as the performer sheepishly waves, jogging back to his position with the microphone safely secured, accompanied with laughter from both the performers and the audience. They are all in on the joke.

There is an obvious metatheatricality to Middle Child's use of gig theatre, in that the mechanics of the theatrical event are as evident as the wires and amps onstage, and this metatheatrical nature is, in part, used to – as *Beneath the Albion Sky*, *End to End* and *Wanderlust* before it – (re)centre the act of storytelling. Graham's MC serves as an explicit narrator, taking us through the piece with a knowing wink. His storytelling also aids in setting up the overarching sensibilities of 1987/1997, 2007 and 2017 at the beginning of each act respectively through a lyrical take on the key political movements of the time. 'The Berlin Wall falls ... we head to New Labour euphoria in '97, stopping at 'Broken Britain' in 2007 and hurtle head first into 2017's Brexit Britain' (Slobodian 2017), all of which is also underscored by a continuously evolving musical score which pastiches elements of popular music from each era, from 1980s pop-rock to Britpop to indie. Frewer's evocative composition and Barnes's clever reworking of popular lyrics, however, is not mere nostalgic appropriation but a reconstructive pastiche that uses lyrics and slogans of the respective periods in a way that imbues them with a double meaning. In 1987, for example, we hear the cast pronounce a refrain that is essentially optimistic in an individualistic sense of success alongside undertones of how Thatcher's anti-state ideology permeated British politics at the time: 'I wanna dance with somebody/'Cos nothing's gonna stop us now/There's no such thing as society/ And heaven is a place on earth' (Barnes 2017: 1). It is a paradoxical positioning – including an exuberant hope for a better future – which, as will become clear in the following, is an essential element to the story of problematic millennial protagonists Chris and Leah – with the current, contemporary knowledge of the lasting damage done to Britain (particularly to Chris and Leah's own generation and that of their parents) through the legacy of Thatcherite policy. In the second half of Act One's 1997 Cool Britannia, this hopeful drive is intensified with the lyrical reference to R. Kelley's belief in flying and Blair's simultaneous principle that things can only get better (Barnes 2017: 4). At the beginning of Act Two, we get indie guitars and lyrical references to reluctant hit-makers MGMT, whilst the MC describes a generation of 'Broken Britain … indie kids sitting outside the … shopping centre wearing skinny jeans, playing the Kooks and wanting to go to the seaside' (ibid.: 23). In 2017, the refrain 'We're not going anywhere' (ibid.: 45), sung immediately after the crowd cheer for Hull as the City of Culture, is both a celebratory, political-lite chant of the solidity and solidarity of community and sense of place within the city and a pessimistic acceptance of Chris and Leah's generation's feeling of inadequacy in their lives in comparison to the exuberant hope promised for them in the earlier decade of Act One. Throughout the piece, Frewer and Barnes combine pop culture and political rhetoric from the previous thirty years in such a way that centres dual readings of such lyrics with both the benefit of hindsight and the continual focus on how the millennial generation has been affected by the messages throughout each era. The pair's application of reconstructive pastiche makes use of the popular and the political to re-centre the felt experience of Chris and Leah – and, through this, the millennial audience experiencing the piece. Rather than this effect being purely textual, the pair's use of music also – in a rather indefinable way – bypasses the intellectual aspect of such reconstructive pastiche and, instead, enables a centring of felt experience. As Wilks is able to describe much better than I in their review of the piece at the Bush Theatre in 2018, there's something so magic about music, where it penetrates all the walls you've fought so hard to build, crumbling them down and attacking your soul with a wave of unwanted, yet needed emotion. [*All I Ever Wanted Was Everything*] is a raucous celebration that reminds me of the gigs I used to go to in my youth, and brings back all the happy memories of losing myself in sound. (Wilks 2018)

Middle Child's use of gig theatre as a theatrical methodology therefore allows for a centring of the felt experience of both the fictional millennial protagonists and the audience currently experiencing the gig/performance though the use of metatheatrical post-immersive engagement and reconstructive pastiche. But how *All We Ever Wanted Was Everything* exemplifies a metamodern theatrical aesthetic is not only in its form – and not all gig theatre is necessarily metamodern – but the story of the piece is also inherently metamodern in its narrative focus on the generational experience of the children of postmodernism. This is gig theatre for the gig economy, Middle Child proclaim (Slobodian 2017), and it is Chris and Leah's hauntological experiencing of their generation's lost futures that really exemplify Barnes's metamodern storytelling.

'This is the millennial story' Barnes says of his script, 'We were promised the world under Tony Blair and graduated into David Cameron's austerity, forcing us to live in a world of broken dreams, unable to feel like we are enough, and – given the narrative of capitalism – envy everyone else's lives' (Barnes 2018). The narrative of *All We Ever Wanted Was Everything* follows two millennials in Hull, one middle-class (Chris) and one working-class (Leah) and how they both work out 'how to live in this disappointing world' (ibid.). Barnes's focus on this is initially largely structural, with Leah and Chris's narratives dealing with a majority of the generational scarring detailed in Chapter 3, which principally coalesces around the pair's own dealing with the weight of expectations placed on them by their parents throughout the relative prosperity of the 1990s and early 2000s. Whilst the 'two children grow up under very different social circumstances' (Bonar 2017), they are joined through their shared generational experiences – uniting in a mutual generational structure of feeling: 'Both read Harry Potter [for example] and are told they can be anything they want' (ibid.). 'You can do anything' says Kimberly to her son Chris in 1997, 'If you can dream it, you can do it. You just have to work' (Barnes 2017: 7). Brian similarly informs his daughter that she could 'live a life better than Dad … If you work hard enough' (ibid.: 10), and ten-year-old Leah's innocent response being that she will do everything she can to achieve this promise of a better life. However, throughout the next two acts – in a decade and then twenty years' time, respectively – we find that Chris and Leah are 'dissatisfied with the world because their parents wanted them to have everything, and when barriers arose – personal or circumstantial – that prevented them from having it, there is only a struggle' (Walker 2017). Whilst Leah's A-level results precluded her from university, Chris struggles to cope with Higher Education – crippled by the anxiety that he is not living up to his mother's expectations: 'I work FUCKING hard ... I'm not just saying that. It's just ... I'm not actually very bright. And that mixed with the promised joy my mother gave me makes me lose sleep at night ... How do you tell someone who's invested all their life in you that you're actually not worth it?' (Barnes 2017: 26). Floundering in an economic, academic and social reality that is antithetical to that promised to them by their parents, Chris and Leah 'make mistakes, they get drunk, they end up in 2017 in their thirties both disillusioned, unhappy and a bit lost' (Bowie-Sell 2017). It is interesting to note that critics labelled Barnes's writing as 'at times a touch too sentimental' (Walker 2017) or 'slightly too earnest at times' (Slobodian 2017) when they also note that the story of Chris and Leah is so relatable – it 'struck a definite chord with this '80s kid I can tell you' continues Slobodian (ibid.) in her review. Bowie-Sell similarly notes that 'it's a story that you've probably heard before' (Bowie-Sell 2017) – but this is the precise aim of Barnes's piece. By exemplifying overly familiar generational experiences through both the felt experience of each character and through a reconstructive pastiche of generational, cultural touchstones – mentions of the Nokia 5110 received cheers from the audience in some performances (ibid.) – Barnes oscillates between the structural and the sentimental, the underlying societal issues and the inner felt experience of these characters within this. Chris and Leah are avatars for the entire millennial generation. As Barnes details, the question that drove the writing of *All We Ever Wanted Was Everything* was finding out what united the millennials as a demographic (Barnes 2018). The company spent a week with 'theatre makers, DJs, club owners, party people, drug lovers, actors, musicians and people our age' (ibid.) to attempt to find a uniting experience before they realized that 'we all felt unable to live within our skin. We all felt we were, on some level, failing. We all wished we were someone else, whilst dealing with a certain amount of anxiety that we couldn't articulate. We felt like we were told we were special and then had a hard time realising that we weren't' (ibid.).

Barnes's script, however, goes deeper than simply manifesting a generational structure of feeling through the characters of Leah and Chris. It also provides important and nuanced exploration of the intergenerational conflicts engendered by the millennials' being haunted by lost futures through a simultaneous focus on both the parents of Leah and Chris and the effects upon the incoming Generation Alpha through the millennials' relationships with their own children. As Mountford explains in her review of the piece at the Bush Theatre in 2018, 'There's a poignant through-line [in the show] about parental wishes for/pressures on children' (Mountford 2018), and Walker describes the piece as, essentially, an 'excellent commentary on intergenerational relationships' (Walker 2017). Whilst, throughout university, Chris begins to suffer anxiety around being unable to live up to the expectations placed on him by his mother as well as those self-created by Chris in the shadow of his deceased father's absence ('I tell her everything's fine. Even though I spend all my time telling myself that I'll never be as good as Dad' [Barnes 2017: 30]), his mother becomes despondent for the diminishing connection with her son as he grows apart from her throughout the decades. 'I'm your kid!', Chris exclaims when she divulges that she feels like she hasn't got anyone. 'Then act like it', she retorts, 'I'm old and alone. Be a son. Don't talk to me like I'm a hindrance. I gave you everything' (Barnes 2017: 53). Chris replies with a scoffed thanks – 'That worked out well didn't it' (ibid.). In a more heated exchange (see Figure 5.2), a 'brutal, powerful, pivotal scene' (Mountford 2018) sees Leah lay fault on her struggling father Brian for her own lack of success:

Figure 5.2 Joshua Meredith as Brian (left), Alice Beaumont as Holly (centre, silhouette) and Bryony Davies as Leah (right) in Luke Barne's *All We Ever Wanted Was Everything* (directed by Paul Smith for Middle Child, the Paines Plough Roundabout @ Summerhall, 2017)

Source: Wullie Marr for Middle Child. Reproduced with kind permission from © Middle Child.

I could have been rich but you fucked it before I was even born. Holly's got a good job and money because her parents gave her everything and you gave me nothing ... Every bad day I have is because of you. I'm fucked because you were fucking fat and lazy and too fucking sub-par to be anything other than a bouncer. Everyone else's dads ... provide for their family. They work so their kids can do stuff. And you just exist. You're just alive. Not for me. Just to survive. (Barnes 2017: 40)

As an audience who have been privy to Brian's inner monologue as he struggles to provide for his daughter as a single father, juggling the guilt of working nightshifts with the need to put food on the table, this comes across as a cruel attack from his daughter. His response – to calmly give Leah her birthday present and go to bed, makes the moment even more tortuous, as does the moment Leah then opens the gift to find he had saved up to buy her the newly released iPhone 1 (ibid.: 41). And yet, the text also allows us to understand Leah's inner feeling of inadequacy, whether her anger is directed towards the right place or not. Barnes continues to explore the disturbing generational cycles inflicted through such an intergenerational blame game when Chris, now a thirty-year-old father in 2017, attempts to prevent his son Collin 'from making the same mistake of wishing and scheming, Chris discourages Collin from dreaming' (ibid.: 46):

Collin   Nanny said 'if I can dream it, I can do it'.
Chris   She shouldn't say that.
Collin   Why not?
Chris   Because the world doesn't work like that. (ibid.: 56)

Through Barnes's complicated positioning of intergenerational conflict throughout Chris and Leah's narrative, whilst these proxies for the millennial generation are the default protagonists of the story Middle Child are telling and reflective of the intended audience of the piece, both they and their beliefs are not treated as sacrosanct, but revealed to be flawed and, in some cases, hurtful. Through this, Barnes does not offer a simple solution or take a particular position in this intergenerational conflict. Instead, he offers insight into the inner experiences of both generations equally – 'We wish we were our parents', state Leah and Chris. 'And us, their parents', Kimberly tells us, 'sit, alone, wishing we were our children' (ibid.: 64).

Whilst such a complex, nuanced and multifaceted story appears, in some ways, to eschew a metamodern aesthetic in favour of a more modernist-leaning drama, Barnes throws a curveball into the mix, toying 'with the concept of destiny, of inevitable outcomes, of circumstances written in the stars' (Walker 2017) through the telling of this tale, heightened by the inclusion of a comet. This incoming Armageddon hurtles towards us throughout the play, anthropomorphized in both the MC's telling of the comet's own desire to eradicate the earth and in Smith's staging of the comet as a Daft-Punk-esque DJ – looming over the nightclub throughout the entire piece. The inclusion of an inevitable apocalypse, as Walker describes, 'deviates from the play's realism, yet serves a greater purpose of diminishing our trivial problems, and reminding us how finite, and therefore valuable, our time is' (Walker 2017). The inescapable knowledge of the story ending badly – of which we are privy to right at the start of the piece, in a way that reflects Sam Ward's *we were promised honey!* (2022) later in this volume – adds another layer of complexity to the millennial audience's (and creative team's) engagement with the inherent feeling of lost futures within Chris and Leah's generational experience – in that, when positioned against the enormity of the ending of everything, our disappointment in our current lived reality seems preposterous. And yet, albeit paradoxical, for both Leah and Chris, this disappointment is still their lived reality. As the asteroid crashes to earth, the pair share the fact that their 'plastic' lives don't feel 'real', that the only thing that does is the lack of love in their lives, the lack of compassion and kindness and truth (cf. Barnes 2017: 64). And yet, the comet reminds the audience, if not the characters, that these two proxies for their generation *do* have love in their lives – Leah, a doting father who tried his best to provide for her, and Chris, a loving wife and son – which he is responsible for bringing into the world. But it is too late. The comet hits, and as 'the universe is clogged with people screaming what they would have done differently, humanity dies' (Barnes 2017: 66). Rather than a cynical postmodern statement about the hopelessness of it all, however, as the heavy guitar-led rock music reaches a crescendo, Graham's MC ends the piece with a rallying cry to the audience standing with him in The Welly:

> And now we, together in this club, can see it in our fallen heroes' world that there's just no need for this bullshit. That all we need to do is make it count right now. All of us, just forget how well we're all doing and just look up and live with spirit in your hearts. Stand up for kindness and joy and hope. Just fucking stand up for each other. And if we've got a song let's sing it as loud as we fucking can. LIVE YOUR LIFE! I fucking dare ya! (*All We Ever Wanted Was Everything* 2017)

Through *All We Ever Wanted Was Everything*'s reconstructive pastiche of the popular music and politics of Britain over a span of thirty years, Barnes and Middle Child stage a personification of, through the avatars of Chris and Leah, the millennial generation's pining for lost futures. The gig-theatre framing enables a space for the felt experience of the audience to be central to this, but Barnes's script also spends time revealing the felt experience of several of the characters throughout the piece, not just the difficult millennial protagonists. Barnes is both sympathetic towards and sceptical of his millennial counterparts, presenting both sociological and political factors that engendered Chris and Leah's underlying anxieties of inadequacy, whilst also blithely undercutting their obsession with the antagonistic insertion of the incoming comet, which reduces their inner conflicts to insignificance in the face of the world-ending apocalypse that only we – as the audience – know is just around the corner. Whilst this could initially be seen as inherently hopeless – making the human-level concerns of Chris and Leah, and therefore the entire millennial generation, pointless – the MC's call-to-arms at the end of this reframes such impending doom as imbued with both hopelessness for the future and hopefulness for a better present. Therefore, the piece centres on our current felt experience of the here and now. Rather than embracing an inherently hopeless understanding of the fact that, in comparison to the whims of an anthropomorphized Daft Punk meteor, none of this matters *or* an inherently postmodernist ironic 'who cares?' understanding of the fact that none of this matters, *All We Ever Wanted Was Everything* embraces a metamodern focus on felt experience – asking, in a reflection of Dember's understanding of a similar narrative moment in the 2022 film *Everything Everywhere All At Once*, 'how we can retain our sense of humanity in the face of either or both of [these interpretations? How can we] stare into the face of either of those overwhelming realizations, and ask: where is the place for our sense of individual human-ness?' (Dember 2022). As Charlie Wilks explains in their review, *All We Ever Wanted Was Everything* is 'a piece that's full of hope, yet absolutely hopeless at the same time' (Wilks 2018). In its handling of the millennials' 'desperately searching for something more than what we've got' (ibid.), Middle Child's production is inherently hope/less.

I want to believe (all of this is true): Poltergeist's *Lights Over Tesco Car Park*

As we take our seats, we have been enthusiastically singing along to early 2000s pop-punk boyband Busted's *Year 3000*, encouraged by the young company members of Poltergeist Theatre onstage – irresistibly 'pumping up the crowd' (Ferguson 2018) before, suddenly – jarringly, the cast's expressions turn serious. The lighting dims. We stop singing. A company member stands in a spotlight, looking down at a latex alien mask – the kind of thing you might buy from a fancy-dress shop for Halloween. She appears to silently get the audience to dare her to put it on. She does. She stands there – green mask over her head, staring out at us with blank, wet, black eyes. She appears unsure what to do. She does a little twirl. She shrugs. Was that alright? The audience laughs. She turns to look at a projected sentence that appears on the wall behind her:

ALL OF THIS IS TRUE

it reads. Poltergeist Theatre formed in 2016 whilst studying at Oxford University. On graduating, the company realized that – as students – they had existed within a social bubble, seemingly ignorant to the external life of the city around them. *Lights Over Tesco Car Park* (2018), the company's fifth show together, was devised throughout the course of a year by the cast and then written and directed by Jack Bradfield, in an attempt to, as Bradfield describes, 'make contact, and even make a few new friends ... to explore the ways communities create their own realities' (Bradfield 2018: vii). The company gained initial support from The Yard Theatre in East London to present an early version of the work in December 2017, then redeveloped the piece with assistance from The North Wall Arts Centre, before becoming one of New Diorama Theatre's Graduate Emerging Companies the following year, meaning that the piece was able to transfer to the National Student Drama Festival, before enjoying a well-received Edinburgh Festival Fringe run that summer, transferring to The Pleasance in Islington in the autumn (Malldon 2018) and, eventually, winning the Samuel French New Play Award in 2018.

The piece, in part, follows the format of metatheatrical docu-theatre – described by some reviews as a 'docu-comedy' (Ferguson 2018) – in that the form of *Lights Over Tesco Car Park* is largely concerned with authentic, metatheatrical storytelling reminiscent of The Gramophones' *End to End* as the show itself is an attempt to retell the initial experiences that generated the material to make the show. The main narrative of this retelling concerns the group's interactions with a man named Robert. Through their recounting of these interactions, the cast choose to foreground as authentic a telling of these events as possible; each performer plays themselves, and have similarly chosen not to offer what would be an inauthentic representation of Robert through attempting to act as a version of him onstage – in fact, Bradfield insists in the published text of the piece that, if others are to perform it, there is 'one rule ... that we urge you not to break: Robert should never appear onstage' (Bradfield 2018: vii). Instead, Robert is represented through archival material of the company's encounters with him. We see screenshots of his original reaching out to them; hear a recording of the voice call between the four group members and Robert following this email; read snippets of their WhatsApp chats; and even, once, are privy to a blurry, covert, slightly ethically dubious photo of the man himself shopping in Tesco as two members of the group – because of some detailed Facebook-stalking – recognize him from afar. The furthest the group get towards staging Robert is representing him onstage in the form of a cap balanced precariously on a microphone stand, through which the group enable a physical presence for Robert in their recreation of moments in which they met in person. However, the group never aim to recreate such conversations – instead, the narrative concerning Robert is wholly centred in a group-based storytelling. As Bradfield makes clear, the piece is not concerned with inauthentic representation or recreation but is based in the truth of the fact that the 'show takes place in a theatre. There is never a moment when it pretends to take place anywhere else' (ibid.).

The group's interaction with Robert starts innocuously enough. It becomes clear that he reached out to the company after they posted an advert in their local paper asking for any people living in Oxford that had any experiences with UFOs or unexplained phenomena and would be up for sharing their story with a group of young theatre makers. In the preliminary phone conversation between Robert and Poltergeist – the recording of which opens the show – the group illustrate his recounting of seeing unexplained lights over the Tesco car park through a clever use of their phone torch lights. 'I don't know why', we hear Robert's voice tell us over the phone, 'but I looked up, and I saw this light' (Bradfield 2018: 4). A performer shines their phone torch at the audience. 'It was a reddish light', Robert continues (ibid.), and the performer covers their phone torch with their finger – the light continuing to shine through their skin with a dull, red glow. The audience laughs. Robert recounts the light splitting into four, and the cast all bring out their phones, torches on, covered by their fingers. It is at once eerie and, in its staging, slightly ridiculous. But the use of Robert's recording imbues this silliness with a continually underlying authenticity. Later in the piece, after we are privy to a re-creation of the group's own visit to the Tesco car park to ensure the veracity of Robert's story (i.e. to check there were no cranes around, the lights of which could have been mistaken for UFOs) (see Figure 5.3), we catch up with Robert in a Costa Coffee. Whilst performers Rosa Garland and Alice Boyd re-create their own roles in the conversation live onstage, Robert's words are projected piece by piece on the wall behind them:

144   *Metamodernism in Contemporary British Theatre*

Figure 5.3 (L–R) Rosa Garland, Alice Boyd, Julia Pilkington and Callum Coghlan (whose role was taken on by Will Spence later that year) in Jack Bradfield and Poltergeist Theatre's *Lights Over Tesco Car Park* (directed by Jack Bradfield, National Student Drama Festival, De Montfort University and The Curve Theatre, Leicester, 2018)

Source: Aenne Pallasca. Reproduced with kind permission from © Aenne Pallasca.

> I think I've been
> um
> I think I've been
> contacted
> **Alice** *returns with some sugar.*
>
> (Bradfield 2018: 19)

Through a conversation that fluctuates between the seemingly impossible premise of alien contact and the innocuous – such as which podcast they would recommend – Robert reveals that he believes he has been contacted by an extraterrestrial through his phone in response to his own advertising for a lodger: 'He said hi he said I heard about the room I am coming to stay see you soon' (Bradfield 2018: 29–30). It is at this point, as put by Allin in her review of the piece at the Edinburgh Festival Fringe, that the group become worried 'as we [the audience] are, that this might turn into a big joke, and that Robert will be the butt of it' (Allin 2018). Nevertheless, the group agree to meet with Robert at the prescribed time of what he expects to be the alien's arrival. The group's telling starts to shift innocuously to second person at points throughout the following scene in a way that slowly and unwittingly implicates us as individual audience members (or perhaps a collective singularity representative of Robert) within the retelling, and it is through this form of inclusive and authentic retelling of these events that we become acutely aware that 'we are not just in Robert's spare room. We are also in a theatre; two places at once. Both here and also not here. Someone might', Allin posits, 'mistake us for aliens' (ibid.). It is in this ghost-like, liminal space between the spare room and the theatre, between the past and the retelling, between audience and storyteller, that the impossible happens:

Rose The radio crackles.
Will   The lights flicker out.
Alice And like a pixelated picture.
Julia Like dial-up.
  The alien appears.

(Bradfield 2018: 66)

The group replicate their interaction with this alien by returning to the image of four phone torch lights, covered with their thin, translucent fingers. Through this quiet, fragile, visual representation, the group describe the being as a thin and delicate thing, floating in front of them and looking, somehow, tired. And because they are unsure what to do – and in a suitably British fashion – they offer it some tea.

Whilst the group's interactions with Robert – leading to their inexplicable encounter with an unknown entity – form the main narrative woven throughout the piece, there are actually three threads to the performance, running 'in parallel but always intersecting' (Allin 2018); that of Robert and the car park; that of the metatheatrical retelling of Poltergeist's own process of developing the piece; and that of four participatory stories of other documented alien encounters. Poltergeist specializes in what John Chapman calls 'puzzle-box productions [or] what writer/director Jack Bradfield describes as collage theatre' (Chapman 2020). This patchwork-like pastiche of various threads and performance styles interwoven throughout a piece is in service of a metatheatrical and post-immersive dialogical engagement that serves to centre on the shared felt experience between company and audience members. As Chapman describes, rather than audience interaction, *Lights Over Tesco Car Park*'s post-immersive dialogical engagement is better described as 'audience collaboration' (ibid.). After we are introduced to Robert's narrative at the start of the piece, the tone suddenly shifts again, as Alice silently tempts an audience member out of their seat with the promise of a flying saucer sweet.

This is followed by a silent call and response, in which it slowly becomes clear that Alice is asking the audience member to copy her simple movements. When the audience member has got the hang of this, the tone suddenly shifts again – the lights become harsh and flashing, and the four performers stand around the stage – arms outstretched – each offering the audience member their own flying saucer. The audience member hesitates, and then chooses one, plucking the sweet from the chosen performer's outstretched hand. This action reveals that each of the four sweets are tokens by which to choose the order that the group retell four true stories of an extraterrestrial encounters that they have found through their research – with help from the (at this point unwitting) audience-member-turned-volunteer. Throughout these four re-enactments, each audience member is gently guided through their part in these mini performances, never becoming 'stooges' to the performers (Chapman 2020). Instead, 'the answers which the selected audience member gives when questioned guide the form of the narrative which therefore alters each time the piece is performed [, reflecting] the shifting nature of perceived truth' (ibid.) threaded throughout the show. In one retelling of these incidents, 'an audience member has an identity forced upon them, is patronized by an interrogator, and, since they do not know what the actors will ask them and must therefore improvize, they unwittingly fill the position of a traumatized victim trying to recollect what they saw' (Britton 2017). In another, 'someone finds themselves blindfolded and experiencing a literally hair raising moment as a mini fan and static from a balloon are used to replicate the feeling of an alien sighting' (Chapman 2020). Whilst on the surface such encounters sound quite daunting, the care, reassurance and compassion that Poltergeist's company members offer to their volunteers throughout this participation, instead, imbues every encounter with a supportive, friendly atmosphere. Each participant – and the audience at large – is softly encouraged to feel 'in on the joke' with the company members, rather than their participation being the joke itself. Later, when three of the company members offer their flying saucers with outstretched hands, the audience already knows what to do; one of us makes the journey to the stage to choose a sweet, and the next story begins. The piece is structured in such a way, therefore, that the show could not continue without at least one audience member per story making the active decision to come onstage, choose a flying saucer and become part of each re-enactment. For Britton, this is 'audience participation done right' (Britton 2017) – describing the show's dedication to audience involvement as being central to the narrative, rather than played for laughs, as its most well-executed asset (ibid.). Between these stories – one of which is never actually chosen throughout each piece, meaning that in each performance of *Lights Over Tesco Car Park* one actor's re-enactment is left out (the jealousy, annoyance or relief of which plays into their interaction with the rest of the cast throughout the remainder of the play) – the narrative of Robert and the alien is also intercut with other metatheatrical moments concerned with the making of the piece itself. In this intermediate level of metamodern metatheatricality (Level B), we experience 'more abstract scenes like a conspiracy theory dance number called "Articles We Found in Our Research"' (Carlson 2017) in which the group energetically share some of their favourite findings, asking us to 'remember, people actually wrote these' (Bradfield 2018: 35) before intercutting the beat – and their dancing – by bellowing article titles into the microphone such as 'Forget the moon-landing hoax … because the moon doesn't exist!' (ibid.: 37) and 'Over twelve million Americans believe that lizard people run their country' (ibid.) before, following the latter, the music immediately cuts out so that Julia can remind us that 'that's actually really messed up' (ibid.).

Following the group's retelling of their encounter with an unexplained presence in Robert's spare bedroom, they then reveal to us that they left his house in a state of confusion, making their way to the eponymous Tesco. It is at this moment that the group describe their own experience of incredible lights over the car park, again using their phones – covering the torches with their fingers – to illustrate the red glow of the impossible light they observed. Through the gentle interaction that they have coaxed the audience into throughout the past hour, when they describe the light softly splitting into two – three – four, audience members begin to raise their own phone torches from within their seats, also covering the lights with their fingers. The lights above Tesco car park split, through this audience involvement, into eight – ten – twenty – a *hundred* lights filling 'up the skies over Headington' (Bradfield 2018: 68) and the raised seating in unison. The group then ask for our help, 'because what happened next is really hard to describe' (ibid.). As they recount how the lights came down from the sky to envelop them, they gently encourage the audience to come down onto the stage, bringing their phones with them. Detailing his nervousness during this encounter, performer Will Spence states that he held someone's hand – 'Maybe your hand?' he asks an audience member – leading them, too, down to the stage space (ibid.). The audience fill up the pitch-black stage, their finger-covered phone torches creating a sky filled with dots of extraterrestrial light. The performers stand with them. 'I feel them all around me', states Julia, referring simultaneously to her alien encounter and the audience currently surrounding her, 'shuffling and breathing and being' (ibid.: 69). After a pause, Alice speaks from within the crowd, with her words echoing the strong bonds she and her castmates forged during this incredible encounter, as well as, equally, the binds forged in the current moment between the actors and audience being together onstage:

Alice   And I think, if we are feeling this together,
If we are in this moment together,
Maybe that's enough. (ibid.)

At this stage, the audience occupy a liminal representative state, being at once alien – both figuratively, as a stand in for the extraterrestrial encounter, and literally, as strangers to both each other and the company members sharing the space with them – and, simultaneously, part of a temporary community – a group of people who decided to take the leap of faith and be included in what, if we are honest, is something quite silly: with us all holding up our phone torches pretending to be aliens. But despite – or perhaps because of – this silliness, the genuine wonder, awe and intensity of this moment, and the bond forged between the company members through this event, is portrayed with the utmost sincerity. It is at once wholly ridiculous and wholly sincere. As reviewer Jack Ferguson describes, it is 'in its own odd and silly way, very poignant' (Ferguson 2018).

Slowly, as we stand there, the alien arrives: Rosa – in her latex mask from the beginning of the show. 'I feel an ending coming on', she warns us, 'and I wonder if I'll ever be the same afterwards' (Bradfield 2018: 69). A crackle and a distorted-sounding version of David Bowie's *Life on Mars* starts playing, as though transmitted from lightyears away. She offers her hands to the nearest audience member and begins slowly dancing with them. They laugh. The other company members offer their hands out too and begin dancing with other members of the audience. Soon, all of the audience who are onstage, still lit only by the dim twinkle of their phone torches, are dancing and laughing together – caught up in both the ridiculousness of the situation and the sheer joy in the act of a group of people dancing to David Bowie at the end of a performance about alien contact. Then, as the chorus hits, Rosa turns to look at a projected sentence that appears on the wall behind her:

NONE OF THIS WAS TRUE

it reads. It is a comedic moment, but it is also a shocking twist for an audience that has slowly become quietly invested in Poltergeist's tale. The company's empathetic, storytelling-centric framing of the performance as authentic, metatheatrical docu-theatre gently encouraged us to believe 'We know that not *all* of this can be true', writes Allin in her review, 'Aliens are not real. And yet. We are not in a car park. And yet. UFO sightings are made up stories. And yet, we still believe, just for a second' (Allin 2018). After all, we have heard Robert's 'voice on the phone. His sincerity' (ibid.). As Jürs-Munby et al. describe, the 'use of authentic texts and personages [is] self-validating, in the sense that its legitimacy is vouchsafed by direct link to external reality made by the use of authentic material' (Jürs-Munby, Carroll and Giles 2016: 26). Through the use of 'audio recordings, projections of transcripts [and] re-enactment of their interactions' (Carlson 2017), Poltergeist managed to portray the 'disbelief, awkwardness and tentative enthusiasm of such an unusual turn of events' (ibid.) that led to an alien encounter in such a way that 'genuinely' (ibid.) drew the audience into the story *as if* such impossible events could have been true. The company 'playfully invit[e] us to ask what we *choose* to believe' (Rees 2018, emphasis my own) *as if* it could, for an hour at least, be somewhat real.

Lights Over Tesco Car Park oscillates between the personal and the alien, altering the roles of audience and the performer, and blurring the lines between the real and the fake. It is also inherently silly – the 'endearingly kitsch and creatively low-tech' (ibid.) design emphasizing the company's use of the aesthetics of the quirky. There is something joyfully ridiculous about an alien spaceship being represented by a thumb-covered phone torch, of the deadpan comedy of a latex-masked alien in a tie-die playsuit and bum-bag. Even the childlike costumes donned by the cast – including overalls, shorts and backwards caps – not only emphasize the young ages of the company members at the time but imbue the proceedings with an almost child-like innocence, making the belief in the impossible all the more imaginable. And through this quirky silliness, the show treats the concept of belief with absolute sincerity – asking the audience to believe in the impossible if only for the duration of the show. 'In a distressing time of post-truth and polarization,' states Rees, in a way that reflects both the metamodern oscillation between the silly and the serious and the desire to be sincere *within* a continual state of irony, *Lights Over Tesco Car Park* is an 'ideal antidote [that] never takes itself too seriously and treats the audience with nothing but love and respect – it feels like nowadays one of the most radical things you can do is simply be unashamedly and unironically lovely' (ibid.). In the end, it doesn't actually matter what, if any, of Poltergeist's docu-comedy was 'true' – 'it was made real for us on stage, regardless of whether or not it actually happened' (Carlson 2017). Whilst the show is framed around encounters with extraterrestrial beings, it is inherently about re-evaluating the interactions we have with each other, 'looking into the connections and communication needed for belief: whether the belief that you have indeed seen a UFO or the bravery necessary to tell the world about your experience' (ibid.). Through an un/believable story about encounters that are un/real, Poltergeist treat the silly with sincerity through a silly performance. Through an unironic empathy towards both the (non/fictional) reporters of alien sightings and the audience experiencing the piece in the theatre at that precise moment, it becomes clear that the crux of the piece is about our embodied felt experience as we (attempt to) connect with others. As Daniella Harrison (2018) brilliantly describes, 'Maybe it's not about the aliens, or whether it's true. Maybe it's about being in a room together, holding our phones' torches in the air, listening to stories and, just for a moment, believing'.

Playful participation and (im)possible political realities: Feat.Theatre's *The Welcome Revolution* and Hidden Track's *Drawing the Line*

As we enter the inviting warmth of Gerry's Café – an initiative run by Theatre Royal Stratford East between 2016 and 2018 – we wander about the space, choosing a comfortable sofa or bean bag on which to lounge on, and, if we wish, accept the offer of tea and biscuits from a smiling young woman. As Jason Rosario (2018) describes, 'There is no traditional start or finish of [this] show, nor is there a clear distinction between performance/performer and audience.' The young woman, who you would be forgiven for thinking is a volunteer for the theatre but is actually one half of the two-woman company Feat.Theatre, then comes to the front of the space and calmly and quietly begins the show. 'Does everybody have a hot drink that wanted one?', she asks, 'I'm going to tell you the story [but] first things first, can we all shake hands with everyone nearest to us and introduce ourselves?' (Davies and Marie Sophie 2018: 3). As Rosario states, this surprise beginning could be jarring, 'but is executed with such warmth and ease that it is not in the least jarring or unpleasant [and] this fluid way of moving through the space and interacting with the audience persists throughout the show, making it feel a little bit more like a gathering in which everyone is involved rather than a traditional performance' (ibid.). Once we are all acquainted with our immediate neighbours, the young woman, who introduces herself as Lara, begins to tell us about her late grandfather. She shows us his old joke book and invites an audience member, if they would like, to read a joke out for the group. The audience member laughs and gives it a go.

Feat.Theatre's *The Welcome Revolution* (2018) imagines 'a world where inviting strangers for cups of tea is no longer a radical act' (Theatre Royal Stratford East 2018). The production was created as a response to the increase in anti-immigrant rhetoric that company members Josie Davies and Stella Marie Sophie observed upon returning to Britain from a period in Germany, as well as being directly inspired by the *Welcome Is a Radical Act* conference at Goldsmiths University, London (2017), which engaged with the increase in nationalism and rise in hostility towards refugees and migrants immediately following 2016's Brexit referendum. The *Welcome Revolution* itself is divided into two halves over the period of a few days. First comes a participatory tea party, in which the public are invited to engage in discussions and practical workshops; and, in the days following, an interactive performance piece is presented that is formed around the material generated within the previous section. In the first half, members of the local community are invited to a tea party at the respective theatre or arts centre the company are currently based at. They share tea, cake and biscuits; participate in family-friendly arts and craft activities; and engage with discussions led by Davies and Marie Sophie about how 'welcome' they feel and what community means to them (Theatre Royal Stratford East 2018). The company both welcome the community into a public sphere in order to engage in a dialogue regarding their own thoughts on the issues surrounding the idea of 'being welcome' and, through this, gather material from the participants in order to craft their show. This tea party formula evolved from the group's concern about the ethical problems in collecting and appropriating local communities' input. As Davies explained to me, in curating the workshops, the pair were trepidatious about there being 'such a fine line between platform and just appropriation ... what's the more equal exchange? Can we actually facilitate these ... workshops in a fair way and who is it for? Is it for us or is it for the participants?' (Davies 2018). The pair decided that there would have to be some form of transaction between them and the participants: 'If we give them something like a cup of tea or a biscuit, then maybe a conversation for that is a more equal exchange and feels more fair and feels less exploitative,' as Davies (2018) explains. The second part of the project sees the audience sitting on sofas, sharing more tea and biscuits, a few days after the initial tea party event. On a stage filled with bunting and origami sculptures created by the tea party participants, Marie Sophie's 'Lara' takes us through her journey towards political engagement through an appreciation of her late grandfather's engagement with his community – an engagement that she feels that her generation has sadly lost. Later, it is revealed that her grandfather's focus on being welcoming stems from his being evacuated to the countryside as a child – joining over a million children in being removed from their homes in major British cities, which were targets for Nazi bombs in the Second World War, to be looked after by welcoming host families in the safety of the British countryside. At the climax of a show that has dealt with multiple reactions to Britain's contemporary response to the refugee crisis (which continues to increase in pertinence over the years since the production) *Feat.Theatre*'s reflection on the blitz spirit, here, is a jolting reminder of the hypocrisy of the populist nationalism that has flourished in Britain through and beyond the

Brexit referendum – forever paradoxically proud of the twentieth-century evacuation project and simultaneously hostile towards twenty-first century refugees.

Throughout Lara's story, we are invited to play particular characters without having to leave the comfort of our sofa (or our cup of tea) (see Figure 5.4). One audience member reads Lara's grandfather's recounting of being an evacuee in a moment which – through such unplanned delivery – somehow emphasizes the emotionality and poignancy of the text; another acts as Lara's school friend; another Lara's parent who 'pushes' her on a swing. It is a paradoxical mix of the authentic and the imaginary. Interwoven throughout this apparently first-hand recounting of a political awakening is material collected from the preceding tea party. Projected photos of these events and scans of handwritten input lend a deeper sense of authenticity to 'Lara's' tale – in fact, states Rosario in their review, it was so authentic 'that I was shocked to find the actress playing Lara is in fact not named Lara at all … it felt [so] deeply real and autobiographical' (Rosario 2018). Whilst Lara is a fiction, the material generated by the workshops is, of course, authentic, some of which is incredibly emotional. In one memorable example, an audience member reads out input the company received from a

Figure 5.4 Stella Marie Sophie (left) interacts with a participant in Feat.Theatre's *The Welcome Revolution* (devised by the company, York Theatre Royal, 2018)

Source: Kirkpatrick Photography. Reproduced with kind permission from © Feat.Theatre.

mother talking about her six-year-old daughter, who had recently seen the tragic photo of two-year-old Alan Kurdi, whose body had washed ashore on the Turkish resort of Bodrum as one of at least twelve refugees who had drowned attempting to flee from Syria to Greece (Smith 2015). The image had quickly gone viral under the hashtag #KiyiyaVuranInsanlik – 'humanity washed ashore' (ibid.). When the child saw this photo, she told her mother that 'when she grew up, she wants to be a mermaid to rescue these children … she knows her father was a refugee. Last week she said, mummy … I am afraid of war, so am I gonna be refugee?' (Davies and Marie Sophie 2018: 20). Despite such harrowing text, as Rosario describes, Marie Sophie 'does not milk the pathos or attempt to get a rise out of us, [instead] she reads [such quotes] calmly, which somehow makes it all the more affecting' (Rosario 2018). When similar quotes are read out by the audience, the unprepared delivery switches between awkwardness at having to read out loud and shocked emotionality. In both Marie Sophie's and the audience's delivery, there is no performance of emotions, instead, the framework of *The Welcome Revolution* elicits authentic reactions to the authentic material gathered by the company.

Fluctuating again between the real and the imagined, though, the tone of the piece shifts, and we suddenly find ourselves drawn into Lara's 'Welcome Revolution' – staged within an imagined land built from a reconstructive pastiche of well-known British literary exports, as Peter Pan, Harry Potter and Alice in Wonderland stage a revolt across a fictionalized Britain. Such shifts between the presentation of material gathered from the public and Lara's story make *The Welcome Revolution* feel at once wholly real and wholly unreal, fluctuating between the observably authentic and the performative deconstruction of such authenticity.

The Welcome Revolution also exhibits explicit interrogation of its own processes: a simultaneously genuine belief *and* disaffected critique of its own methods of engagement. The company extols the act of welcoming as an activist act, of sharing stories and listening to the local community as positive political protest, but are critical of the next steps of their engagement and of their position within the power dynamics created by facilitating such a dialogical space – weaving such critique into the piece itself. Around the time that I experienced the piece in Stratford, which sits within the London Borough of Newham – an area of extremely high deprivation (Newham Council 2019), data was revealed by Arts Council England that the borough had the lowest level of adult arts engagement in London (ArtsProfessional 2018). In response to this, Feat.Theatre told me that a range of participants attended the tea party in Stratford that year and contributed to the later performance, including European migrants, a member of Hackney Council and a homeless participant. The group describe the attendance of the homeless person as creating a juncture in their approach:

> We were like, 'The tea party's irrelevant now. Let's just give this person a hot drink and food, if that will help.' That was a turning point … we were talking about displacement and the refugee crisis in terms that were quite broad. Then, you just have a person, a rough sleeper, who's actually in your life. Okay, well, we're not going to ask him our questions, for example, because that feels inappropriate. Then you have this whole internal conflict of if it's not appropriate to ask them, who is it appropriate to ask? (Davies 2018)

This is a moment returned to in the performance of *The Welcome Revolution*, when Marie Sophie addresses what they saw as shortcomings in their approach to this participant – 'I show him how to make an origami heart with a napkin because I find there's very little I can say' (Davies and Marie Sophie 2018: 13). In the Stratford performance, where over 80 per cent of the local area at the time was classed as being in the second and third worst levels of the ten-level Index of Multiple Deprivation Scale (Newham Council 2019), it was not surprising to hear stories of social isolation, inequality, poverty and homelessness that felt antithetical to the collective and communal 'feel-good' experience curated for the audience through the first half of the production. Whilst some of these responses explicitly addressed the fact that the participants enjoyed their time at the tea party itself, others offered insights into issues that the company admit they could not address. It is here that *The Welcome Revolution* evidences a self-awareness of the dichotomy between hope/lessness within its own construction. The company address the show's shortcomings: of being unable to affect change, of appropriating participants' stories, of the failure to create an extended relational platform between the tea party and the performance. *Feat.Theatre* strive to curate a public sphere as an effectual communicative forum between local communities, to perform the act of welcoming as a radical act of political defiance, but their onstage attentiveness to the limitations of their process conveys an awareness and acceptance of the critiques that could be levied at their work.

Towards the end of the performance, Lara has asked us all to close our eyes. She describes the possible futures we might undertake immediately after our time at the café has ended. We are told to imagine that we 'start going to marches and protests [and] have a cup of tea with a friend who needs to be listened to' (Davies and Marie Sophie 2018: 31) – imagining our increasing engagement with the act of welcoming on a political and personal level. Then the narrative seemingly bends time and space as we, in second person, are told that we enter the venue we are currently sitting in – we see 'a room full of people, all drinking tea and weirdly, they all have their eyes shut ... This', we are told, 'is how revolutions start' (ibid.: 32). *The Welcome Revolution*, as it oscillates between the real and the fictitious, the personal and the political, the hopeful and the hopeless, strives towards utopia, whether through participatory practice or through imagined narrative, whilst overtly admitting that it almost expects to fail. For the company, despite its faults, such theatre 'can be galvanizing, even though it's hopeless' (Davies 2018).

It is pitch black. We sit across a traverse stage space in the Deptford Lounge, London, each holding in our hands a card that simply proclaims 'No, Thank You!'. A voice booms out from the stage. 'In the beginning,' it proclaims, 'there was ... *The Line*' (*Drawing the Line* 2019). A white line appears projected on the wall to the side of us whilst dim lights reveal a thick rope bisecting the stage – separating us from the other audience members opposite. Little do we know how much this line, this boundary between the known and the unknown, between us and them, will come to mean to us throughout the next two hours.

Hidden Track's *Drawing the Line* (2019) was initially created as a scratch performance at Camden People's Theatre in 2018, before being commissioned for development by The Albany in 2019. The company, led by Elliot Hughes and Anoushka Bonwick, create interactive game theatre described as 'pioneering adventures in theatre form that tell accessible political stories' (Hidden Track 2023). Their focus on audience participation through gaming dynamics centres post-immersive participation developed through the values of care, agency, access and – importantly – the ability to opt in or out depending on individual audience member's choice (hence the cards we are currently holding). *Drawing the Line* was advertised as giving the audience the 'chance to roll up their sleeves, get involved and create their own country' (My Theatre Mates 2019), combining storytelling, gaming and group decision making by dividing the audience into two rival nations pitted against each other for land and resources. The company's work is heavily influenced not only by the mechanics of board games but by Live Action Role Play (LARPing) and Role-Playing Games (RPGs) and, as such, whilst game-mechanics are essential in their methodology, the act of storytelling is just as significant in their work as in the work of Feat.Theatre, Poltergeist and The Gramophones. *Drawing the Line* itself begins with the three performers telling the audience an invented creation myth in which 'all in this world, audience included, is separated into two halves by The Line' (Halpin 2019). As the two halves become nations, we – each a half-audience – become part of creating this narrative. We choose our national fauna, name our nation's

Figure 5.5 Nisha Cole (far left) as Lineswoman with audience participants in Elliot Hughes's and Hidden Track's *Drawing the Line* (directed by Anoushka Bonwick, Deptford Lounge, London, 2019)

Source: Rosie Powell. Reproduced with kind permission from © Hidden Track.

'guardian spirit' – as represented onstage by one of two actors – and build our national landmarks out of cardboard boxes (see Figure 5.5). The interaction develops when we are given the chance to earn points by carrying out specific tasks or undertaking challenges, with the nation that earns the most points becoming 'entitled to move the line in their favour whilst making increasingly significant decisions that affect the other nation' (Meloni 2019). As Meloni describes in her review of the piece, this is the point at which the game begins to feel like a social experiment, when 'all of a sudden, aggressive reactions are provoked from both sides [and] the previous light-hearted approach to the first skirmish changes as we realize that peace is irreparably broken' (ibid.). A sense of belonging and nationalism is instilled in our competing sides whose 'members fight for an identity that a few hours earlier didn't even exist' (ibid.). As the playfulness of the game develops to become more competitive, we are pressured to 'focus on earning points without questioning the rather questionable ethics that feed the process' (ibid.). Several audience members are recruited as supervisors to enforce rules that 'are no longer transparent' (ibid.) or fair to both sides, and those who have migrated from the weaker nation are in a 'constant condition of being disadvantaged' (ibid.) – consistently silenced by those who offered them asylum in exchange for obedience. The nations that exist towards the end of the performance, as Meloni describes are 'alarming and yet very familiar' (ibid.).

In Act Two, the winning nation's population increase has meant that resources are now limited. As audience members of the losing nation seek refuge by crossing the line, they are met with disapproval from their new neighbours, who state that they have nothing left to give. The Lineswoman, a character who's control over the balance of 'The Line' has fallen apart throughout the show, confronts the two Guardian Spirits as they blame a 'failing system' on this inequality:

Lineswoman   The system is not failing, this is exactly what the system is designed to do.
Guardian Spirit   So it's hopeless then?
Lineswoman   No, it's not hopeless. We just need some new rules.

(*Drawing the Line* 2019)

The company's use of the modalities of play within *Drawing the Line* facilitates a performative game that, as Carroll et al. describe in terms of postdramatic political theatre, opens 'up a space for alternative realities to come into view [... through] the way that norms of discourse and representation are disrupted' (Carroll, Jürs-Munby and Giles 2013: 23). By drawing on semiotics of anti-immigration, nationalism and the redefining of borders (Drayton 2022: 117), the company generate new political playgrounds that, as the piece draws to a close, feel all too recognizable in a post-Brexit Britain. Reflective of Feat.Theatre's work, *Drawing the Line* is both 'altruistic in its use of performance processes that compel an audience to interact socially and playfully with one another' (ibid.) and aware of the paradox inherent within this – of the unobtainability of the 'fleetingly "collective" theatre situation['s]' (Carroll, Jürs-Munby and Giles 2013: 23) ability to enact progressive, political change. As such, Hidden Track's theatrical modalities are reflective of artist Luke Turner's understanding of the metamodern as an attempt to describe 'a climate in which a yearning for utopias, despite their futile nature, has come to the fore' (Turner 2015). As Jen Harvie critiques, 'Participation is not intrinsically politically progressive' (2013: 10) and yet, although performative and playful dialogical engagement does not necessarily enact utopic change, Hidden Track may open up space for such alternative realities to be discussed, imagined and put into play.

Both *The Welcome Revolution* and *Drawing the Line* are exemplary of theatre in which metamodernism is threaded throughout their overtly political positionings. The two shows attempt to facilitate the creation of alternative political realities through playful, post-immersive dialogical engagement with their audience and a (re)centring of the act, and power of, participatory storytelling within theatre. Each piece approaches their audience with the promise of belief *as if* their time together within these participatory processes can make an actual impact; whether in the hope that exploring the act of welcoming can encourage new, inviting spaces for those that need such, or whether the translating of the ethics of international borders onto an in-person, live action, multiplayer RPG might give Brexit voters some pause for thought. Each company is inherently critical of their ability to enact eudemonic or utopic change, whilst continuing, paradoxically, to be optimistic. They exhibit an inherently metamodern hope/lessness in participatory political theatre's ultimate efficacy – a paradoxical positioning of (im)possibility.

The (meta)narrative you can(not) stage: Arinzé Kene's *Misty*

Playwright and performer Arinzé Kene groans as he pulls on one side of a giant cube that sits, monolithically, on the stage of The Bush Theatre, London. Both he and the cube are flanked by two musicians – playing the drums and synths respectively. With considerable effort, he succeeds in pulling the wall of the cube down and recoils at what he finds inside. The scene is recognizable as Kene's study – the one in which he wrote the piece he is currently performing – but everything is covered in orange balloons. Sitting at his desk, re-writing the play currently being performed, is a little girl of around ten years of age. As he gasps, the girl turns around in the swivel chair and addresses Kene as though he were her little brother. Her voice is a deep, demonic nightmare.

Arinzé Kene's *Misty* was commissioned by The Bush Theatre, premiering in the spring of 2018, before transferring to Trafalgar Studios for a limited run later that year. Written and performed by Kene, with music co-written by him, Shiloh Coke and Adrian McLeod, and directed by Omar Elerian, the piece became famous as marking only the fourth time a play by a Black British playwright had transferred to London's West End – following Mustapha Matura's *Play Mas* (1974), Ray Harrison Graham's *Gary* (1990) and Kwame Kwei-Armah's *Elmina's Kitchen* (2003). *Misty* was later nominated for the Best New Play Olivier Award, and in 2023 the show was restaged at The Shed in New York City. The piece is the most traditionally 'successful' of the projects discussed in this book, certainly the most well-known and definitely the one with most budget. Whilst my focus in this volume is on theatre produced by companies working within Britain's Fringe Theatre circuit, I include *Misty* as a vital example of an inherently metamodern piece of millennial-written theatre that garnered significant mainstream success.

The piece, variably described as 'a blend of gig-theatre, spoken word [and] live art' (Kene 2018) or a 'qausi-musical' (Meyer 2023), employs metatheatrical storytelling to intertwine two narratives – shifting sporadically between the story of a young, Black man's experience of gentrification in Hackney, East London, and the story of Kene dealing with the criticism levered upon him during the writing of this piece. In Level C – the central *mis-en-abyme* – of this metatheatrical narrative, the character of Virus finds his sense of place within his local area erased and, in order to deal with such violent displacement by 'glorified cultural tourists' (Kene 2018: 34), lashes out at both his loved ones and the local community. In Level B – the semantic level – Kene's immediate family, friends and stakeholders chastise him for writing what they refer to as an '*urban* play' (ibid.: 18) or – when not dressed up in thinly veiled, racist white niceties, a 'n____ play' (ibid.); a piece that glorifies Black trauma and the trope of the angry young Black man in a way that replicates the way 'that some black writers "conveniently" wanna write narratives that majority white audiences are interested in seeing about black people' (ibid.: 44). Through this oscillation between both the play Kene has written and the metatheatrical glimpses of the complicated processes undertaken in the writing of it, Kene finds himself – as storyteller in Level A – stuck within a yes/but, hope/less scenario in which the piece invariably becomes focussed on the story he wants to tell and his desire to tell this particular story whilst also being acutely aware of the issues inherent within the performance of 'Blackness' on the British stage. Throughout the piece, Kene variously shares the stage space with orange balloons, representative – as he describes – 'mostly [of] the resistance I experience as an artist [of the] stress ... the anxiety' (Best 2023). In one instance, Kene attempts to hide these stage-invaders under his shirt. In another, he struggles to escape from inside a one giant balloon. At one point, he is pelted with orange water balloons – attempting to dodge them before succumbing to the soaking punishment. The unpredictability of the balloons, with their ability to pop or deflate at any moment (ibid.), become an apt silly-yet-serious metaphor for Kene's creative instinct, ego or ability to cope with dichotomous criticism levied upon him by those around him.

The piece begins in spoken verse, detailing the beginning of the story of Virus as he sits on the night bus – feeling insecure as the singular 'virus' (apart from the bus driver) amongst a crowd of 'blood-cells' – a purposefully thinly veiled racial metaphor. Kene raps the sections focussed on Virus throughout the piece, donning a red beanie to distinguish between his performance as this character and his bare-headed self. As this initial section hits a crescendo – with Virus, provoked by a shove from some 'Drunk prick ...

happy slapping him, blood cell spattering/Batter him, nothing else mattering' (Kene 2018: 16) – the tone of the piece suddenly shifts. The music cuts off, and the spoken-word form is replaced by the two musicians recreating a voicemail on Kene's phone left by his friends Raymond and Donna, who offer critique on the play he is currently performing. 'I looked around', says Raymond, 'and most of the audience were … most of them don't look like us' (ibid.: 17). Donna condemns the piece as 'nothing but a modern minstrel show' (ibid.: 18), but the predominantly white audience? 'They seemed to love it!' (ibid.). Soon after this criticism, Kene is also confronted by his producer – portrayed in the original London runs by sound bites of Morgan Freeman and then from audio clips of Barack Obama for the New York transfer. The producer undercuts Kene's uncertainty about the narrative of his piece following the previous criticism, asking if Kene 'question[s] my judgement, my competence, my intelligence[?]' (ibid.: 27). If this part were played by Kene himself, or one of the performer-musicians onstage, the metatheatrical struggle in Kene's conscious would still be clear. By utilizing archival audio material in a form of reconstructive pastiche, however, Kene creates a scenario in which not only is his producer telling him what will work but, by proxy, the most successful Black actor in Hollywood and, in later performances – arguably (during his term) – the most powerful Black man in the world, are enforcing upon him the requirements he must adhere to in order to be successful. There is an irony in the 'palatability' of both Freeman and Obama as those that impose the conditions upon Kene's success as both are 'acceptable', 'safe' expressions of Blackness (cf. Jackson 2014) to the white sensibility. Morgan Freeman was considered – at one point – the most 'trustworthy' celebrity in America (Pomerantz 2012) and Obama's campaign was famously concerned with the duality of his being 'characterized as a race-neutral candidate [to garner support across the white community] but when necessary emphasiz[ing] his blackness to maintain the support of the African American community' (Johnson et al. 2011: 135). Kene's reconstructive pastiche, here, therefore further problematizes the overarching questions regarding the agency of a Black storyteller within a predominantly white entertainment business.

At the end of Act One, Kene is continually challenged about his intentions behind his telling the story of Virus's experience in East London replicating white-friendly narratives of Black trauma. 'What about people who actually live this shit life, Arinzé?' (Kene 2018: 41), he is queried, 'Have you asked them how they feel about you telling this story?' (ibid.). In response to this, Kene produces a dictaphone, and the audience becomes privy to a recorded conversation between Kene and a man called Lucas. As we listen to the pair talk, it becomes clear that the events that Lucas describes – 'it started on the nightbus' (ibid.: 42) – are the exact events that Kene has fictionalized in the spoken-word excerpts throughout the piece so far. The character of Virus is revealed to be based on real-life interviewee Lucas, who sums up his view of the gentrification of his local area as ' "blood cells and viruses" stuff, it's just the way I see the world' (ibid.). The reveal is framed as a surprise to the audience and as a point scored for Kene in the continual battle fought between him and his critics throughout the piece. It also leads to an upturning of the Virus/Young-Black-Man versus Blood-Cell/White-Gentrifiers metaphor: 'I realised that I heard it wrong', states Kene, 'Lucas was saying that *he* was the blood cell and *they* were the viruses ... If viruses invade the body ... Lucas and I have witnessed viruses invade our area' (ibid.: 47). As such, Kene renames Virus (the fictional stand in for Lucas) as Blood Cell in the remainder of the tale. However, as soon as we begin Act Two, the power lent to Lucas/Blood Cell's story through this proven veracity is immediately challenged by Kene's friends Raymond and Donna – their voicemail re-enacted again by *Misty*'s musician duo, Coke and McCleod: 'So what', says Raymond, 'It doesn't matter if it's a true story. It doesn't make it okay to tell a story, cos it's true' (ibid.: 44). He argues that Kene is feeding on the commodification of Black Trauma for white audiences, writing 'just another hood story' (ibid.), notwithstanding the authenticity of the narrative. In another oscillation between these critical polarities, Kene counters:

> I don't think you can dismiss Lucas's story on account of…
> it being depressing as fuck.
> I grew up with him and,
> he'd never been to see any of my work and when I asked why …
> Well … you know what he said would make him come to the theatre?
> He wanted to see himself there. (ibid.: 46)

Is he so wrong, Kene asks, for putting Lucas's story on the stage? Don't people like Lucas deserve to have their stories told, too? (ibid.). Neither his friends, or Kene himself, have an answer.

We then return once again to Kene's staging of Lucas/Blood Cell's tale through the energetic track 'Geh-Geh', which the script instructs is performed as though it's *'the moment an hour into a hip-hop concert where the artist is drenched in sweat, the stage is theirs. The audience is theirs'* (ibid.: 61). Through the lyrics, Blood Cell reveals that, in a fit of anxiety-filled confusion as he evades police following his assault on the man on the night bus, he kidnaps his niece from her school and takes her to the local zoo. Here, the police inevitably catch up with him. As they Taser him and he drops to the ground, in all too familiar language, Blood Cell tells us that he is, 'Struggling to breathe/Geh-geh/They're folding me like a long sleeve/Geh-geh/My ears pop/Geh-geh/Everything stops' (ibid.: 65). The band abruptly halt playing, the house lights come on, Kene pulls the wire from the mic and, in another sudden tonal shift, we return to the recording on Kene's interview with Lucas, who describes the feeling of his being Tasered, before an impossible reveal: 'That's when I died' (ibid.: 66), Lucas tells us. On the recording, Kene is heard asking how, if Lucas is dead, he could be talking to him now.

>   **Lucas**   I don't know haha. You wrote this. You tell me.
>   **Arinzé** (*on Dictaphone*)   I wrote this?
>   **Lucas**   Yes.
>   **Arinzé** (*on Dictaphone*)   So, I just made all this depressing shit up. … WHY?
>   **Lucas**   Haha I don't know. Ask yourself. (ibid.: 66–7)

The live, onstage Kene is now addressed by his previous/fictional/recorded self; 'Arinzé, why man?'. There is a pause. 'I don't know', the onstage Kene replies (ibid.: 67). In an escalation of the conflict between Kene's desire to tell a certain story and 'interrogating the conundrum Kene faces as a Black artist' (Kumar 2023), Kene has finally turned on himself. It is an seemingly inescapable conundrum that is sincerely addressed in a section that serves to de-authenticate the original reasons Kene offered for telling the story of Lucas – now revealed as entirely fictitious – and further centre Kene's own conflict within this challenge, all achieved through a moment that is inherently ridiculous – a fictional/past recording of Kene able to somehow traverse time and confront to the real/future version of himself onstage. And yet, the staging of this impossible moment allows the centring of the sincerity of Kene's inner conflict. Utilizing the inherently silly enables Kene to be completely sincere.

Kene's metatheatrical, lyrical storytelling oscillates between such ironic-sincere aesthetics, between the real and the fake, between the impassioned and the hopeless, between a Black Trauma play and a play centring on the problematics of Black Trauma plays. It offers no easy answers and never settles on one opinion. When Kene, as Blood Cell, is hitting the crescendo of a particularly impassioned track about the redevelopment of Hackney – 'Call it virus invasion/Call it gentrification … It's nothing but modern-day colonisation' (Kene 2018: 54) – he is suddenly interrupted by the ringing of a mobile phone in the auditorium. He breaks character and confronts an audience member, asking them to switch it off before he 'realises' that the noise is coming from his phone somewhere onstage. 'Ah shit, my bad', he tells us, 'I was texting at the interval' (ibid.: 55). The scripted phone call that immediately follows reveals that this is all, in fact, part of the show, and the seemingly embarrassing interruption of Kene's incredibly heartfelt call-to-arms against the purging of the community from his local area serves to intercut the sincerity with an ironic laugh. Kene's structuring of *Misty's* metatheatrical aesthetic means that he is never able to latch onto a definite position in an argument that gradually becomes more complex. Instead, reflecting Vermeulen and van den Akker's metamodern oscillation, both Kene and the piece are constantly pulled as by 'a pendulum swinging between 2, 3, 5, 10, innumerable poles' (Vermeulen and van den Akker 2010: 6). Kene does not allow himself, or the audience, to hold a specific position on the debate. However, within such an 'intellectual discussion' (Meyer 2023), Kene is careful to always centre himself – and his own felt experience as a playwright, a performer, a Londoner and a Black man – throughout this oscillation. This comes to a head when Kene responds angrily to a two-pronged attack from his Producer and his Agent (who, in keeping with the continual undercutting of sincerity by always including an ironic, metatheatrical element, is voiced through a pastiche of audio clips of Maya Angelou) about what they see as the Black playwright's 'attitude' problem – 'can't this just fucking exist? … Can't it just be a play? Can a play from a person like me just be a fucking play already?' (Kene 2018: 58). Through Kene's use of metatheatrical storytelling, centred throughout on his own felt experience as a Black British playwright and performer, *Misty* questions the purpose, impact and responsibility of stories – and who is allowed to tell them – whilst simultaneously extolling the power of such stories on the stage.

The audience as storytellers at the end of the world: YESYESNONO's *we were promised honey!* and Nathan Ellis's *work.txt*

We sit around a bare, circular stage, waiting for the performance to start. A man, sitting next to us, has begun telling us a story about someone who once stole a plane. Slowly, the rest of the audience quietens their pre-show chat to listen. He finishes the story and speaks to the entire audience. 'The show that we're about to do,' says the man 'is the story of our future … It's a story we are going to tell together.' A pause. 'I hope that sounds okay' (*we were promised honey!* 2022).

Commissioned by Soho Theatre, with further support from New Diorama Theatre and Arts Council England, *we were promised honey!* was the fourth production by YESYESNONO – made up of writer/performer and producer duo Sam Ward and Rhian Davies respectively. The show premiered at the

Edinburgh Festival Fringe in 2022 before transferring to the Soho Theatre for a limited run that winter, touring throughout the United Kingdom and transferring to 59E59 Theatres in New York City the following year. The entire premise of *we were promised honey!*, written and performed by Ward with additional directing by Atri Najeree, is based around Ward playing a version of himself – Sam – telling the audience stories. Through Sam's gentle and reassuring inclusion of audience participation throughout this, the piece centres the act of storytelling as being one of embodied collectiveness based on the joint process of sharing and of communal trust. We are constantly reminded, through both the structure of the piece and the themes within Sam's stories, that we are here, together, in this moment – centring, protecting and solidifying our felt experience as audience members watching/participating-in/creating this performance. However, such a collective feeling is continually underpinned by the knowledge, and continual reminders, of the fact that this show will end. The stories Ward (and the audience) tell(s) all revolve, in various ways, around the first story Sam tells us – the real-life tale of 29-year-old Richard Russell, an airport worker in Seattle who, on the tenth of August 2018, stole a seventy-six-seater commercial airliner and flew it over the skies of the city for over an hour. Although he was not a pilot, Russell performed barrel rolls and loop-the-loops that the CEO of the airline later described as 'awesome' and explained that he was able to control the plane because of his time spent playing flight simulator videogames. Air traffic control was concerned; when they asked him if he knew how to land the plane safely, Russell replied that he hadn't thought that far ahead yet.

At this point, Sam pauses in his telling of this story, and we are left – for the time being – to imagine the inevitable ending. 'As the writer of this show', Sam tells us, 'I want to tell you now that the story we're going to tell, the story of our future/Doesn't have a happy ending' (ibid.: 10). Considering he has now – in his own words – spoiled the ending, Sam gives us a choice: do we want to continue with the story even though we know that it will not end well? As reviewer Sallon describes, Sam proposes that 'we can sit here in silence until the advertised runtime of the show is over, or, even though you already know it's going to end badly, you can hear what happens next' (Sallon 2022). Sam 'asks us to take a breath[, to] give our consent to start the story. In these moments,' describes Pereira, 'the collective energy is palpable' (Pereira 2022). All it takes, for a choice to be made, is for one audience member to say, 'I would like to begin'. 'I would like to begin' somebody says, and the show begins. It is through centring the inevitability of the fact that it will not end well for us (Ward 2022: 10) that we become constantly aware of a future that, as Katie Hawthorne surmises in her introduction to the published playscript, 'isn't a fixed point, but somehow mutable' (ibid.: ii) as Sam begins to tell us stories about our own im/possible future(s) (see Figure 5.6). He starts with the immediate, seemingly quite convincingly possible futures following this performance:

> Three minutes after the end of this show one of you will still be in your seat staring thoughtfully at the stage, hoping that somebody on the other side will notice you and think, 'Look how deep in thought that person is; I bet they're having interesting thoughts'. (ibid.: 16)

Sam's telling then shifts further into the future, where more speculative, abstract and increasingly ridiculous futures are laid out for us, such as the implied fact that 'in forty years one of you will wake up one morning filled with the divine revelation that you are the Christ' (ibid.: 17). These stories begin to, as Hawthorne describes, splinter the audience 'into shards of possibility. We're the protagonists … and with every prophecy, dispensed with the jaunty yet cryptic tone of a tabloid horoscope, there is the option to claim it – to think, maybe that one's about me' (ibid.: ii). These prophecies shift into three longer stories – each involving at least one audience member existing in a future that Sam projects for them, each begun with the repeated

Figure 5.6 Sam Ward in *we were promised honey!* (additional directing by Atri Najeree, the Paines Plough Roundabout @ Summerhall, 2022)

Source: Mihaela Bodlovic. Reproduced with kind permission from © Mihaela Bodlovic.

choice as to whether we – as a collective – want to continue. In his gentle encouragement towards this post-immersive participation, Ward builds on YESYESNONO's established 'ethos of care, and a practice of taking the audience extremely seriously' (ibid.: iii). As Karen Marquis describes in her review of the piece at the Edinburgh Festival Fringe, this 'direction of the audience is so clear and direct that it inspires trust' (Marquis 2022).

The first of these three gently participatory stories implicates a volunteer in a projected future – fifty years after the end of the show – in which they, through a rather ridiculous set of circumstances, eventually end up carrying a pregnant person on their back to the top of a lighthouse where, 'using nothing but your hands and a manual on dolphin pregnancies you will have found in a cupboard downstairs' (Ward 2022: 21), they will help deliver a baby. The story is absurd, and inherently comedic, and yet – at the climax of this silliness – Sam reiterates that 'in fifty years you will be holding a brand new human being, [participant's name]. A little thing that you will stand up to support with your arm like this' (ibid.), Ward motions as though holding a new-born child in the crook of his arm and looks down towards the imaginary baby. 'And for reasons that you don't completely understand', Sam reveals, the audience member will tell this new-born that 'by the time you're grown, this world will be a better place for you to be' (ibid.). It is a moment of stillness at the end of Sam's energetic description of an absurd im/possible future that promises – in some small way – hopeful optimism, despite the knowledge, underpinning all of this, of inevitable tragedy. By focusing on one of the arguably most intensely *human* experiences – that of holding an entirely brand new and helpless baby in your arms, and the inherent future of a life-yet-to-be-lived that is implied by the bodily presence of this tiny human – Ward injects a sobering moment of sincere conflict between hope and hopelessness into what has, so far, been an inventive, incongruous tale underpinned by a (performance of) belief in a hope that we inherently know to be false: 'When you say those words on top of a lighthouse in fifty years,' states Sam, 'they will *feel* very true' (ibid., emphasis added). Even though, as will become clear, this is not the case.

Sam snaps out of it. 'That was the start', he announces, 'Went well, I thought. Thank you,' he addresses the previous volunteer, 'I thought you were very interesting' (ibid.: 23). The show continues along the same lines, with Sam fluctuating between continuing to tell chapters of the inevitably tragic tale of Richard Russell's flight before asking the audience if they would like to continue, and then gently imbricating another participant in the ensuing tale of their possible future. As he continues, Sam's storytelling delves further into a forthcoming dystopia that is at once terrifyingly real in its focus on the impending devastation of the climate crisis and simultaneously satirically absurd. We, the audience, are projected to live for hundreds, if not thousands of years. One of us will become a CEO with an office at the top floor of a skyscraper that now sits in empty, uninhabitable desert. Another will become a security guard for an underground shopping mall, tasked with protecting the valuable supplies of mini fridges. Towards the climax of this dystopian absurdity, there is a particularly touching moment in which two audience members are asked to each read, unprepared, from a script. Through their dialogue, we find that their story weaves together several disconnected threads that have been running throughout Sam's storytelling over the course of the previous hour. According to the text they read, after meeting for the first time at this precise moment, reading these exact lines, the pair go on to be friends, then lovers, then spouses until – hundreds of years in the future – one of them abruptly leaves. As they read out this dialogue, they simultaneously perform their own existence at the time of their first meeting and, paradoxically, their later meeting several thousand years in the future, standing in an underground mall between different models of mini fridges after an incredibly long period apart:

A   ... This building used to be a theatre. This is the exact same spot where you and I met for the first time.
B   Did we meet in a theatre? I don't remember that ... I don't really like plays.
A   I don't think you liked this one.
    Both of us had to read something onstage. (Ward 2022: 43)

In a reflection of our ghost-like presence in Robert's spare room alongside the company of *Lights Over Tesco Car Park*, this moment implicates us – both through its form and its content – simultaneously within the reality of the show we are experiencing and an imagined im/possible future. 'Tell me that you love me', one participant asks of the other, 'It doesn't have to be real; you can just imagine it' (ibid.: 45). It is a sentiment that is true across both realities – in the pair's imagined future, in which they reconnect thousands of years after a failed relationship, and in their unrehearsed performance of Ward's pre-prepared lines.

As *we were promised honey!* continues, both Richard Russell's flight and our own imagined futures become increasingly overwhelming in their continual slide towards catastrophe. And yet, continuing to gently guide us through these disastrous tales, each time Sam asks us if we want to continue, one audience member always answers 'yes'. As promised, Russell's story ends in tragedy as he fatally crashes. Whilst Russell was living wholly in the moment, this was underscored by the inevitable consequences of his actions.

On a grander scale, of course, this is understandably representative, in Ward's performance, of humanity in the Anthropocene. 'It's exhausting, isn't it?', Sam asks the audience:

> I always get to this point in the story ... where I want to say something different to what's actually written down ... that Richard never crashed ... I want to pretend that things got better. But I can't. Because that's not how the story goes ... So instead I keep going with his story/Just as we keep going with ours. Not because we think things will get better ... But because/What choice do we have but to keep going, even when we already know the end? (ibid.: 47–8)

Sam's admission, here, is at once a surrender to reality and to the structure of a pre-written script – that, of course, also paradoxically contains Ward's (written) aversion to continuing the telling of the tale. In an echo of metamodernism's inherent emergence from postmodernism's binding to Fukuyama's proclamation of the end of history, Ward frames his impulse against such surrender as in opposition to those 'that say that history is finished, that say everything that could ever happen has already happened, that say the end has already been decided, the end is here already, that we only have to wait' (ibid.: 47). But, despite Ward's sentiment, as Richard Russell's story ended in disaster, so must ours. At the penultimate section of *we were promised honey!* Sam takes us through an increasingly overwhelming overview of the next hundred, thousand, million, billion, trillion years following the end of this show. We hear glimpses of imagined, im/possible futures that oscillate between the terrifyingly portentous – describing how the humans that are left will watch the Anthropocene collapse – and the hilariously absurd – describing how, twenty-thousand years into the future, a member of the audience will finally receive a text from their crush apologizing for their slow reply (Ward 2022: 54). These overlapping moments, fluctuating between im/possibility and hope/lessness, become increasingly overwhelming as they interweave with the design of Carmel Smickersgill's prodigious sound and David Doyle's subtle lighting until:

'We made it!', Sam tells us (ibid.: 58). It is the end of the show. 'Congratulations' (ibid.). He lets us know the current time, happy that we are on schedule. He tells us what the weather is like outside. He reminds us of our immediate futures – that we will exit this space in roughly two minutes. But, for now, we are here, together, in this space, 'waiting for the show to end' (ibid.). And then, in both a dramatic contrast to the overwhelming sense of the incoming and devastating end of it all that Sam has taken us through, John Denver's song *Take Me Home, Country Roads* starts quietly playing, and Sam proposes that singing along to this might be a nice way to end. Whilst Poltergeist presented one final switch from the sincerity of our felt experience as we danced together to David Bowie's *Life on Mars* at the end of *Lights Over Tesco Car Park* in the ironic reveal that the show was based on a lie, Ward, instead, ends *we were promised honey!* on a somewhat cheesy – almost clichéd – moment of simple joy and connection – of a group of people singing along to a song that we all (at least) know the chorus of. Through this unassuming act, Ward provides a moment of pure, simple, unadulterated togetherness before the inevitable dissipating of the audience as we leave the theatre and continue our separate journeys towards our preordained unhappy end. Perhaps Marquis best describes this oscillation between together/apartness, between hope/lessness, between the present and the im/possible futures yet/never to come when they state, in their review of the piece, that 'we're not watching this, we're in it, travelling to the last moment we will spend alive. And when that moment arrives, the show does something so moving with a song, that it's as life affirming as it is devastating' (Marquis 2022).

The stage is filled with oversized yellow Jenga blocks stacked in precarious arrangements – half finished towers, bridges to nowhere, collapsed house-like structures. We sit facing these ruins. There is no one onstage. Instead, a woman speaks from the audience. She is reading lines that are projected onto the upstage wall. She says that two volunteers raise their hands. They do. She says that they wait for two copies of the script to finish printing. A pause. We all wait for the printer – which is also onstage – to complete its job. The woman says that the two volunteers take these scripts and position themselves onstage. The volunteers do this. The woman says that the audience imagine an office. We imagine an office (Ellis 2022: 14).

work.txt, written by Nathan Ellis, premiered at the Vaults Festival, London in March 2020. Due to the imminent arrival of the global pandemic, the piece was reworked as a Zoom-based performance (aptly retitled *work_from_home*) later that year before returning to the stage in a revised version, at the Soho Theatre in spring 2022. My focus in this analysis is on this final, third iteration which has toured internationally – translated into Italian, German and Portuguese for subsequent runs. Advertised 'as a show about work, but the workers aren't here, so it's down to you' (Ellis 2022), *work.txt* is essentially a performance with no actors, initially pitched by Ellis to producer Emily Davis as a desire to 'make a show about work that is performed entirely by the audience' (Unlocked with Olivia Bright 2020: 09:51). Inspired by a combination of David Graeber's *Bullshit Jobs* (2015) and Mark Fisher's writing on labour within late-stage capitalism (Fisher 2009), Ellis became interested in the work that was happening in a theatre when there were no actors (Thompson 2022), as well as the 'always on' attitude of contemporary work life – particularly in the post-pandemic work landscape, and concerns about automation: '[if] jobs can be done by a robot, why are they worth saving,' says Ellis, '[if] they're not a job that actually gives satisfaction in any meaningful way, and the robot could do them better[?]' (ibid.).

The form of *work.txt* forces the audience to become collaborative storytellers. As we enter the auditorium, we are greeted by a projection on the far wall which not only instructs us what to do and what to read out loud but also who should be doing this work. The piece begins with the following projected:

A member of the audience reads the following out
This is a play.
It is performed entirely by us …

The whole audience
Cool!
This is exciting!
I love it when a performance involves participation. (Ellis 2022: 5)

Whilst we begin as a collective, we soon 'learn and infer more about each other as we tell a story together' (Solloway 2022), with the projector soon asking only certain demographics of people to read particular lines; those who work in an office, those who are self-employed, people who earn over thirty thousand pounds a year, people who earn less than thirty thousand pounds a year ('Don't worry!', this latter group are instructed to say, 'That's ok! We aren't bitter!' [Ellis 2022: 6]). As Sanders explains, it feels like there's a 'surge of excitement', within the audience as we discover our 'collective control' (Solloway 2022). True to the metamodern sensibility running throughout this collection of performances, though, *work.txt* is quick to exhibit an awareness of critiques about its own form when it addresses the 'people who would rather this were a normal play and are already bored of this and were maybe brought by someone else and are maybe hoping this play will be quite short and were absolutely not informed it was going to be like this' (Ellis 2022: 6), or when the following scripted exchange is read out:

An enthusiastic member of the audience
I hoped it would be like this and that we would be involved for once!

A pessimist replies
I'd just like to say

For the record
I am not having fun yet. (ibid.: 7)

Quite quickly, the dichotomy between the 'feeling' that we are participating in this collective storytelling and the fact that all we are doing is responding to instructions provided to us onscreen leads to the audience 'questioning' who is in charge: 'There's someone back there pressing the buttons to control lights and things. They must be in charge' (ibid.: 8). The stage manager, to whom this was addressed, responds that they're not responsible. The audience, reading from the projected script, then question the usher, who confesses that this isn't really their thing, and they'd much rather be at home watching *Gilmore Girls* on Netflix. Of course, all of this interaction is read out by the audience, the stage manager and the usher from the pre-written projections that appear one by one on the back wall – and the stage manager addresses this fact whilst, of course, still reading the following from the projected script: 'In fact, being honest, I'm not even in charge of what I'm saying now. I haven't even seen *Gilmore Girls*. It's just what's projected for the stage manager character to say' (ibid.: 9). *work.text* is at once focused on the actual experience that the collective audience (as well as the actual stage manager and usher) are currently going through, whilst – at the same time – being entirely fictitious. At this point, the piece has not only blurred the boundaries between spectator and performer, and between theatre-worker and performer, but between the performance and the performed, between the real and the fictitious.

Through this oscillation between the un/real, a story begins to emerge, and one audience member unwittingly becomes the main character in this tale, playing the role of a worker who – at the start of the working day – decides to simply lie down in the lobby of their work building. Throughout the narrative, this action becomes viral – travelling around the world, and to various characters performed intermittently by audience members, in the form of an internet meme. It feels hope/lessly apt that the action of withdrawing their labour – which, in the show's narrative, destabilizes the company as the character is the one employee with access to certain important computer files – does not instigate a revolution, but, instead, is reduced to just one of many images shared across social media that day. Intercutting this main narrative, smaller stories are performed by pairs of volunteers reading scripts from, variously, the back-wall projections, the printer onstage or from lines fed through headphones. As this participation develops, the work the piece asks the audience to undertake means that, as Solloway (2022) describes, we begin to 'feel responsibility to [our] fellow audience members to make the show a good one'. However, the piece remains paradoxically critical of this act. When two audience members portray the role of an art curator and a gallery attendant who have just become aware of the viral image of the main character's prostrate protest, the curator suggests that this 'art project' should be replicated in the gallery or, even better – 'we could use this as some sort of engagement project, so that people can engage with the art, requesting people, suggesting to them, that they might engage, by lying down' (Ellis 2022: 30). Such is the ironic self-awareness of the text, as this is exactly what the text has already asked an audience member to do in order to represent the main character. However, the self-criticism of the show then goes further when the projection instructs 'a person who hasn't spoken very much yet' to say the following:

> Can I just say something. I'm still working from home, you know, so I came to this show to try and have fun. To take my mind off things. I love the theatre but this absolutely isn't theatre. (ibid.: 32)

A 'team-player' is then instructed to respond with:

> It said at the beginning that nobody was in charge but all these lines are scripted for us. Even those criticisms were obviously scripted. I'd like someone to say something unscripted now. (ibid.)

There is a pause, until the projection informs the audience that they feel 'a deep discomfort' (ibid.). We are reminded of our paradoxical position within this experience – that we are at once in charge and beholden to the instructions fed to us through the projector. Even in our (scripted) reactions to (un)scripted moments, instructions tell us what to do, what to say and, now, what to feel. 'What if we all refused to play along?', questions Solloway, suggesting that it is 'certainly an option, the right to withhold labour [and the] thought crosses our hive mind' (Solloway 2022) but, inevitably, even this is addressed by the projected instructions – 'Maybe,' the text on the wall states, 'everyone gets up and walks out' (Ellis 2022: 32–3). In a way that feels inevitable, though, we don't. *work.txt* serves to replicate, as Saville describes, 'the sense of togetherness that comes from pulling together to perform a task, even as it makes the nature of work itself feel more and more problematised and futile' (Saville 2022). Throughout its metatheatrical, post-immersive collective storytelling manifest as silly play, the piece is sincerely critical of the work practices it interrogates and its own form. 'I have to be back at work on Monday,' a member of the audience is instructed to shout at one point, disrupting the scene that is currently being performed by two other audience members on the stage, 'real work, not like you standing around chatting about thoughts and feelings, about whether work is good or bad or pointless.

Of course I hate my job. Everyone does. But you have to work. What else would you do?' (Ellis 2022: 27). However, as Anna James's review of the piece describes, the show continuously 'points out that for all the critique of modern work, we are still a group of people doing what we're told, following instructions' (James 2022).

Alongside getting the audience to work as prosumers (as per Harvie 2013: 29), *work.txt* also inherently centres our felt experience throughout this participation. In what has fascinatingly become a theme throughout this collection of metamodern pieces, following the ending of the penultimate scene of the show – which sees two volunteers pretending to be on a cruise ship – the opening lyrics to Celine Dion's *My Heart Will Go On* are projected, in time, on the wall. Karaoke music kicks in and we find ourselves joining together to sing along to that song from Titanic. Following this ridiculous collective act, we return to the audience member lying on the stage – representing the protest action of the main character. They are instructed to tell us they would like to stop – reading out dozens of reasons for this desire that oscillate between the seemingly serious and the ostensibly surreal: 'I want to stop because I tripped and wanted it to look like I did it on purpose … because I don't eat gluten … because I am so lonely … because this is stupid … because life is too short' (Ellis 2022: 44). Their requests speak at once to the work they are currently undertaking – that of lying on the floor and reading these words to an audience – and to our collective experience of work within late-stage capitalism. When they eventually do stop, we are told (by the projector) that the printer will now take over the work. Onstage, the printer begins printing blank sheets of paper as a text-to-voice recording – performing some form of printer-based-Artificial-Intelligence – takes us through to the end of the story. Further mirroring the finale of *we were promised honey!*, *work.txt* then similarly descends towards a dystopian future that is at once scarily, realistically prophetic and absurd. 'Two hundred years after the end of the working day', the printer informs us, 'Jeff Bezos dies on Mars' (ibid.: 47) and 'Four thousand years after the end of the working day, nature stays late at the office again' (ibid.). The audience are now obsolete, the machines have now taken over the work – have taken over the storytelling – until they, too, eventually switch themselves off. 'Applause', the printer demands (ibid.: 48) as its lights blink for the final time.

Conclusion

The performances described throughout this chapter exhibit a shared central sensibility – an embodied *feeling* – that differs from previous 'traditional' postmodern practice in ways that reflect a metamodern cultural structure of feeling, indicating a methodological and aesthetic shift beyond postmodernity whilst continuing to make use of certain postmodern strategies. The performances' applications of metamodernism follow the form of metamodern theatrical practice as defined in Chapter 4, with each of these performances exhibiting the overarching sensibilities of oscillation between modern and postmodern predilections and a concern with centring, solidifying or developing the felt experience of the writer/performer or the audience/participant. These sensibilities are manifest in several aesthetic strategies used variously throughout the productions: an interest in the authentic; the use of metatheatrical devices; a centring of the act of storytelling; appropriating and utilizing disparate forms or cultural artefacts through a form of reconstructive pastiche; post-immersive audience participation and dialogical engagement; and the aesthetics of the quirky. Additionally, these millennial-led productions explore several narrative themes that also exhibit intersecting millennial and metamodern concerns: that of believing in certain narratives as if they were true, the time-twisting of being haunted by lost futures and the desire for belonging and community within an increasingly polarized and individually complex and lonely contemporary experience.

Central to each of these performances is a metamodern re-application of the act of storytelling – and the power of stories – as a fundamental theatrical tenet. This metamodern (re)appreciation of storytelling is used variously: as a metatheatrical device in which to consider the development of the story being told, as a collective act of post-immersive participation or as a way in which to highlight the inherent in/authentic paradox within metatheatrical theatre. Each performance exhibits a shift away from postmodern pastiche, distancing and disconnect, towards an attempt at the re-application of sometimes disparate elements and forms of performance that engender a centring of the felt experience of the theatre maker and/or audience that would not be able to be expressed in such a way without the metaphorical 'space' that is created by the tent-pole effect of metamodern reconstructive pastiche. Such spaces-of-felt-experience become evident in the pieces focusing on moments of embodied (often emotional) connection and an engagement with the inherently communal act of theatre that is inherently concerned with honesty, authenticity and sincerity whilst *also* continuing to fluctuate to an opposing force of imitation, inauthenticity and irony. This is manifest in, for instance, the performances use of collaborative storytelling, or in the act of including an awareness of the audience's experience of the piece within the content and form of the piece itself, or – in the case of a number of these examples – in something as modest and unassuming as the simple act of a group of strangers coming together to dance or sing to a suitably clichéd pop song.

Perhaps the most accessibly evident metamodern aesthetic threaded throughout these performances, and that which clearly indicates a palpable shift away from previous postmodern predilections, is the central oscillation between disparate polarities that impacts, and is created by, both the form and content of each. This may be evident through their forms oscillating between connect and disconnect or between the performed and the real – often engendering a liminal space of un/reality that consciously asks us (often clearly and out loud) to not suspend disbelief, per se, but allow ourselves to (paradoxically) believe at the same time as accepting that everything is fake. Metamodern theatre exploits this paradoxical un/reality – and our own comprehension of this – to deliver work that can be at once silly and serious, at once ironic and sincere, at once wholly detached and wholly emotional. It offers a place in which we can(not) believe in aliens; in which we exist – at once – within multiple layers of (un)reality; in which we can come together, for a brief moment, and both wholly ironically and wholly sincerely enjoy the act of communal karaoke.

Such oscillation may also be evident in the content of such performances, with the examples here exhibiting an integral oscillation between an attempted enjoyment in our experiencing the present moment and the pervasive apprehension, even terror, about the incoming future. Or it might be evident in the fluctuation between a hopeful application of theatre and storytelling as a power for good and the inescapable understanding that of course theatre (in *these* forms, at *this* time and in *these* circumstances) is not an affective political or social force. These shows are ironest and hope/less, they offer no easy answers and they are questioning and critical of their own existence. Yet they continue to offer hope in the power of possibilities *as if* such theatre could answer these questions/could change the world/could affect its audience – even if we expect it to fail. At the centre of this hope/less metamodern theatrical practice is an im/possible strive towards an affective connection between those in the theatre space at the time of the encounter (and sometimes beyond) when, outside of this space, outside of this time, we are increasingly and overwhelmingly disconnected. But, for now, they propose, in this moment at least, in a space that is at once now and not-now, here and not-here, un/real, and hope/less, we sing, we dance, we perform and we join in, together.

Afterword: (Im)Possible Futures

This book has sought to understand how contemporary theatre is reflective of and affected by, as well as – in turn – influences and develops, the metamodern structure of feeling. It argues for the applicability of the term metamodernism within mainstream theatre scholarship and criticism, suggesting its usage as a heuristic label or shared language in which we can understand contemporary theatre's position of porosity and power in a post-postmodern cultural landscape. As Elinor Fuchs sought for a language through which to give words to her experience of the shifts in theatrical aesthetics in the latter half of the twentieth century, I too was seeking for a language through which to describe the shifts I was observing in the first part of the twenty-*first* century. In detailing the metamodern in relation to contemporary theatre throughout this volume, metamodernism now provides that language.

This book, however, is not a manifesto. I do not propose that theatre makers finish this volume, put it back on the shelf and return to the studio with the express aspiration to create intentionally metamodern theatre. Metamodern theatre does not strive to be metamodern – it simply is. My use of the term relates to work that is created within a particular cultural turning point and that responds to, affects and challenges particular shifts through and beyond the postmodern episteme within wider contemporary culture. As argued throughout this book, whilst metamodern theatre is not the express domain of millennial theatre makers, there is an inevitable synchronicity between the developmental shift from postmodernity to metamodernity and the formative experiences of the millennial generation from the Children of Postmodernism to the young adults of the permacrisis. In this sense, metamodern theatre is not *only* created by millennial theatre makers, and not *all* millennial theatre makers make metamodern theatre. However, the influence of the social, political, economic, educational, cultural and generational positioning of the millennial generation has materialized in aesthetics, strategies and preoccupations that serve to enhance, build upon, reflect and emphasize metamodern elements within their work. As such, when we understand both as structures of feeling, the metamodern and the millennial – particularly within the field of theatre – are inherently interconnected. It is important to note, however, that the examples of theatre analysed throughout this book would still exist as is without the nomenclature metamodernism. My application of the term is descriptive rather than prescriptive. I do not seek to push any particular theatrical or artistic agenda or indicate that theatre created by millennial theatre makers is necessarily 'better' or more 'developed' than that made by other generations, or those whose work still distinctly resides comfortably within the realm of postmodern performance practice. Instead, I appropriate the term metamodernism as a heuristic label through which to define, discuss and delineate shifts that have already happened within contemporary theatre.

I have subtitled this short afterword '(Im)Possible Futures' in reference to the preoccupation, within the millennial structure of feeling, towards hauntological lost futures and, within the metamodern structure of feeling, of a recurrent strive towards utopia despite a seemingly inherent impossibility of achieving such. However, the title also refers to the impossibility of predicting the fluid, future developments of theatrical practice. Metamodernism – as defined in this volume – is an attempt to discern a structure of feeling throughout contemporary performances created in the context of a certain time. Whilst the effects of the coronavirus pandemic on the landscape of theatre and performance are yet to be fully realized, the economic and cultural ramifications will undeniably shift certain economic structures, areas of accessibility and cultural sensibilities. Therefore, whether metamodernism will continue to be a viable framework of understanding these sensibilities remains to be seen. However, the impact of recent changes to Gen Z's educational, political, social and cultural experiences means that their formative adult years will be affected by similar or – in all likelihood – much worse crises than affected us millennials at a similar age. As such, the metamodern tendencies displayed in the theatre practice in this book, that – in some cases – are direct responses to the millennial structure of feeling, may continue to be replicated by an emerging generation of theatre makers whose experience of generational precarity and loss is even more amplified than that of the millennials. Or, of course, such structures may soon be supplanted by something entirely new, developed in response to such circumstances. At this point, however, the oscillatory and paradoxical nature of metamodern theatre appears to be thriving, with shows such as Hannah Maxwell's semi-autobiographical *Nan, Me and Barbara Pravi* (2023) – 'Entirely fictional. And completely true' (Camden People's Theatre 2023) – and Adam Lenson's similarly semi-autobiographical, multiversal-lost-futures-obsessed *Anything That We Wanted to Be* (2023) becoming standout hits at the Edinburgh Festival Fringe at the time of writing, indicating a continual development of metamodern performance practice beyond this volume. The often-repeated metaphor positions theatre as a mirror to society. As we continue to exist within the paradoxically positioned metamodern episteme, developments in theatre will also reflect this oscillatory, contradictory existence that is at once ironic and sincere, apathetic and optimistic, together and apart, honest and fake, hopeful and hopeless.

References

A Younger Theatre. (2010) 'Forced Entertainment: Too Forced?'. *A Younger Theatre*. https://www.ayoungertheatre.com/forced-entertainment-too-forced/ (accessed 15 August 2023).

Abramson, Seth. (2015) *Metamodernism, #5: Reading Frederic Jameson Against Mas'ud Zavarzadeh*. https://metamoderna.org/situating-zavarzadean-metamodernism-5-reading-frederic-jameson-against-masud-zavarzadeh/ (accessed 9 April 2024).

Abramson, Seth. (2018) *On Metamodernism*. https://medium.com/@Seth_Abramson/on-metamodernism-926fdc55bd6a (accessed 15 August 2023).

Ahmed, Kamal. (2018) 'Up to a Third of Millennials "Face Renting Their Entire Life"', *BBC*, Tuesday 17 April. https://www.bbc.com/news/business-43788537 (accessed 16 August 2023).

All We Ever Wanted Was Everything. (2017) [Theatrical Production] Middle Child. Dir. Paul Smith. Hull: The Welly, 16–17 June.

Allin, Eve. (2018) 'Edinburgh Review: *Lights Over Tesco Car Park* at Pleasance Jack Dome', *Exuent Magazine*, Sunday 5 August. https://exeuntmagazine.com/reviews/edinburgh-review-lights-over-tesco-car-park-pleasance-jack-dome/ (accessed 17 August 2023).

Andrewes, Thom. (2020) 'In Search of London's Independent Music Theatre Scenes', in M. Rebstock (ed.) *Freies Musiktheater in Europa / Independent Music Theatre in Europe*. Bielefeld: transcript Verlag, 111–46.

Anything That We Wanted To Be. (2023) [Theatrical Production] Adam Lenson. Dir. Hannah Moss. Edinburgh: Summerhall, Cairns Lecture Theatre, 2–27 August.

Arquilla, John. (2011) 'The (B)end of History', *Foreign Policy*, Thursday 15 December. https://foreignpolicy.com/2011/12/15/the-bend-of-history/ (accessed 16 August 2023).

ArtsProfessional. (2018) 'Data Map Reveals Levels of Arts Engagement across England'. https://www.artsprofessional.co.uk/news/data-map-reveals-levels-arts-engagement-across-england (accessed 17 August 2023).

Ashcroft, Ria. (2016) [Interview with the Author] Sunday 24 April 2016, in T. Drayton 'Towards a Listening Theatre: Metamodernism, Millennials and Contemporary Political Theatre'. PhD Thesis. University of East London.

Auslander, Phillip. (1997) *From Acting to Performance: Essays in Modernism and Postmodernism*. Abingdon: Routledge.

Auslander, Phillip. (2004) 'Postmodernism and Performance', in S. Conner (ed.) *The Cambridge Companion to Postmodernism*. Cambridge: Cambridge University Press, 97–115.

The Author. (2009) [Theatrical Production] Tim Crouch. Dir. Karl James and a smith. London: Royal Court Theatre Upstairs, 23–4 September.

Bakhtin, Mikhail. (1982) *The Dialogic Imagination: Four Essays*. Translated by M. Holquist. Texas: University of Texas Press.

Bakk, Ágnes. (2016) 'On Audience Outreach and Gaming: Conversation with Kirsty Sedgman', *The Theatre Times*, Saturday 3 December. https://thetheatretimes.com/audience-outreach-gaming-conversation-kirsty-sedgman/ (accessed 17 August 2023).

Barnes, Luke. (2017) *All We Ever Wanted Was Everything*. London: Oberon Modern Plays.

Barnes, Luke. (2018) 'Meet the Writer: Luke Barnes Q&A'. https://www.bushtheatre.co.uk/bushgreen/meet-the-writer-luke-barnes-qa/ (accessed 17 August 2023).

Barthes, Roland. (1967) *The Death of the Author*. Aspen: *The Magazine in a Box*, 5+6. Available at: http://www.ubu.com/aspen/aspen5and6/index.html (accessed 5 April 2024).

Bauman, Zygmunt. (2000) *Liquid Modernity*. Cambridge: Polity Press.

BBC News. (1999) 'UK Politics Tony Blair's Speech in Full', *BBC*, Tuesday 28 September. http://news.bbc.co.uk/1/hi/uk_politics/460009.stm (accessed 16 August 2023).

BBC News. ([1997] 2016) 'How David Bowie Used "Cut Ups" to Create Lyrics – BBC News' [YouTube Video]. https://youtu.be/6nlW4EbxTD8 (accessed 16 August 2023).

Beinborn, Nele Frieda. (2016) 'Places of Becoming: Gathering Urgency in Contemporary Political Theatre'. MA diss. Utrecht University. https://studenttheses.uu.nl/handle/20.500.12932/24406 (accessed 9 April 2024).

Bellaera, Lauren, Weinstein-Jones, Yana, Ilie, Sonia, and Baker, Sarah T. (2021) 'Critical Thinking in Practice: The Priorities and Practices of Instructors Teaching in Higher Education', *Thinking Skills and Creativity*, 41 (4): 100856.

Beneath the Albion Sky. (2013) [Theatrical Production] Write by Numbers/Eager Spark. Dir. Charlie Whitworth. Exeter, The Bike Shed Theatre, 4 June.

Best, Tamara. (2023) 'Inside '*Misty*,' the Play That Puts Gentrification on Trial: "The Play Isn't Saying 'You're Good,' 'You're Bad'— It's Shedding Light on What Gentrification Does to a Place," Playwright Arinzé Kene Says. "I Don't Want Anyone to Feel Judged."', *The Daily Beast*, Wednesday 22 March. https://www.proquest.com/docview/2789535454?accountid=17234&forcedol=true (accessed 17 August 2023).

Beswick, Katie. (2020) 'Feeling Working Class: Affective Class Identification and Its Implications for Overcoming Inequality', *Studies in Theatre and Performance*, 40 (3): 265–74.

Blake, Aaron. (2014) 'The "Participation Trophy" generation', *The Washington Post*, Wednesday 20 August. https://www.washingtonpost.com/news/the-fix/wp/2014/08/20/meet-the-participation-trophy-generation/ (accessed 22 August 2023).

Blumenau, Ralph. (2001) 'Kant and the Thing in Itself', *Philosophy Now*. https://philosophynow.org/issues/31/Kant_and_the_Thing_in_Itself (accessed 17 August 2023).

Bogart, Anne. (2014) *What's the Story: Essays about Art, Theater and Storytelling*. Abingdon, Routledge.

Bolton, Ruth N., Parasuraman, A., Hoefnagels, Ankie, Nanne, Migchels, Kabadayi, Sertan, Gruber, Thorsten, Komarova Loureiro, Yuliya and Solne, David (2013) 'Understanding Generation Y and Their Use of Social Media: A Review and Research Agenda'. *Journal of Service Management*, 24 (3): 245–67.

Bonar, Amy. (2017) '*All We Ever Wanted Was Everything* (Middle Child)', *Three Weeks Edinburgh*, Sunday 27 August. https://threeweeksedinburgh.com/article/all-we-ever-wanted-was-everything-middle-child/ (accessed 17 August 2023).

Bourriaud, Nicolas. (2005) *Keynote Speech: Modern, Postmodern, Altermodern?*, Art Association of Australia & New Zealand Conference, 7 July, Sydney.

Bourriaud, Nicolas. (ed.) (2009) *Altermodern. Tate Triennial 2009*. London: Tate Publishing.

Bowie-Sell, Daisy. (2017) 'Edinburgh Review: *All We Ever Wanted Was Everything* (Summerhall)', *Whats On Stage*, Wednesday 9 August. https://www.whatsonstage.com/news/edinburgh-review-all-we-ever-wanted-was-everything-summerhall_44328/ (accessed 17 August 2023).

Bradfield, Jack. (2018) *Lights Over Tesco Car Park*. London: Samuel French.

Brief Interviews with Hideous Men. (2012) [Theatrical Production] Andy Holden and David Raymond Conroy. Dir. Andy Holden and David Raymond Conroy. London, ICA, 30–31 August.

Britton, Charles. (2017) '"Lights Over Tesco Carpark" Review – "Equal Parts Inspired and Bonkers"', *Cherwell*, Wednesday 8 November. https://cherwell.org/2017/11/08/review-lights-over-tesco-carpark/ (accessed 17 August 2023).

Broadribb, Benjamin. (2022) 'Lockdown Shakespeare and the Metamodern Sensibility', in G. K. Allred, B. Broadribb, and E. Sullivan (eds), *Lockdown Shakespeare: New Evolutions in Performance and Adaptation*. London, Bloomsbury, 45–65.

Brown, Jennifer, Apostolova, Vyara, Barton, Cassie, Bolton, Paul, Dempsey, Noel, Harari, Dan, Hawkins, Oliver, McGuinness, Feargal, and Powell, Andrew. (2017) Briefing Paper Number CBP7946, 11 April 2017, 'Millennials'. London: House of Commons Library.

Brown, Wendy. (1999) 'Resisting Left Melancholy', *boundary 2*, 26 (3): 19–27.

Bunnell, N. (2015) 'Oscillating from a Distance: A Study of Metamodernism in Theory and Practice', *Undergraduate Journal of Humanistic Studies*, Spring 2015 (1): 1–7.

Byrne, Bryony. (2010) '*The Thrill of It All*'. *Aesthetica*. https://aestheticamagazine.com/the-thrill-of-it-all/ (accessed 15 August 2023).

Cahill, Alex. (2015) 'The Theatrical Double Reflexivity Complex: How the Spectator Creates Metatheatre'. *Studia Dramatica*, 2015 (2): 173–88.

Cairns, James. (2017) *The Myth of the Age of Entitlement: Millennials, Austerity and Hope*. Toronto: University of Toronto Press.

Camden People's Theatre. (2023) 'Hannah Maxwell Presents *Nan, Me and Barbara Pravi*'. https://cptheatre.co.uk/whatson/Nan-Me-Barbara-Pravi (accessed 6 September 2023).

Campanella, Eduardo, and Dassù, Marta. (2019) 'Brexit and Nostalgia', *Survival*, 61 (3): 103–11.

Carlson, Katie. (2017) '*Lights Over Tesco Car Park*: Is Anyone Out There?', *The Oxford Student*, Friday 3 November. https://www.oxfordstudent.com/2017/11/03/lights-tesco-car-park-anyone/ (accessed 17 August 2023).

Carroll, Jerome, Jürs-Munby, Karen, and Giles, Steve. (2013) 'Introduction: Postdramatic Theatre and the Political', in K. Jürs-Munby, J. Carroll and S. Giles (eds), *Postdramatic Theatre and the Political: International Perspectives on Contemporary Performance*. London: Methuen, 1–30.

Carsmile, Steve. (2010) 'Forced Entertainment – *The Thrill of It All*'. *Freaky Trigger*. http://freakytrigger.co.uk/ft/2010/10/forced-entertainment-the-thrill-of-it-all (accessed 4 September 2023).

Cearns, Liz. (2016) 'Camden People's Theatre Plays All the Right Notes', *Broadway World*, Thursday 22 September. https://www.broadwayworld.com/uk-regional/article/Camden-Peoples-Theatre-Plays-ALL-THE-RIGHT-NOTES-20160922 (accessed 24 August 2023).

Ceriello, Linda, and Dember, Greg. (2013 – Present) *What Is Metamodern?* https://whatismetamodern.com (accessed 15 August 2023).

Chan, Szu Ping. (2022) 'The Devastating Cost of Britain's Loneliness Epidemic', *The Telegraph*, Monday 26 December. https://www.telegraph.co.uk/business/2022/12/26/devastating-cost-britains-loneliness-epidemic/#:~:text="One%20in%20five%20millennials%20don,women%20reporting%20feelings%20of%20loneliness. (accessed 23 August 2023).

Chapman, Ben. (2019) 'Millennials More Likely to Face Working-Age Poverty than any Previous Generation, Report Finds', *The Independent*, Wednesday 22 May. https://www.independent.co.uk/news/business/news/millennials-working-age-poverty-statistics-baby-boomers-resolution-foundation-a8924286.html (accessed 16 August 2023).

Chapman, John. (2020) '*Lights Over Tesco Car Park* (#30plays30days – 21)'. https://2ndfrombottom.wordpress.com/2020/04/22/lights-over-tesco-car-park-30plays30days-21/ (accessed 17 August 2023).

Collins, Tim. (2019) 'Millennials and Gen Z Really Are Snowflakes: Scientists Find People Aged 18 to 25 Are the Most Upset When They're Labelled Narcissistic, Entitled and Oversensitive', *The Mail Online*, Wednesday 15

May. https://www.dailymail.co.uk/sciencetech/article-7033111/Millennials-Gen-Z-really-snowflakes.html (accessed 22 August 2023).

Colquhoun, Matt. (2020) *Egress: On Mourning, Melancholy and the Fisher-Function*. London: Repeater.

Cooper, Brent. (2017) '"Beyond" Metamodernism: The Meta-Turn Has Come Full Circle'. https://medium.com/the-abs-tract-organization/beyond-metamodernism-c595c6f35379 (accessed 16 August 2023).

Cooper, Brent. (2018) 'The Metamodern Condition: A Report on "The Dutch School" of Metamodernism'. https://medium.com/the-abs-tract-organization/themetamodern-condition-1e1d04a13c4 (accessed 15 August 2023).

Corlett, Adam, and Judge, Lindsay. (2017) 'Home Affront: Housing across the Generations', *Intergenerational Commission*. https://www.resolutionfoundation.org/app/uploads/2017/09/Home-Affront.pdf (accessed 16 August 2023).

Critchley, Simon. (2016) *On Bowie*. London: Profile Books.

Crouch, Tim. (2009) 'An Article by Tim Crouch'. http://www.timcrouchtheatre.co.uk/shows2/the-author/the-author (accessed 17 August 2023).

Cunningham, Katie. (2012) '*End To End* (The Gramophones Theatre Company / PBH's Free Fringe)', *Three Weeks Edinburgh*, Friday 24 August. https://threeweeksedinburgh.com/article/end-to-end-the-gramophones-theatre-company-pbhs-free-fringe/ (accessed 17 August 2023).

Curan, Thomas, and Hill, Andrew P. (2017) 'Perfectionism Is Increasing Over Time: A Meta-Analysis of Birth Cohort Differences between 1989 To 2016', *Psychological Bulletin*, 145 (4): 410–29.

Davies, Josie. (2018) [Interview with the Author] Monday 5 March 2018. in T. Drayton (2020) 'Towards a Listening Theatre: Metamodernism, Millennials and Contemporary Political Theatre'. PhD Thesis. University of East London.

Davies, Josie, and Marie Sophie, Stella. (2018) '*The Welcome Revolution*'. [Unpublished Script shared with the author].

Defraeye, Piet. (2007). 'Postdramatic Theatre (review)', *Modern Drama*, 50: 644–7.

Dember, Greg. (2017a) 'How to Be Ironic and Earnest, with J. P. Sears ("Ironesty")', *What Is Metamodern?*, https://whatismetamodern.com/religion-spirituality/j-p-sears-ironesty-metamodernism/ (accessed 16 August 2023).

Dember, Greg. (2017b) 'I Coined the Word IRONESTY'. https://icoinedthewordironesty.com (accessed 16 August 2023).

Dember, Greg. (2018) 'Eleven Metamodern Methods in the Arts', *What Is Metamodern?*. https://medium.com/what-is-metamodern/after-postmodernism-eleven-metamodern-methods-in-the-arts-767f7b646cae (accessed 12 December 2023).

Dember, Greg. (2019) 'Punk Rock for Sissies: Metamodernism and the Return of Affect in Early 21st Century American Indie Rock', *What Is Metamodern?*.

https://medium.com/what-is-metamodern/punk-rock-for-sissies-74e57c103 96a (accessed 15 August 2023).

Dember, Greg. (2022) 'Everything Metamodern All at Once', *What Is Metamodern?*. https://whatismetamodern.com/film/everything-everywh ere-all-at-once-metamodern/ (accessed 24 August 2023).

Dember, Greg. (2023) 'Metamodernism; Oscillation Revisited', *What Is Metamodern?*. https://medium.com/what-is-metamodern/metamodernism-oscillation-revisited-b1ae011abf3c (accessed 16 August 2023).

Dempsey, Brendan Graham. (2023) *Metamodernism: Or, The Cultural Logic of Cultural Logics*. Minnesota: ARC Press.

den Dulk, Allard. (2020) 'New Sincerity and Frances Ha in Light of Sartre: A Proposal for an Existentialist Conceptual Framework', *Film-Philosophy*, 24 (2): 140–61.

Derrida, Jaques. (1994) *Spectres of Marx, the State of the Debt, the Work of Mourning, & the New International*. Translated by Peggy Kamuf. London: Routledge.

Dimock, Michael. (2019) 'Defining Generations: Where Millennials End and Generation Begins', *Pew Research* Centre. https://www.pewresearch.org/short-reads/2019/01/17/where-millennials-end-and-generation-z-begins/ (accessed 9 April 2024).

Djupe, Paul A. (2021) 'QAnon, Millennials, and Gen Z – a Match Made in Heaven?'. https://onetwentyseven.blog/2021/03/17/qanon-millenni als-and-gen-z/ (accessed 16 August 2023).

Drawing the Line. (2019) [Theatrical Production] Hidden Track. Dir. Elliot Hughes. London: The Albany, 9 May.

Drayton, Tom. (2018) 'The Listening Theatre: A Metamodern Politics of Performance', *Performance Philosophy Journal*, 4 (1): 170–81.

Drayton, Tom. (2022) 'Can I Join In? Playful Performance and Alternative Political Realities', in A. Koubová, P. Urban, W. Russell and M. MacLean (eds), *Play and Democracy: Philosophical Perspectives*. Abingdon: Routledge, 108–24.

Duncan, Pansy. (2015) *The Emotional Life of Postmodern Film*. Abingdon: Routledge.

Duvall, John N. (1999) 'Troping History: Modernist Residue in Fredric Jameson's Pastiche and Linda Hutcheon's Parody', *Style*, 33 (3): 372–90.

Economic Affairs Committee. (2018) 'Treating Students Fairly: The Economics of Post-School Education 2nd Report of Session 2017–19 – Published 11 June 2018 – HL Paper 139', https://publications.parliament.uk/pa/ld201719/ ldselect/ldeconaf/139/13902.htm (accessed 16 August 2023).

Eggington, William. (2003) *How the World Became a Stage: Presence, Theatricality, and the Question of Modernity*. Albany: State of New York University Press.

Ellis, Nathan. (2022) *work.txt*. London: Methuen.

Ellis, Vicky. (2012) 'Review: *End to End* – The Gramophones – 06.11.2012', *Blackpool Social Club*, Wednesday 7 November. https://www.blackpoolsocial.club/1180-review-end-to-end/ (accessed 17 August 2023).

Elmina's Kitchen. (2003) [Theatrical Production] Kwame Kwei-Armah. Dir. Angus Jackson. London: The National Theatre, 29 May–25 August.

Eltringham, Joanne. (2013) 'Gramophones Theatre Company in "*End to End*"'. https://arts.caithness.org/article/1206 (accessed 17 August 2023).

End to End. (2012) [Theatrical Production] The Gramophones. Dir. Tilly Branson. Edinburgh: PBH's Free Fringe, August 2012.

Eshelman, Raoul. (2008) *Performatism or the End of Postmodernism*. Aurora: The Davies Group.

Eversmann, Peter. (2004) 'The Experience of the Theatrical Event', in V. A. Cremona, P. Eversmann, H. Van Maanen, W. Sauter and J. Tulloch (eds), *Theatrical Events: Borders, Dynamics, Frames*. Amsterdam: Rodopi, 139–74.

Everything Everywhere All at Once. (2022) [Film] Dir. Daniel Kwan and Daniel Scheinert. New York City: A24. 25 March.

Farquharson, Cristine, McNally, Sandra, and Tahir, Imran. (2022) 'Education Inequality', *Institute for Fiscal Studies*, Tuesday 16 August. https://ifs.org.uk/inequality/education-inequalities/ (accessed 17 August 2023).

Fathadhika, Sarentya, Hafiza, Sara, and Rahmita Nanda, Rizki. (2019) 'Are You Millennial Generation? The Effect of Social Media Use toward Mental Health among Millennials', *Proceedings of the 1st International Conference on Psychology (ICPsy 2019)*, 1: 49–54.

Ferguson, Jack. (2018) '*Lights Over Tesco Car Park*', *The Student*, Sunday 12 August. https://studentnewspaper.org/lights-over-tesco-car-park/ (accessed 17 August 2023).

Fermor, Patrick Leigh. (1977) *A Time of Gifts: On Foot to Constantinople: From the Hook of Holland to the Middle Danube*. London: John Murray.

Field Agent. (2015) 'Millennials, Boomers, & 2015 Resolutions: 5 Key Generational Differences'. https://blog.fieldagent.net/millennials-boomers-new-years-resolutions-5-key-generational-differences (accessed 16 August 2023).

Fisher, Mark. (2009) *Capitalist Realism: Is There No Alternative?* Alresford: Zero Books.

Fisher, Mark. (2014) *Ghosts of My Life: Writings on Depression, Hauntology and Lost Futures*. Alresford: Zero Books.

Flight, Thomas. (2023) 'Why Do Movies Feel So Different Now?' https://www.youtube.com/watch?v=5xEi8qg266g (accessed 15 August 2023).

Foster, Hal. (1985) 'Postmodernism: A Preface', in H. Foster (ed.), *Postmodern Culture*. London: Pluto Press, 3–15.

Foucault, Michel. (1970), *The Order of Things*, London: Tavistock.

Foucault, Michel. (1986) 'Of Other Spaces: Utopias and Heterotopias'. Translated by Jay Miskowiec. *Diacritics*, 16 (1) (Spring 1986): 22–7. Originally published as Des Espace Autres (Conférence au Cercle d'études architecturales, 14 March 1967). *Architecture, Mouvement, Continuité*, 5: 46–9.

Fragkou, Marissia. (2018) *Ecologies of Precarity in Twenty-First Century Theatre: Politics, Affect, Responsibility*. London: Methuen.

Freinacht, Hanzi. (2015) '5 Things That Make You Metamodern'. https://medium.com/@hanzifreinacht/5-things-that-make-you-metamodern-9e45fd97dc9b (accessed 17 August 2023).

Freinacht, Hanzi. (2017) *The Listening Society: A Metamodern Guide to Politics Book One*. Jaegerspris: Metamoderna ApS.

Frieze. (2014) [YouTube video] *What Is Metamodern?*. https://vimeo.com/113901626 (accessed 22 August 2023).

Fuchs, Elinor. (1996) *The Death of Character: Perspectives on Theater after Modernism*. Indiana: Indiana University Press.

Fukuyama, Francis. (1989) 'The End of History?' *The National Interest*, 16: 3–18.

Fukuyama, Francis. (2012) 'The Future of History: Can Liberal Democracy Survive the Decline of the Middle Class?' *Foreign Affairs*, 91 (1): 53–61.

Funk, Wolfgang. (2015) *The Literature of Reconstruction: Authentic Fiction in the New Millennium*. London: Bloomsbury.

Furness, Corrinne, and Whitworth, Charlie. (2013) '*Beneath the Albion Sky*'. [Unpublished Script shared with the author].

Gardner, Lynne. (2010) '*The Thrill of It All* – Review'. *The Guardian*. Wednesday 27 October. https://www.theguardian.com/stage/2010/oct/27/the-thrill-of-it-all-review (accessed 15 August 2023).

Gardner, Lynne. (2019) 'Putting on a Fringe Show Is More Than Just Tough – It Takes a Miracle', *The Stage*, Monday 27 May. https://www.thestage.co.uk/opinion/lyn-gardner-putting-on-a-fringe-show-is-more-than-just-tough--it-takes-a-miracle (accessed 17 August 2023).

Gardner, Lynne. (2021) 'How Indie Companies Are Coping with Covid-19: "We're Like Cockroaches – We're Hard to Squash"', *The Stage*, Wednesday 10 June. https://www.thestage.co.uk/long-reads/how-indie-companies-are-coping-with-covid-19-were-like-cockroaches--were-hard-to-squash (accessed 17 August 2023).

Gary. (1990) [Theatrical Production] Ray Harrison Graham. Dir. Roy Winston. London: Arts Theatre, 1990.

Gerosa, Alessandro. (2024) *The Hipster Economy: Taste and Authenticity in Late Modern Capitalism*. London: UCL Press.

Gessen, Masha. (2017). 'The Invention of a New Kind of Political Party in Sweden'. *The New Yorker*. 1 December 2017. https://www.newyorker.com/news/our-columnists/the-invention-of-a-new-kind-of-political-party-in-sweden (accessed 15 August 2023).

Gibbons, Alison. (2014) '"I Agree to This": Third Angel and the Price of Fame', *Notes on Metamodernism*. https://www.metamodernism.com/2014/01/29/i-agree-to-this-third-angel-and-the-price-of-fame/ (accessed 15 August 2023).

Gibbons, Alison. (2017) 'Contemporary Autofiction and Metamodern Affect', in R. van den Akker, A. Gibbons and T. Vermeulen (eds), *Metamodernism: History Affect and Depth after Postmodernism*. Lanham: Rowman & Littlefield, 117–30.

Gibbons, Alison, Vermeulen, Timotheus, and van den Akker, Robin. (2019) 'Reality Beckons: Metamodernist Depthiness beyond Panfictionality', *European Journal of English Studies*, 23 (2): 172–89.

Goodhart, David. (2021) 'Tony Blair Is Still Wrong on His 50% University Target', *unHerd*, Tuesday 8 June. https://unherd.com/thepost/tony-blair-is-still-wrong-on-his-50-university-target/ (accessed 17 August 2023).

Gorynski, Maxi. (2018) 'Moral Archipelagoes — an Interview with Timotheus Vermeulen'. *Wonk Bridge*. https://medium.com/wonk-bridge/moral-archipelagoes-an-interview-withtimotheus-vermeulen-6dfc1c907c47 (accessed 15 August 2023).

Graeber, David. (2015) *Bullshit Jobs: A Theory*. New York City: Simon & Schuster.

Green, Andy. (2017) *The Crisis for Young People: Generational Inequalities in Education, Work, Housing and Welfare*. London: Palgrave Macmillan.

Gritzner, Karoline. (2008) '(Post)Modern Subjectivity and the New Expressionism: Howard Barker, Sarah Kane, and Forced Entertainment', *Contemporary Theatre Review*, 18 (3): 328–40.

Haas, Birgit. (2007) *Plädoyer für ein dramatisches Drama*. Vienna: Passagen Verlag.

Halpin, Sophia. (2019) 'REVIEW! *Drawing the Line* by Hidden Track @ Deptford Lounge'. https://theatreboxblog.wordpress.com/2019/05/13/review-drawing-the-line-by-hidden-track-deptford-lounge/ (accessed 17 August 2023).

Hamera, Judith. (1986) 'Postmodern Performance, Postmodern Criticism'. *Literature in Performance*, 7 (1), 13–20.

Hamilton, Richard. (1983) *Richard Hamilton Collected Words, 1953–1982*. London: Thames & Hudson.

Harrison, Daniella. (2018) 'Review: *Lights Over Tesco Car Park* by Poltergeist Theatre', *Fest*, Tuesday 14 August. https://www.festmag.com/edinburgh/theatre/review-lights-over-tesco-car-park-by-poltergeist-theatre (accessed 17 August 2023).

Harrison, Sara. (2021) 'The Tyranny of Life Milestones', *BBC*. 22 March 2021. https://www.bbc.com/worklife/article/20210315-the-tyranny-of-life-milestones (accessed 15 August 2023).

Harvie, Jen. (2013) *Fair Play: Art, Performance and Neoliberalism*. Basingstoke: Palgrave Macmillan.

Hasted, Michael. (2014) '*Beneath the Albion Sky* at the Everyman Studio, Cheltenham', Friday 20 June. https://stagetalkmagazine.com/p/4190 (accessed 17 August 2023).

Henke, Christoph, and Middeke, Martin. (2007) 'Introduction: Drama and/after Postmodernism', in C. Henke and M. Middeke (eds), *Drama and/after Postmodernism*. Trier: WVT Wissenschaftlicher Verlag Trier, 1–33.

HESA [Higher Education Statistics Agency]. (2019a) 'Higher Education Student Enrolments and Qualifications Obtained at Higher Education Institutions in the United Kingdom for the Academic Year 2005/06'. https://www.data.gov.uk/dataset/8743480b-0383-4f07-a6ac-621d3f41914a/higher-education-student-enrolments-and-qualifications-obtained-at-higher-education-institutions-in-the-united-kingdom-for-the-academic-year-2005-06 (accessed 16 August 2023).

HESA [Higher Education Statistics Agency]. (2019b) 'Higher Education Student Enrolments and Qualifications Obtained at Higher Education Institutions in the United Kingdom for the Academic Year 2012/13'. https://www.data.gov.uk/dataset/f977a0d7-1916-4760-9419-522a6e488bdd/higher-education-student-enrolments-and-qualifications-obtained-at-higher-education-institutions-in-the-united-kingdom-for-the-academic-year-2012-13 (accessed 16 August 2023).

Hidden Track. (2023) 'About Us'. https://hiddentrack.org.uk/aboutus (accessed 17 August 2023).

Higgs, John. (2019) *The Future Starts Here: An Optimistic Guide to What Comes Next*. London: Weidenfeld & Nicholson.

High School Musical. (2006) [Film] Dir. Kenny Ortega. Burbank: Disney Channel, 20 January.

Hoesterey, Ingeborg. (1995) 'Postmodern Pastiche: A Critical Aesthetic', *The Centennial Review*, 39 (3): 493–510.

Hope Leaves the Theatre. (2005) [Theatrical Production] Theatre of the New Ear. Dir. Charlie Kaufmann. Brooklyn: St. Ann's Warehouse, 28 April 2005.

Hornby, Richard. (1986) *Drama, Metadrama, and Perception*. Lewisburg: Bucknell University Press.

Howe, Neil, and Strauss, William. (1991) *Generations: The History of America's Future, 1584 to 2069*. New York: Morrow.

Howe, Neil, and Strauss, William. (2000) *Millennials Rising: The Next Great Generation*. New York: Vintage.

Huber, Irmtraud, and Funk, Wolfgang. (2017) 'Reconstructing Depth: Authentic Fiction and Responsibility', in R. van den Akker, A. Gibbons and T. Vermeulen (eds), *Metamodernism: Historicity, Affect and Depth after Postmodernism*. London: Rowman & Littlefield, 151–66.

Hull City of Culture 2017. (2016) 'Showtime: Hull Throws Open Its Doors to the World with 365 Days of Culture and a Momentous Year for the City'. Hull: Hull UK City of Culture 2017.

Huntley, Rebecca. (2006) *The World According to Y: Inside the New Adult Generation*. Crows Nest: Allen & Unwin.

Hutcheon, Linda. ([1988] 2002) *The Politics of Postmodernism*. London, Routledge.

Ilori, Kemi Atanda. (2014) *The Theatre of Wole Soyinka: Metamodernism, Myth and Ritual*. Leeds: Universal Books.

Ilori, Kemi Atanda. (2016) 'The Theatre of Wole Soyinka: Inside the Liminal World of Myth, Ritual and Postcoloniality'. PhD Thesis. University of Leeds. https://etheses.whiterose.ac.uk/15733/ (accessed 8 April 2024).

In Defense of the Force Awakens. (2017) [YouTube video] Lets Talk about Stuff. https://www.youtube.com/watch?v=XuAvwS9VGKI&t=51s (accessed 15 August 2023).

Independent Voices. (2015) 'Ifs and Buts: The Tories Should Forget Their Impossible Immigration Pledge and Simply Take Asylum-Seekers Out of the Equation', *The Independent*, Thursday 28 August. https://www.independent.co.uk/voices/editorials/ifs-and-buts-the-tories-should-forget-their-impossible-immigration-pledge-and-simply-take-asylumseekers-out-of-the-equation-10475677.html (accessed 17 August 2023).

Ipsos Mori. (2017) 'How Britain Voted in the 2017 Election'. https://www.ipsos.com/ipsos-mori/en-uk/how-britain-voted-2017-election (accessed 16 August 2023).

Jackson, Sarah J. (2014) *Black Celebrity, Racial Politics, and the Press: Framing Dissent*. New York: Routledge.

James, Anna. (2022) '*work.txt* review', *The Stage*, Thursday 3 March. https://www.thestage.co.uk/reviews/work-txt-review-soho-theatre-upstairs-london-nathan-ellis (accessed 18 August 2023).

James, David. (2019) 'Uplift: Contemporary Sentimentalism and the Literature of Amelioration', AHRC Metamodernism Network Conference, Radboud University, Nijmegen, 3–5 July.

Jameson, Frederic. (1991) *Postmodernism: Or, the Cultural Logic of Late Capitalism*. London: Verso.

Jankovic, Bojana. (2013) '*Beneath the Albion Sky*: Walking the Line', *Exuent Magazine*, Sunday 22 September. https://exeuntmagazine.com/reviews/beneath-the-albion-sky/ (accessed 17 August 2023).

Javanović, Smiljka. (2021) 'Metamodernism and the Coronavirus (COVID-19) Pandemic', *INSAM Journal of Contemporary Music, Art and Technology*, 6(1): 57–74.

Jeffries, Stuart. (2021) *Everything, All The Time, Everywhere: How We Became Post-modern*. London: Verso.

Johnson, Tekla Ali, Dowe, Forde, Pearl K., and Fauntroy, Michael K. (2011) 'One America? President Obama's Non-racial State', *Race, Gender & Class*, 18 (3): 135–49.

Jones, Josh. (2015) 'How David Bowie, Kurt Cobain & Thom Yorke Write Songs With William Burroughs' Cut-Up Technique', *Open Culture*, Wednesday 4

February. https://www.openculture.com/2015/02/bowie-cut-up-technique.html (accessed 16 August 2023).

Jordan, Spencer. (2019) *Postdigital Storytelling: Poetics, Praxis, Research*. Abingdon, Routledge.

Jürs-Munby, K., Carroll, J., Giles, S. (2013) *Postdramatic Theatre and the Political: International Perspectives on Contemporary Performance*. London: Methuen.

Kalisch, Eleanore. (2000) 'Aspekte Einer Begriffs – Und Problemgesichte Von Authentizität Un Darstellung', in Erika Fischer-Lichte and Isabel Pflug (eds), *Inszenierung Von Authentizität*. Tübingen: Francke, 31–44.

Kant, Immanuel. ([1781] 1934) *The Critique of Pure Reason*. Translated by J. M. D. Meiklejohn. Letchworth: J.M. Dent.

Kant, Immanuel. ([1784] 1963) 'Idea for a Universal History from a Cosmopolitan Point of View'. Translated by Lewis White Beck. *Immanuel Kant, 'On History*,' Indianapolis: The Bobbs-Merrill.

Kaye, Nick. (1994) *Postmodernism and Performance (New Directions in Theatre)*. London: Palgrave Macmillan.

Kene, Arinzé. (2018) *Misty*. London: Nick Hern Books.

Kester, Grant. (2005) 'Conversation Pieces: The Role of Dialogue in Socially-Engaged Art', in Z. Kucor and S. Leung (eds), *Theory in Contemporary Art Since 1985*. Chichester: Simon & Blackwell, 153–65.

Kester, Grant. (2009) 'Dialogical Aesthetics: A Critical Framework for Littoral Art', *Variant*, 9 (2): 1–8. https://www.variant.org.uk/9texts/KesterSupplement.html (accessed 15 August 2023).

Kirby, Alan. (2006) 'The Death of Postmodernism and Beyond'. *Philosophy Now* (58): 34–7. https://philosophynow.org/issues/58/The_Death_of_Postmodernism_And_Beyond (accessed 15 August 2023).

Kirby, Alan. (2009) *Digimodernism: How New Technologies Dismantle the Postmodern and Reconfigure Our Culture*. New York: Continuum.

Knaller, Susanne. (2012) 'The Ambiguousness of the Authentic: Authenticity between Reference, Fictionality and Fake in Modern and Contemporary Art', in J. Straud (ed.), *Paradoxes of Authenticity: Studies on a Critical Concept*. Bielefeld: Transcript Verlag, 51–76.

Konstantinou, Lee. (2017) 'Four Faces of Postirony', in R. van den Akker, A. Gibbons and T. Vermeulen (eds), *Metamodernism: History Affect and Depth after Postmodernism*. Lanham: Rowman & Littlefield, 87–102.

Kovalova, Mariia, Alforova, Zoya, Sokolyuk, Lyudmyla, Chursin, Oleksandr, and Obukh, Liudmyla (2022) 'The Digital Evolution of Art: Current Trends in the Context of the Formation and Development of Metamodernism', *Amazonia Investiga*, 11 (56): 114–23. https://doi.org/10.34069/AI/2022.56.08.12. (accessed 9 April 2024).

Krüger, Lida. (2016) '"Stop Putting Words in My Mouth!": Undermining the Binary between the Actual and the Fictional', *New Theatre Quarterly*, 32 (3): 244–55.

Krumsvik & Co. (2017) Timotheus Vermeulen on Metamodernism and Fake News. [Podcast] 30 January. https://krumsvik.podbean.com/e/timotheus-vermeulen-on-metamodernism-and-fake-news/ (accessed 15 August 2023).

Kumar, Naveen. (2023) 'Review: In "*Misty*," a Restless Artist Grapples with a Gentrifying City', *New York Times*, Friday 10 March. https://www.nytimes.com/2023/03/10/theater/misty-arinze-kene-the-shed-review.html (accessed 17 August 2023).

Kunzru, Hari. (2011) 'Postmodernism: From the Cutting Edge to the Museum', *The Guardian*, Thursday 15 September. https://www.theguardian.com/artanddesign/2011/sep/15/postmodernism-cutting-edge-to-museum (accessed 16 August 2023).

Lamont, Duncan. (2023) 'What 175 Years of Data Tell Us about House Price Affordability in the UK'. https://www.schroders.com/en-gb/uk/individual/insights/what-174-years-of-data-tell-us-about-house-price-affordability-in-the-uk/ (accessed 16 August 2023).

Landis, Holly. (2020) 'No More Stiff Upper Lip: How Millennials and Gen Z Are Changing the Future of Mental Health', *Rising Issue*, Wednesday 9 September. https://www.risingissue.co.uk/features/no-more-stiff-upper-lip-how-millennials-and-gen-z-are-changing-the-future-of-mental-health (accessed 16 August 2023).

Lavender, Andy. (2016) *Performance in the Twenty-First Century: Theatres of Engagement*. Abingdon: Routledge.

Le Cunff, Anne-Laure. (2019) 'An Introduction to Metamodernism: The Cultural Philosophy of the Digital Age'. https://nesslabs.com/metamodernism (accessed 16 August 2023).

Leach, Robert. (2004) *Makers of Modern Theatre: An Introduction*. Abingdon: Taylor & Francis.

Left Lion. (2014) 'The Gramophones', *Left Lion*, Tuesday 5 August. https://leftlion.co.uk/legacy-content/the-gramophones-6856/ (accessed 17 August 2023).

Left Lion. (2015) 'Inside Out Festival – The Gramophones', *Left Lion*, Sunday 19 April. https://leftlion.co.uk/legacy-content/inside-out-festival-the-gramophones-7388/ (accessed 17 August 2023).

Leggett, Alexander. (2023) 'Quirky Dramaturgy in Contemporary UK Theatre: Autism, Participation and Access'. PhD. thesis. Birkbeck University, London.

Lehmann, Hans-Theis. (1999) Postdramatisches Theater. Frankfurt, Verlag der Autoren.

Lehmann, Hans-Theis. (2006) Postdramatic Theatre. Translated by K. Jürs-Munby. Abingdon, Routledge.

Levin, Sam. (2017) 'Millionaire Tells Millennials: If You Want a House, Stop Buying Avocado Toast', *The Guardian*, Monday 15 May. https://www.theg uardian.com/lifeandstyle/2017/may/15/australian-millionaire-millennials-avocado-toast-house (access 22 August 2023).

Lewis, Paul, Clarke, Sean, Barr, Caelainn, Holder, Josh, and Kommenda, Niko. (2018) 'Revealed: One in Four Europeans Vote Populist', *The Guardian*, Tuesday 20 November. https://www.theguardian.com/world/ng-interact ive/2018/nov/20/revealed-one-in-four-europeans-vote-populist (accessed 17 August 2023).

Lightfoot, Joe. (2021) 'The Liminal Web: Mapping an Emergent Subculture of Sensemakers, Meta-Theorists & Systems Poets'. https://www.joelightfoot. org/post/the-liminal-web-mapping-an-emergent-subculture-of-sensemak ers-meta-theorists-systems-poets (accessed 22 August 2023).

The Life & Loves of a Nobody. (2014) [Theatrical Production] Third Angel. Dir. Rachael Wolton. Sheffield: Sheffield Theatres' Crucible Studio, 21–8 January.

Lights Over Tesco Car Park (2018) [Theatrical Production] Poltergeist Theatre. Dir. Jack Bradfield. Oxford: North Wall Arts Centre, 21 July.

Lipovetsky, Gilles (2005) *Hypermodern Times*. Cambridge: Polity Press.Lopes Ramos, Jorge, Dunne-Howrie, Joseph, Maravala, Peris Jadé, and Simon, Bart. (2020) 'The Post-Immersive Manifesto. *International Journal of Performance Arts and Digital Media*, 16 (2): 196–212.

Love Letters at Home. (2020) [Theatrical Production] Uninvited Guests. Directed by the company. 20 May Online.

Ludford, Samuel. (2021) 'Against Metamodernism'. https://samuelludford.med ium.com/against-metamodernism-51be3cbbe751 (accessed 16 August 2023).

Lutzka, Sven. (2006) 'Simulacra, Simulation and *The Matrix*', in M. D. Diocaretz and S. Herbrechter (eds), *The Matrix in Theory*. Leiden: Brill, 113–29.

Lyotard, Jean-François. (1984) *The Postmodern Condition: A Report on Knowledge*. Translated by G. Bennington and B. Massumi. Manchester: Manchester University Press.

MacDowell, James. (2010) 'Notes on Quirky', *MOVIE: A Journal of Film Criticism*, 1. http://www2.warwick.ac.uk/fac/arts/film/movie/contents/note s_on_quirky.pdf (accessed 16 August 2023).

MacDowell, James. (2012) 'Wes Anderson, Tone and the Quirky Sensibility', *New Review of Film and Television Studies*, 10 (1): 6–27.

MacDowell, James. (2017) 'The Metamodern, the Quirky and Film Criticism', in A. Gibbons, R. van den Akker and T. Vermeulen (eds), *Metamodernism: Historicity, Affect, and Depth after Postmodernism*. London: Rowman & Littlefield, 25–40.

Mahdawi, Arwa. (2023) 'Millennials Aren't Getting More Rightwing with Age. I Suspect I Know Why', *The Guardian*, Tuesday 3 January. https://www.theg uardian.com/commentisfree/2023/jan/03/millennials-radicalism-not-gett ing-more-rightwing-with-age (accessed 16 August 2023).

Malldon, Jon. (2018) 'Review: *Lights Over Tesco Car Park* (Poltergeist Theatre, Home-Stream)'. https://jonsmalldon.wordpress.com/2020/04/06/review-lights-over-tesco-car-park-poltergeist-theatre-home-stream/ (accessed 17 August 2023).

Malzacher, Florain. (2015) 'No Organum to Follow: Possibilities of Political Theatre Today', in F. Malzacher (ed.), *Not Just a Mirror: Looking for the Political Theatre of Today*. Berlin, Alexander Verlag Berlin, 16–30.

Mannheim, Karl. (1928) Das Problem der Generationen, *Kölner Vierteljahreshefte für Soziologie*, 7: 157–85.

Mannheim, Karl. (1952) 'The Problem of Generations', in P. Kecskemeti (trans.), *Essays on The Sociology of Knowledge*. Abingdon: Routledge, 276–320.

Marie Sophie, Stella. (2018) [Interview with the Author (as Stella Von Kuskell)] Monday 5 March 2018, in T. Drayton (2020) 'Towards a Listening Theatre: Metamodernism, Millennials and Contemporary Political Theatre'. PhD Thesis. University of East London.

Marouf, Hala. (2022) 'Welcome to the Age of New Sincerity: "Permacrisis" as the Word of the Year and a Beacon of Hope', *The Mike*. https://readthemike.com/welcome-to-the-age-of-new-sincerity/#:~:text=The%20concept%20of%20New%20Sincerity,%2C%20most%20importantly%2C%20to%20optimism (accessed 16 August 2023).

Marquis, Karen. (2022) 'we were promised honey! Review', *The Wee Review*, Saturday 20 August. https://theweereview.com/review/we-were-promised-honey (accessed 18 August 2023).

Marshall, Colin. (2019) 'How David Bowie Used William S. Burroughs' Cut-Up Method to Write His Unforgettable Lyrics', *Open Culture*, Tuesday 7 May. https://www.openculture.com/2019/05/how-david-bowie-used-william-s-burroughs-cut-up-method-to-write-his-unforgettable-lyrics.html (accessed 16 August 2023).

Marx, Karl, and Engels, Friedrich. (1848) *Manifest der Kommunistischen Partei*. London: Office der Bildungs-Gesellschaft für Arbeiter.

The Matrix. (1999) [Film] Dir. The Wachowski's. Burbank: Warner Bros, 31 March.

The Matrix Resurrections. (2021) [Film] Dr. Lana Wachowski. Burbank: Warner Bros, 22 December.

Matthews, Timothy, Danese, Andrea, Caspi, Avshalom, Fisher, Helen L., Goldman-Mellor, Sidra, Kepa, Agnieszka, Moffitt, Terrie E., Odgers, Candice, L., and Arseneault, Louise. (2018) 'Lonely Young Adults in Modern Britain: Findings from an Epidemiological Cohort Study', *Psychological Medicine*, 49 (2): 268–77.

Mayward, Joel. (2021) '*The Matrix: Resurrections*'. https://cinemayward.com/review/the-matrix-resurrections/ (accessed 15 August 2023).

McGuire, Michelle. (1998) 'Forced on Politics and Pleasure', *Variant*, 2 (5): 11–12. https://romulusstudio.com/variant/pdfs/issue5/forced.pdf (accessed 18 August 2023).

McIntyre, Anthony P. (2015) 'Isn't She Adorkable! Cuteness as Political Neutralization in the Star Text of Zooey Deschanel', *Television & New Media*, 16 (5): 422–38.

Melnick, Jeffrey. (2009) *9/11 Culture*. Chichester: Blackwell.

Meloni, Marianna. (2019) 'Drawing the Line, Deptford Lounge – Review'. http://everything-theatre.co.uk/2019/05/drawing-the-line-deptford-lounge-review.html (accessed 17 August 2023).

Meyer, Dan. (2023) 'How Arinzé Kene Brought a Slice of London to NYC in *MISTY*', *Theaterly*, Friday 17 March. https://www.theatrely.com/post/how-arinze-kene-brought-a-slice-of-london-to-nyc-in-misty (accessed 17 August 2023).

Misty. (2018) [Theatrical Production] Trafalgar Theatre Productions, Jonathan Church Productions, Eilene Davidson and Audible in association with Island Records. Dir. Omar Elerian. London: The Bush Theatre, 15 March.

Mitova, Nina. (2020) 'The Beyondness of Theatre: The Twenty-First-Century Performances and Metamodernism'. MA diss. Utrecht University. https://studenttheses.uu.nl/handle/20.500.12932/37354. (accessed 9 April 2024).

Moonrise Kingdom. (2012) [Film] Dir. Wes Anderson. Universal City: Focus Features. 16 May.

Mould, Oli. (2018) *Against Creativity*. London: Verso.

Mountford, Fiona. (2018) '*All We Ever Wanted Was Everything* Review: Meditation on Success and Failure Asks for Too Much Trust', *The Evening Standard*, Tuesday 6 November. https://www.standard.co.uk/culture/theatre/all-we-ever-wanted-was-everything-review-meditation-on-success-and-failure-asks-for-to o-much-trust-a3981671.html (accessed 17 August 2023).

Mueller, Jason C., and McCollum, John. (2022) 'A Sociological Analysis of "OK Boomer"'. *Critical Sociology*, 48 (2): 265–81.

Murray, Brendan. (2023) 'UK Economy Hits Perilous Stage Lagging Rest of G-7', *Bloomberg*, Thursday 18 May. https://www.bloomberg.com/news/newsletters/2023-05-18/supply-chain-latest-the-uk-economy-has-reached-a-perilous-moment#xj4y7vzkg (accessed 16 August 2023).

My Theatre Mates. (2019) 'NEWS: Interactive Nation-Building Theatre *Drawing the Line* Headlines Albany's REBELS Season'. https://mytheatremates.com/drawingtheline_news_featured/ (accessed 17 August 2023).

Nan, Me and Barbara Pravi. (2023) [Theatrical Production] Hannah Maxwell. Dir. Len Gwyn. Edinburgh: Summerhall, Cairns Lecture Theatre, 5–27 August.

Newham Council. (2019) 'Index of Multiple Deprivation Stratford and New Town'. https://www.newham.info/deprivation/report/view/48c56a8149ef411fa7f11cd2c3528643/E05000492/ (accessed 17 August 2023).

Newport, Cal. (2012) 'Solving Gen Y's Passion Problem', *Harvard Business Review*, 18 September. https://hbr.org/2012/09/solving-gen-ys-passion-problem (accessed 16 August 2023).

Nicholas, Tom. (2019) 'Roots and Routes: Kingston-upon-Hull-upon-Stage During UK City of Culture 2017', *European Journal of Theatre and Performance*, 1. https://journal.eastap.com/2019/01/21/roots-and-routes-kingston-upon-hull-upon-stage-during-uk-city-of-culture-2017/ (accessed 17 August 2023).

Ng, Eddy S. W., and Johnson, Jasmine McGinnis. (2015) 'Millennials: Who Are They, How Are They Different, and Why Should We Care?', in R. J. Burke, C. Cooper and A. Antoniou (eds), *The Multi-generational and Aging Workforce: Challenges and Opportunities*. Cheltenham: Edward Elgar Publishing, 121–37.

Niven, Alex. (2019) *New Model Island: How to Build a Radical Culture beyond the Idea of England*. London: Repeater.

Notes on Metamodernism. (2023) Notes on Metamodernism. https://www.metamodernism.com (accessed 18 August 2023).

O'Grady, Sean. (2018) 'Millennials Need to Stop Complaining about the Housing Crisis – Us Baby Boomers Had It Much Worse', *The Independent*, Friday 16 February. https://www.independent.co.uk/voices/our-voices/housing-crisis-millennials-stop-complaining-baby-boomers-worse-britain-a8213606.html (accessed 22 August 2023).

O'Leary, Majella, and Chia, Robert. (2007) 'Epistemes and Structures of Sensemaking in Organizational Life', *Journal of Management Inquiry*, 16 (4) 392–406.

ONS [Office of National Statistics]. (2022) 'Marriages in England and Wales: 2019'. https://www.ons.gov.uk/peoplepopulationandcommunity/birthsdeathsandmarriages/marriagecohabitationandcivilpartnerships/bulletins/marriagesinenglandandwalesprovisional/2019 (accessed 15 August 2023).

ONS [Office of National Statistics]. (2023) 'More Adults Living with Their Parents'. https://www.ons.gov.uk/peoplepopulationandcommunity/populationandmigration/populationestimates/articles/moreadultslivingwiththeirparents/2023-05-10 (accessed 16 August 2023).

The Oscillator's Stone (2023) [Podcast] 'The Oscillator's Stone #011: What Is Metamodernism? (w/ Greg Dember)'. https://podbay.fm/p/the-oscillators-stone-podcast/e/1680463396 (accessed 15 August 2023).

Owen, Rob. (1999) *Gen X TV: 'The Brady Bunch' to 'Melrose Place'* Syracuse: Syracuse University Press.

Owens, Katheryn, and Green, Chris. (2020) 'Performing Millennial Housing Precarity: How (Not) to Live Together', *Studies in Theatre and Performance*, 40 (1): 44–53.

Owls at Dawn. (2017) 'Owls at Dawn. "The Metamodern Condition"', Episode 32. 16 March 2017. http://www.owlsatdawn.com (accessed 15 August 2023).

Paillard, Elodie, and Milanezi, Slivia. (2021) *Theatre and Metatheatre: Definitions, Problems, Limits*. Berlin: Walter de Gruyter.

Parkinson, Hannah Jane. (2017) '"Sometimes You Don't Feel Human' – How the Gig Economy Chews Up and Spits Out Millennials', *The Guardian*, Tuesday

17 October. https://www.theguardian.com/business/2017/oct/17/sometimes-you-dont-feel-human-how-the-gig-economy-chews-up-and-spits-out-millennials (accessed 16 August 2023).

Pereira, Daniel. (2022) 'we were promised honey! 4 Star Review', *Broadway Baby*, Thursday 11 August. https://broadwaybaby.com/shows/we-were-promised-honey/761149 (accessed 18 August 2023).

Peterson, Jordan, B. (2018) *12 Rules For Life*. New York: Random House.

Pilcher, Jane. (1994) 'Mannheim's Sociology of Generations: An Undervalued Legacy', *The British Journal of Sociology*, 45(3): 481–95.

Play Mas. (1974) [Theatrical Production] Mustapha Matura. Dir. Donald Haworth London: The Royal Court, 10 July–3 August.

Playful Acts of Rebellion. (2013) [Theatrical Production] The Gramophones. Dir. Christopher Neil. Exeter: The Bike Shed Theatre, 29 April–3 May.

Pomerantz, Dorothy. (2012) 'Morgan Freeman Tops Our List of the Most Trustworthy Celebrities', *Forbes*, Wednesday 15 August. https://www.forbes.com/sites/dorothypomerantz/2012/08/15/morgan-freeman-tops-our-list-of-the-most-trustworthy-celebrities/?sh=7bef5b9a335c (accessed 25 August 2023).

Prassl, Jeremias. (2018) *Humans as a Service: The Promise and Perils of Work in the Gig Economy*. Oxford: Oxford University Press.

Primack, Brian, Shensa, Ariel, Escobar-Viera, César G., Barrett, Erica L., Sidani, Jaime E., Colditz, Jason B., and Everette James, A. (2017) 'Use of Multiple Social Media Platforms and Symptoms of Depression and Anxiety: A Nationally-Representative Study among U.S. Young Adults', *Computer in Human Behaviour*, 69: 1–9.

Purchase. (2022) 'The Infamous iPad Kid'. https://sites.psu.edu/ist110pursel/2022/01/23/the-infamous-ipad-kid/ (accessed 16 August 2023).

Purdy, Jedediah. (2000) *For Common Things: Irony, Trust, and Commitment in America Today*. New York: Knopf Doubleday Publishing Group.

Radchenko, Simon. (2019) '*Bleeding Edge* of Postmodernism: Metamodern Writing in the Novel by Thomas Pynchon', *Interlitteraria*, 24 (2): 495–508.

Radchenko, Simon. (2020) 'Metamodern Gaming: Literary Analysis of *The Last of Us*', *Interlitteraria*, 25 (1): 246–59.

Raphael, Sarah. (2019) 'We All Know Social Media Can Seriously Harm Your Mental Health. So, What Now?', Vice, 4 January. https://www.vice.com/en_in/article/wj3ypy/we-all-know-social-media-can-seriouslyharm-your-mental-health-so-what-now (accessed 16 August 2023).

Reay, Diane. (2005) 'Beyond Consciousness?: The Psychic Landscape of Social Class', *Sociology*, 39 (5): 911–28.

Rees, Liam. (2018) '*Lights Over Tesco Car Park*', *Broadway Baby*, Friday 17 August. https://broadwaybaby.com/shows/lights-over-tesco-car-park/733800 (accessed 17 August 2023).

Robinson, Dave. (1999) *Nietzsche and Postmodernism*. Cambridge: Icon Books.

Rosario, Jason. (2018) 'The Welcome Revolution: Feat.Theatre', *FreingeReview*, Tuesday 14 August. https://fringereview.co.uk/review/edinburgh-fringe/2018/the-welcome-revolution/ (accessed 17 August 2023).

Rowland, Antony. (2021) *Metamodernism and Contemporary British Poetry*. Cambridge: Cambridge University Press.

Rushmore. (1998) [Film] Dir. Wes Anderson. Burbank: Touchstone Pictures, 17 September.

Russell, Bertrand. (1998) *The Autobiography of Bertrand Russell*. Abingdon: Routledge.

Rustad, Gry. (2011) 'The Joke That Wasn't Funny Anymore'. http://www.metamodernism.com/2011/02/10/the-joke-that-wasnt-funny-anymore (accessed 15 August 2023).

Ryan, A. (2005) 'New Labour and Higher Education', *Oxford Review of Education*, 31 (1): 87–100.

Sallon, Miriam. (2022) 'We Were Promised Honey! at the Soho Theatre', *thespyinthestalls*, Wednesday 23 November. https://thespyinthestalls.com/2022/11/we-were-promised-honey/ (accessed 18 August 2023).

Saltz, Jerry. (2010) 'Sincerity and Irony Hug It Out', *New York Magazine*, 27 May. http://nymag.com/arts/art/reviews/66277/ (accessed 15 August 2023).

Samuels, Robert (2010) *New Media, Cultural Studies, and Critical Theory after Postmodernism: Automodernity from Zizek to Laclau*. London: Palgrave Macmillan.

Saner, Raymond. (2001) 'Postmodern Theater: A Manifestation of Chaos Theory?', *Chaos Theory and Its Applications*, 12 February. https://paricenter.com/library/chaos-theory-and-its-applications/postmodern-theater-a-manifestation-of-chaos-theory/ (accessed 4 September 2023).

Santos, Christina. (2020) 'Mental Health Apps Are Taking Over Traditional Therapy Among Millennials'. https://medium.com/@csantos314/mental-health-apps-are-taking-over-traditional-therapy-among-millennials-f0c3be9b1d65 (accessed 16 August 2023).

Saville, Alice. (2022) 'Redux Review: *work.txt* and work_from_home', *Exuent Magazine*, Thursday 11 August 2022. https://exeuntmagazine.com/reviews/redux-review-work-txt-work_from_home/ (accessed 18 August 2023).

Savyna, Anna. (2021) 'Metatheatrical Aspects in "*The Author*" by Tim Crouch', *Scientific Journal of Polonia University*, 49 (6): 69–74.

Schechner, Richard. (1979) 'The End of Humanism'. *Performing Arts Journal*, 4 (1/2): 9–22.

Schechner, Richard. (1992) 'A New Paradigm for Theatre in the Academy', *TDR*, 36 (4): 7–10.

Schuhbeck, Birgit. (2012) 'Less Art, More Substance – New Tendencies in Contemporary Theatre'. *Notes on Metamodernism* http://www.metamodernism.com/2012/02/22/less-art-moresubstance-new-tendencies-in-contemporary-theatre/ (accessed 15 August 2023).

Schulze, Daniel. (2017) *Authenticity in Contemporary Theatre and Performance*. London: Methuen.

Scott, Joanne. (2022) 'A Datalogical Reading of Online Performance', *International Journal of Performance Arts & Digital Media*, 18 (1): 69–89.

Second Life. (2003), [Videogame] Dis. Phillip Rosedale. San Francisco: Linden Lab, 23 June.

Sedgman, Kirsty. (2018) *The Reasonable Audience: Theatre Etiquette, Behaviour Policing, and the Live Performance Experience*. London: Palgrave.

Sennet, Richard. (2012) 'The Architecture of Cooperation', lecture, Graduate School of Design, Harvard University, delivered 28 February. https://www.gsd.harvard.edu/event/richard-sennett-the-architecture-of-cooperation/ (accessed 17 August 2023).

Shaffi, Sarah. (2023) ' "It's the Opposite of Art": Why illustrators Are Furious about AI', *The Guardian*, Mon 23 January. https://www.theguardian.com/artanddesign/2023/jan/23/its-the-opposite-of-art-why-illustrators-are-furious-about-ai (accessed 22 August 2023).

Sharp, Andy. (2020) *The English Heretic Collection: Ritual Histories, Magickal Geography*. London: Repeater.

Shcherbak, Nina. (2023) [Online Lecture] 'Metamodernism or New Sincerity', Thursday 16 March, St Petersburg: St Petersburg University.

Shrimpton, Hannah, Skinner, Gideon, and Hall, Suzanne. (2017) 'The Millennial Bug: Public Attitudes on the Living Standards of Different Generations'. https://www.resolutionfoundation.org/app/uploads/2017/09/The-Millennial-Bug.pdf (accessed 16 August 2023).

Sibthorpe, Nathan. (2018) 'The Effect of Embodied Metafiction in Contemporary Performance', MFA Thesis, Queensland University of Technology.

The Sims 2. (2004) [Videogame] Redwood City: Electronic Arts, 14 September.

Slobodian, Claire. (2017) 'Review: *All We Ever Wanted Was Everything* at Reading Fringe', *Explore RDG*, Friday 21 July. https://www.explorerdg.com/heritage-culture/all-we-ever-wanted-was-everything-review/ (accessed 17 August 2023).

Smith, Helena. (2015) 'Shocking Images of Drowned Syrian Boy Show Tragic Plight of Refugees', *The Guardian*, Wednesday 2 September. https://www.theguardian.com/world/2015/sep/02/shocking-image-of-drowned-syrian-boy-shows-tragic-plight-of-refugees (accessed 25 August 2023).

Snaith, Emma. (2019) 'High Rents Are Stopping Young People Moving Away from Small Towns for Better-Paid Work, Report Finds', *The Independent*, Thursday 6 June. https://www.independent.co.uk/news/uk/home-news/rent-young-people-millennials-move-work-cities-small-towns-england-report-a8947156.html (accessed 17 August 2023).

Sofa Shakespeare. (2021) *Hamlet*. https://www.youtube.com/watch?v=9uhlCCmM_Ac (accessed 15 August 2023).

Solloway, Jack. (2022) 'work.txt', *Voice Magazine*, Thursday 11 August. https://www.voicemag.uk/review/11561/worktxt (accessed 18 August 2023).

Sontag, Susan. (1969) *Against Interpretation* (2nd ed.). New York: Dell Publishing.

Statista. (2022) 'Number of People Unemployed (Aged 16–65) in the United Kingdom from 1992 to 2022, by Generation'. https://www.statista.com/statistics/1393558/unemployment-figures-uk-by-generation/#:~:text=In%202022%2C%20among%20the%20working,Millennials%2C%20and%20295%2C593%20Gen%20Z (accessed 17 August 2023).

Stein, Joel. (2013) 'Millennials: The Me, Me, Me Generation', *Time Magazine*, Monday 20 May. https://time.com/247/millennials-the-me-me-me-generation/ (accessed 16 August 2023).

Stone, Hannah. (2016) [Interview with the Author] Sunday 24 April 2016, in T. Drayton (2020) 'Towards a Listening Theatre: Metamodernism, Millennials and Contemporary Political Theatre'. PhD Thesis. University of East London.

Strayed, Cheryl. (2012) *Wild*. London: Atlantic Books.

Taylor, Chloe. (2019) 'British Millennials Still 'Scarred' by 2008 Financial Crisis, Researchers Say'. *CNBC*, Monday 13 May. https://www.cnbc.com/2019/05/13/british-millennials-scarred-by-2008-financial-crisis-research-says.html (accessed 16 August 2023).

Taylor, Edward, and Roberts, Andrew. (2010) '*The Thrill of It All*'. *Total Theatre Magazine*, 22(4). http://totaltheatre.org.uk/archive/reviews/thrill-it-all (accessed 15 August 2023).

Theatre Royal Stratford East (2018) 'Making the World a Better Place – the Welcome Revolution'. https://www.stratfordeast.com/news/making-the-world-a-better-place-the-welcome-revolution (accessed 17 August 2023).

Thompson, Jessie. (2022) 'work.txt at Soho Theatre: The Show about Working that Audiences Have to Perform Themselves', *The Evening Standard*, Monday 28 February. https://www.standard.co.uk/culture/theatre/work-txt-soho-london-nathan-ellis-interview-workplace-flexible-working-mental-health-b984418.html (accessed 18 August 2023).

Thompson, Lucas. (2016) '"Sincerity with a Motive": Literary Manipulation in David Foster Wallace's *Infinite Jest*', *Critique: Studies in Contemporary Fiction*, 57 (4): 359–73.

Thompson, Rachel. (2018) 'Millennials Aren't Entitled. It's Employers that Need to Change', *Mashable*. https://mashable.com/article/millennials-entitled-workplace-culture (accessed 16 August 2023).

Thorne, Jesse. (2006) 'A Manifesto for the New Sincerity'. https://maximumfun.org/news/manifesto-for-new-sincerity/ (accessed 16 August 2023).

The Thrill of It All. (2010) [Theatrical Production] Forced Entertainment. Dir. Tim Etchells. Brussels: Kaaitheater, 7 May.

Timmer, Nicoline. (2010) *Do You Feel It Too?: The Post-Postmodern Syndrome in American Fiction at the Turn of the Millennium*. Leiden, Brill Academic Pub.

Timperley, Chloe. (2020) *Generation Rent: Why You Can't Buy a Home or Even Rent a Good One*. Chicago: Canon.

Turner, Luke. (2012) 'David Foster Wallace's Hideous Men & London's Olympic Epiphany', *Notes on Metamodernism*. https://www.metamodernism.com/2012/09/12/david-foster-wallaces-hideous-men-londons-olympic-epiphany/ (accessed 15 August 2023).

Turner, Luke. (2015) *Metamodernism: A Brief Introduction*. http://www.metamodernism.com/2015/01/12/metamodernism-a-brief-introduction/ (accessed 15 August 2023).

Turner, Victor. (1990) 'Are There Universals of Performance in Myth, Ritual, and Drama?', in R. Schechner and W. Appel (eds), *By Means of Performance*. Cambridge: Cambridge University Press, 8–18.

Unframe. (2021) 'Collage Art: The Second Generation'. https://unframe.london/collage-art-pop/ (accessed 16 August 2023).

Unlocked with Olivia Bright. (2020) [Podcast] 'Episode 5 – Unlocking *work.txt*'. Monday 21 December. https://www.unlockedpodcast.co.uk/post/5-unlocking-work-txt (accessed 18 August 2023).

Urban, Tim. (2013) 'Why Generation Y Yuppies Are Unhappy'. https://waitbutwhy.com/2013/09/why-generation-y-yuppies-are-unhappy.html (accessed 16 August 2023).

Usborne, Simon. (2017) 'Just Do It: The Experience Economy and How We Turned Our Backs on "Stuff"'. *The Guardian*, Saturday 13 May. https://www.theguardian.com/business/2017/may/13/just-do-it-the-experience-economy-and-how-we-turned-our-backs-on-stuff (accessed 16 August 2023).

van den Akker, Robin. (2017) 'Metamodern Historicity', in R. van den Akker, A. Gibbons and T. Vermeulen (eds), *Metamodernism: History Affect and Depth after Postmodernism*. Lanham: Rowman & Littlefield, 21–5.

van den Akker, Robin; Gibbons, Alison and Vermeulen, Timotheus (2017) *Metamodernism: History Affect and Depth after Postmodernism*. Lanham: Rowman & Littlefield.

van den Akker, Robin, and Vermeulen, Timotheus. (2017) 'Periodising the 2000s, or, the Emergence of Metamodernism', in R. van den Akker, A. Gibbons and T. Vermeulen (eds), *Metamodernism: History Affect and Depth after Postmodernism*. Lanham: Rowman & Littlefield, 1–20.

van Poecke, Niels. (2017) 'Authenticity Revisited: The Production, Distribution, and Consumption of Independent Folk Music in the Netherlands (1993–Present)'. PhD Thesis. Erasmus University, Rotterdam. https://repub.eur.nl/pub/102670/Authenticity-Revisited-dissertation-Niels-van-Poecke-Final-version-.pdf (accessed 18 August 2023).

Vázquez Rodríguez, Lucía Gloria. (2017). '(500) Days of Postfeminism: A Multidisciplinary Analysis of the Manic Pixie Dream Girl Stereotype in Its Contexts'. *Revista Prisma Social*, (2): 167–201.

Vermeulen, Timotheus, and van den Akker, Robin. (2010) 'Notes on Metamodernism', *Journal of Aesthetics & Culture*, 2(1). doi: 10.3402/jac.v2i0.5677.

Vermeulen, Timotheus, and van den Akker, Robin. (2015a) 'Misunderstandings and Clarifications'. *Notes on Metamodernism*, 3 June 2015. https://www.metamodernism.com/2015/06/03/misunderstandings-and-clarifications/ (accessed 15 August 2023).

Vermeulen, Timotheus, and van den Akker, Robin. (2015b) 'Utopia, Sort of: A Case Study in Metamodernism', *Studia Neophilologica*, 87 (1): 55–67.

Voegelin, Eric. (1989) 'Equivalences of Experience and Symbolization in History', in E. Sandoz (ed.), *The Collected Works of Eric Voegelin*, vol. 12. Baton Rouge: Louisiana State University Press, 115–33.

Vogel, Erin A., Rose, Jason P., Roberts, Lindsay R., and Eckels, Katheryn. (2014) 'Social Comparison, Social Media and Self-Esteem'. *Psychology of Popular Media Culture*, 3 (4): 206–22.

Walker, Sophie. (2017) 'Theatre Review: *All We Ever Wanted Was Everything* [Middle Child]', *Soundsphere*. https://www.soundspheremag.com/news/hull/theatre-review-one-life-stand-middle-child/ (accessed 17 August 2023).

Wallace, David Foster. (1993) 'E Unibus Pluram: Television and U.S. Fiction'. *Review of Contemporary Fiction*, 13 (2): 151–94.

Wallace, David Foster. (1996) *Infinite Jest*. Boston: Little, Brown.

Wallace, David Foster. (1999) *Brief Interviews with Hideous Men*. Boston: Little, Brown..

Wanderlust. (2014) [Theatrical Production] The Gramophones. Devised by the company. Mansfield: Create Theatre, 25 July.

Ward, Sam. (2022) *we were promised honey!* London: Methuen.

Warren, Ellis. (2017) 'Star Wars Episode VIII: The Last Jedi Review'. https://elliswarrensite.wordpress.com/2017/12/23/star-wars-episode-viii-the-last-jedireview/ (accessed 20 November 2022).

Watkins, Alfred. ([1925] 1988) *The Old Straight Track: The Classic Book on Ley Lines*. New York City: Abacus.

we were promised honey! (2022) [Theatrical Production] YESYESNONO. Dir. Sam Ward and Atri Najeree. Edinburgh: Paines Plough Roundabout @ Summerhall, 3–28 August.

Welcome Is a Radical Act: An Action/Reflection Event on the Arts and Refugees. (2017) [Conference]. London: Goldsmith's University of London, Thursday 9 November. https://www.gold.ac.uk/calendar/?id=11138 (accessed 9 April 2024).

The Welcome Revolution. (2018) [Theatrical Production] Feat.Theatre. Dir. Josie Davies and Stella Marie Sophie. Stratford: Gerry's Café, 21 February.

Wessendorf, Markus. (2003) 'The Postdramatic Theatre of Richard Maxwell'. https://www2.hawaii.edu/~wessendo/Maxwell.htm (accessed 15 August 2023).

West-Knights, Imogen. (2019) 'Life in the Electoral Wilderness'. *The New Statesman*, Wednesday 27 November. https://www.newstatesman.com/politics/uk-politics/2019/11/life-electoral-wilderness (accessed 16 August 2023).

Westling, Carina E. I. (2020) *Immersion and Participation in Punchdrunk's Theatrical Worlds*. London: Methuen.

Wilks, Charlie. (2018) 'Review: *All We Ever Wanted Was Everything*, Bush Theatre', *Broadway World*, Wednesday 7 November. https://www.broadwayworld.com/westend/article/BWW-Review-all-we-ever-wanted-was-everything-Bush-Theatre-20181107 (accessed 17 August 2023).

Williams, Alex. (2015) 'Move Over, Millennials, Here Comes Generation Z', *New York Times*, Friday 18 September. https://www.nytimes.com/2015/09/20/fashion/move-over-millennials-here-comes-generation-z.html (accessed 16 August 2023).

Williams, Holly. (2017) 'Could Playwrights Save Pop Music? The Rise of "Gig Theatre"', *The Telegraph*, Thursday 1 June. https://www.telegraph.co.uk/music/what-to-listen-to/could-playwrights-save-pop-album-rise-gig-theatre/ (accessed 17 August 2023).

Williams, Raymond. (1952) *Drama from Ibsen to Eliot*. London: Chatto & Windus.

Williams, Raymond. (1965) *The Long Revolution*. Harmondsworth: Penguin.

Williams, Raymond. ([1961] 1969) *Drama from Ibsen to Brecht*. Oxford: Oxford University Press.

Williams, Raymond. (1977) *Marxism and Literature*. Oxford: Oxford University Press.

Williamson, Tom, and Bellamy, Liz. (1983) 'Ley-Lines: Sense and Nonsense on the Fringe', *Archaeological Review from Cambridge*, 2: 51–8.

Wilson, Shaun, and Ebert, Norbert. (2013) 'Precarious Work: Economic, Sociological and Political Perspectives'. *Economic and Labour Relations Review*, 24 (3): 263–78.

Winn, Raynor. (2018) *The Salt Path*. London: Penguin Michael Joseph.

work.txt. (2022) [Theatrical Production] Nathan Ellis and Emily Davis. Dir. Nathan Ellis. London: Soho Theatre, 28 February.

Wright, Joe. (2013) 'The Legacy of Blair's 50% University Target: The High-Skilled Service Can't Find Good Work for Everyone'. https://civitas.org.uk/2013/11/20/the-legacy-of-blairs-50-university-target-the-high-skilled-services-cant-find-good-work-for-everyone/ (accessed 17 August 2023).

The Wonderful Story of Henry Sugar. (2023) [Film] Dir. Wes Anderson. Los Gatos, Netflix.

Zuleeg, Fabian, Emmanouilidis, Janis A., and Borges de Castro, Ricardo. (2021) 'The Age of Permacrisis'. *Euractiv*, Tuesday 13 April. https://www.euractiv.com/section/future-eu/opinion/the-age-of-permacrisis/ (accessed 22 August 2023).

Index

Abramson, Seth 30–1, 51, 109–10
affect 20, 26, 56, 60–1, 93, 113
The Albany 155
Anderson, Wes 107–8
Anthropocene 167–8
apocalypse 139–41, 164–5, 166–8, 173
Ashcroft, Ria 126–31
as if 30, 77, 79–81, 109–12, 125, 149, 174 *see also* Kant, Immanuel
authenticity
  and culture 35, 53, 79–82
  and metamodern theatre 22, 25, 96–7, 123–4, 127, 129, 142–3, 148–9, 152, 160–3, 164, 171–2, 174
  and millennials 79–82
  and theatre 6–7, 25, 32–6, 62
Auslander, Phillip 13, 15–16, 84
autofiction 121, 124

Bakhtin, Mikhail 105
Barnes, Luke 132–3, 137
Barthes, Roland 3, 16
Battersea Arts Centre 120
Baudrillard, Jean 3
Bauman, Zygmunt, 31
belief 62–3, 110–11, 122–4, 149–50, 166
Beinborn, Nele Frieda 42–4
Beswick, Katie 74
Bike Shed Theatre 22, 120, 126
Bogart, Anne 29–31, 43, 102–3, 125
Bourriaud, Nicholas 49
Bowie, David 63, 148
Bradfield, Jack 142, 144–5
Brexit 40, 78, 112, 135, 151–2, 157–8
Broadribb, Benjamin 23–6, 46–7
Britain
  (broken) 132, 134–5, 151–2, 169–70

geography of 120–2, 126, 129
government 71, 78, 81, 134–6 *see also* Labour
history of 124, 151, 153 *see also* myths
The Bush Theatre 135, 158

Cahill, Alex 42, 61
Cairns, James 82, 85
Camden People's Theatre 133, 155
Ceriello, Linda 7, 14, 50
childhood 4, 10, 20, 79, 83
  extended 74–6, 81
climate crisis, *see* apocalypse
Coke, Shiloh and Adrian McLeod 158, 161
community 135, 148, 151, 153, 159–60, 174
Covid-19 23, 76, 79, 112, 169, 172, 178
Create Theatre 129
Crouch, Tim
  The Author, 99–100, 102

Davies, Josie 150–5
Dember, Greg 14, 53, 55–63, 65–7, 89–96, 99, 103, 116, 118, 141 *see also* felt experience
The Deptford Lounge 155–6
Derrida, Jacques 80, 112–15 *see also* lost futures
dialogical engagement, *see* post-immersive
Duncan, Patsy 20
Dutch school 51

Eager Spark, 86
  Beneath the Albion Sky, 120–6
East London 150, 153–4, 159–60

Index

Edinburgh Festival Fringe 126, 129, 142, 144, 164, 166, 178
Elerian, Omar 158
Ellis, Nathan
  work.txt 169–73
embodiment 9, 20, 27, 34, 92, 105, 150, 164
engagement 26, 32, 37, 41, 44, 61–2, 95, 106, 130, 145, 153 *see also* Lavender, Andy
epistemes 14
Eshelman, Raoul 49, 62, 99, 123
The Everyman Theatre 123

Feat.Theatre
  The Welcome Revolution 150–5
felt experience 24, 53, 58–61, 92–5, 125, 129, 136, 141, 147–8, 150, 159–63, 164–5, 168–9, 171–3, 174–5
fiction, *see* storytelling, un/reality.
Fisher, Mark 80–1, 112–15, 169 *see also* lost futures
Forced Entertainment 85
  The Thrill of It All, 1–4, 18–19
Foster, Hal 31
Foucault, Michel 14, 43
Fragkou, Marissia, 105
Freinacht, Hanzi 51, 56, 116
Frewer, James 132
fringe theatre 86–7, 108, 119
Fuchs, Elinor 15–16, 27, 177
Fukuyama, Francis 52, 113, 168
Funk, Wolfgang 79
Furness, Corinne 120–5

Gardner, Lynne 18, 86
generations 70–3
  baby boomers 69, 72
  gen alpha 78, 137, 139, 178
  gen X 72, 74–5, 115
  gen Z 72, 76, 78–9, 178
  intergenerational relationships 121, 137–9
  see also millennials
Gibbons, Alison 40, 60–1
gig theatre 133–4
The Gramophones
  End to End 126–9
  Playful Acts of Rebellion 22, 25–6, 34
  Wanderlust 129–32

Haas, Birgit 36
Hamera, Judith 16, 21
Harvie, Jen 130, 157, 173
hauntology, *see* lost futures
Hidden Track
  Drawing The Line 155–8
Higgs, John 73, 75
higher education, *see* students
Holdon, Andy, and Raymond Conroy
  Brief Interviews with Hideous Men, 37–9
hope/lessness, 37, 74, 78, 81–82, 85, 87, 111–12, 114–15, 127–9, 140–1, 154–5, 157–8, 166, 168–9, 171
Howe, Neil, and William Strauss 71
Hutcheon, Linda 49, 64

Ilori, Kemi Atanda 41–2
immersive theatre, *see* post-immersive
im/possible 115, 145, 147, 165–9, 175
irony 6, 14, 18–19, 21, 26, 29, 31, 33, 38, 53, 55, 59–61, 65–7, 91, 106–7, 149, 163

Jameson, Frederic 50, 60, 63–4, 113
Javanoviç, Smiljka 50–1
Jeffries, Stuart 52, 60, 63
Jürs-Munby, Karen 16–17, 19, 148

Kant, Immanuel, 110–11 *see also* as if
Kaye, Nick 5
Kaufman, Charlie
  Hope Leaves the Theatre, 100

Kene, Arinzé
  Misty 158–63
Kester, Grant 34, 105
Kirby, Alan 4
Knaller, Susanne 34
Konstantinou, Lee 65–6

Labour party
  Blair / New Labour 82–4, 134–6
  Corbyn 40, 80–1, 112
Lavender, Andy 18, 20, 21, 31–33
Leggett, Alexander 108
Lehmann, Hans-Theis 16–18, 25
ley lines 120–2
liminality 5, 41–3, 93, 115, 145, 148, 167, 175
loneliness 24, 77, 116–18, 173–4
lost futures 77, 80–2, 112–15, 136–7, 164, 174
love 23–6, 140, 149, 166
Lyotard, Jean-François 16, 18, 30, 131

MacDowell, James 54, 57, 106–9 *see also* quirky
magical realism 122–4
Malzacher, Florian 43
Mannheim, Karl 70
Marouf, Hala 66
Marx, Karl 112–13
The Matrix 59–60, 122
McGrath, John 133
Melnick, Jeffrey 33
metamodernism 7–10, 13–15, 49–68
  in culture 7–8
  in film 106–7
  misunderstandings of 51
  in politics 111–12
  scholars of 7, 50
metatheatre 39–41, 42
  in metamodern theatre 98–102, 127, 132, 134, 142–4, 154, 159–63, 172, 174
  see also Cahill, Alex; Mitova, Nina

Middle Child
  All We Ever Wanted Was Everything 132–41
Mitova, Nina, 44–5, 102, 130
millennials
  children of postmodernism 10, 72, 74–5, 177
  disappointment 75, 121, 123, 125, 136–7, 139–40
  generational demographic 70–2, 137
  misconceptions 69, 82
  structure of feeling 54, 69–70, 72–82
  see also generations, lost futures, precarity
mise en abyme 99, 101, 134, 159
modernism 14
  liquid modernity 31, 49
  modernist theatre 14
Mould, Oli 85–6
myths 122–4, 153, 155 *see also* storytelling

narrative, *see* storytelling
neoliberalism 52, 104–5, 114
  and mental health 76–8, 85–6
  and the end of history 80, 113
  see also precarity
Newport, Cal 82
New Diorama Theatre 142, 163
new sincerity 37–8, 60, 65–6, 92–5, 111
Nicholas, Tom 132–3
Nordic school 51

optimism 128–9, 140 *see also* hope/lessness
oscillation
  in metamodern culture 19, 37–9, 51, 55–7, 58–61, 66, 74, 81–2
  in metamodern theatre 26, 38, 44–6, 91–3, 124–5, 141, 149, 155, 159, 163, 168, 171, 174–5

Index

Owens, Katheryn and Chris Green 75–6

participation 145–6, 150–8, 164, 170–3 *see also* post-immersive
pastiche 16, 46, 49, 63–5
  in metamodern theatre 103–4, 134–5, 137, 160, 163, 174
performance of belief 62, 99, 110–11 *see also* belief
performatism, *see* Eshelman, Raoul
permacrisis 10, 52, 54, 70, 151, 177–8 *see also* apocalypse
Peterson, Jordan 80
political theatre 36–7, 42–4, 150–8
Poltergeist 86
  Lights Over Tesco Car Park 141–50
Postdramatic 16–17, 84–5
  versus postmodern theatre, 17–18
post-immersive 104–6, 126, 130, 145, 148, 150–1, 155–8, 170–3, 174
postmodernism 14, 17–18
  children of, *see* millennials
  and cynicism 19, 38–9, 60, 66–7
  end of 49, 52–3
  postmodern performance 4–6, 13, 15, 8, 19, 21
  post-postmodern performance 26, 29–36
precarity 78–9
  and culture 114–15, 153
  employment 85–6, 136, 169–70
  housing 75–6, 160–1
  social 86
  and theatre 86–7, 105, 115, 153
  see also permacrisis
Punchdrunk 45

QAnon 112, 117
quirky, 57, 106–9, 128, 149, 153, 155, 158–9

Radchenko, Simon, 89–90, 93, 111, 116–17

reality *see* un/reality
reconstructive pastiche, *see* pastiche
refugees 151–3, 157
Riverside Studios 1
Russell, Richard 164, 167–8

Savyna, Anna 99–101
Schechner, Richard 16, 84
Schuhbeck, Birgit, 36–7, 62
Schulze, Daniel 33–6, 79–80 *see also* authenticity
Scott, Joanne 23–4
Sedgman, Kirsty 92
self-reflexivity 16, 19, 42–3, 61–3, 99, 121
Sh!t Theatre 87
Sibthorpe, Nathan 44, 100–2
sincerity 53, 55, 75, 93–5, 97, 107, 143
  and silliness 7, 49, 108–9, 123, 148–50, 152, 155–7, 159, 166–7, 172
  see also authenticity
singing 135, 161–2
  with the audience 24–5, 140, 141, 148, 168–9, 173 *see also* felt experience
Smith, Paul 132
social media 4, 5, 10, 77, 117, 132, 143
Soho Theatre 163, 169
Sophie, Stella Marie 150–5
Stone, Hannah 126–31
storytelling 29–31, 102–3, 120–1, 125–6, 129–32, 134–5, 143–7, 152–3, 160–3, 163–9, 170–1, 174
structure of feeling 13, 27–9
  of the millennials, *see* millennials
students
  graduate theatre companies 85–6
  in the 2000s 82–4, 136–7
  of theatre in 2000s 1–6, 70, 83–5

Tate, Andrew 80, 82, 117
Theatre Royal Stratford East 150
Third Angel
  The Life & Loves of A Nobody 40–1

Trafalgar Studios 158
Turner, Luke 30, 37–40, 109, 111
Turner, Victor 5

Uninvited Guests
   Love Letters Straight from Your Heart 23
   Love Letters at Home 23–6, 34
university, *see* students
un/reality 122–4, 149, 152, 160–2, 166–7, 171, 175 *see also* as if
Urban, Tim 77
utopia 81, 150, 155, 157–8

van den Akker, Robin, and Timotheus Vermeulen 7, 10, 13, 15, 36, 45, 49–55, 67, 70, 73, 81, 91, 110–12, 117, 163

van Poecke, Niels 33
Vault Festival 169

Wallace, David Foster 37–9, 42, 60, 65, 111 *see also* new sincerity
Ward, Sam *see* YESYESNONO
The Wardrobe Theatre 120
Wessendorf, Markus 17
Westling, Carina 45–6
Whitworth, Charlie 120–5
Williams, Raymond 13, 27–9, 54, 69, 73

Yard Theatre 120, 142
YESYESNONO 86
   we were promised honey! 163–9

Zavrazadeh, Mas'ud 50
Zoom 23–5, 46, 169